To Jamie Brown

From Labor to Reward

Blessing
Martha C. Taylor
7-19-2020

From Labor to Reward

Black Church Beginnings in San Francisco, Oakland,
Berkeley, and Richmond, 1849–1972

Martha C. Taylor

FOREWORD BY
Dwight N. Hopkins

RESOURCE *Publications* · Eugene, Oregon

FROM LABOR TO REWARD
Black Church Beginnings in San Francisco, Oakland, Berkeley, and Richmond,
1849–1972

Resource Publications
An Imprint of Wipf and Stock Publishers
199 W. 8th Ave., Suite 3
Eugene, OR 97401

www.wipfandstock.com

PAPERBACK ISBN: 978-1-4982-3281-4
HARDCOVER ISBN: 978-1-4982-3283-8
EBOOK ISBN: 978-1-4982-3282-1

Manufactured in the U.S.A.

In memory of the late Rev. Dr. James A. Noel, the H. Eugene Farlough, Jr. Chair of African American Christianity, Professor of American Religion at San Francisco Theological Seminary.

Contents

Part II—First Great Migration 1910–1939

Part III—Great Migration 1940-1950

Part IV—Civil Rights Era and Beyond-1950s-1972

Foreword

Black people in the Oakland-San Francisco Bay Area have been pointers toward what the bright future of African American life can be. These communities have Africa in their heart, Canada at their head, Native American nations to their left arm, the Pacific Islands and Asia next to their right arm, and Mexico and South America near their feet. Innovative while affirming traditions from their southern roots and global while planted in their local landscape, Bay Area Blacks offer America an untapped textural road map for how they and the United States can get along together. Black Bay Area residents vibrate with the energy unbounded by the dead mentality of slavery. There are signs that they do not self-police themselves with the invisible, poisonous mindset of "What would white people think if I do this?" or "I can't believe white supremacy is still around." Rather than perpetually dwell in the land of "they keep doing the same thing to us," Black neighborhoods seem much more pro-active; that is to say, they are setting their own agendas, focusing on that agenda, experimenting agilely, and, above all, maintaining an internal energy in harmony and balance. How does one prioritize the stability of the family, the cornerstone of any civilization? How does one accumulate land to feed one's people? How does one self-govern to train the future? And how does one transfer spiritual legacies of fathers, grandfathers, and great-grandfathers, mothers, grandmothers, and great-grandmothers to three generations yet unborn? In other words, there is a meaning in the history of the Black Bay Area of mobilizing the contours of culture in the quest to carve out a better tomorrow than today, and Dr. Martha C. Taylor's *From Labor to Reward: Black Church Beginnings: San Francisco, Oakland, Berkeley, Richmond* maps that meaning magnificently.

Key to that internal energy of harmony and balance and that external management of earth, air, and water has been and remains the Black Church.

Thus Taylor's *herculean project* fills in a huge void in American religious history, Black religious history, and traditions of the Black Church. She now enters the ranks of those experts of Southern, East Coast, and Midwest African-American church history scholars. Anyone now interested in the sojourn of African Americans and its crucial significance for the United States must examine closely West Coast Black faith institutions. Consequently, that instructs us to buy and read Dr. Taylor's break-through scholarship.

The book begins with the little known labor and business acumen of enslaved and free Blacks who flocked to the Bay Area as part of the frontier pressing, 1848 gold rush. Indeed, forever pioneering with daring agency, African Americans convened the First State Convention of the Colored Citizens of the State of California in1855. Held in Sacramento on November 20th at St. Andrew's African Methodist Episcopal Church, the convention was guided by clergy along with other civic leaders. Proudly they proclaimed: African Americans are intent on remaining in California and making it their home for their children and their children's children. The Convention gatherers fought for their voting rights, legal rights, children's right to attend public schools, and the right to testify in court.

The Second Colored Convention gathered in Sacramento at the Seventh Street African Methodist Church during December 10-12, 1856. Mindful of the proverbial truth that the future of any people hangs on the balance of children's well-being, the second assembly focused a great deal on the possibility of constructing a university open to African Americans. Held on October 13, 1857 in the St. Cyprian's African Methodist Episcopal Church, San Francisco, the Third Colored Convention deliberated on another decisive dimension for the nationhood of any citizens: the question of land wealth and everything underneath and on this core materiality. Specifically, proceedings debated taxable properties in mining or agriculture owned by Blacks. These three Convention themes resonate deeply with the keys to African American humanity. In fact roughly ten years later, with the end of the Civil War (1865), we witness similar thematic echoes. Upon emancipation, the Black freed people had three primary goals: to find their families sold off during slavery (i.e., children as a purpose of a people), to learn how to read (i.e., education to think outside of any accepted norm), and to own land (i.e., the wealth of earth, air, and water). And just like steady leadership provided by Black clergy during the beginning of freedom time, African American pastors walked in the lead along the path to a holistic life at the beginning of their people's journey in the Bay Area.

Similar to a Black power base, a hub within a dark nation, the Black Church emerged as the practical, priestly, and prophetic organizing center of new African American life in northern California. Indeed soon after their gold rush arrival, Blacks built Saint Andrews African Methodist Episcopal Church Sacramento, the first known Black Church to be organized in California in 1850; the same year California was admitted to the Union.

Throughout the remainder of the book, Dr. Taylor gifts the reader with the meticulous rendering of the origins, activities, and import of the major Black churches in San Francisco, Oakland, Berkeley, and Richmond. In a refreshing way, she details the roles and leadership of both men and women. From 1849 to 1972, with an eye for detail while maintaining the larger issues at stake, Taylor frames her impressive research and storytelling efforts within the Gold Rush era (1849–1909), the First Migration period (1910–1939), the Second Migration movement (1940–1949), and the 1950–1972 dynamics of civil rights, Black power, and progressive Black Church leadership in the public realm. At the end, her anthropological, historical, and theological bent brings us up into the second decade of the twenty-first century, where the current trend reflects the Black-out migration from the Bay Area and the accompanying decline of Black churches.

From Labor to Reward: Black Church Beginnings: San Francisco, Oakland, Berkeley, Richmond offers crucial insight in the academic studies of Black churches as wrapped in the dynamics of the larger US economic, social, political, cultural, and global dynamics. First, it is pioneering in the sense that it is the first and only book of its kind. Second, avoiding the totalizing approach of a general historical account, the book anchors its analysis in the particularity of interviews and primary archival work from the Bay Area. Third, it successfully defends the claim that the Bay Area remains one of the nation's vibrant, though challenged, centers for Black Church energy. Fourth, this book shifts the Black-Church, narrative pendulum in a more balanced and harmonious way away from the limited frame of Black religious leadership and lay experiences of New England, the South, and the Midwest. Northern California has been and remains a cutting edge laboratory for what is best for Black life and, indeed, for the country. Therefore, and fifth, by including California, specifically the Bay Area, Black Church history has finally become a comprehensive discipline. Finally, perhaps the greatest significance of this study is that we, for the first time, hear from the voices of the people. These are the voices of the left out and the marginalized, the ones who are centered in this major historical story by Dr. Martha C. Taylor.

Dwight N. Hopkins, author of *Being Human: Race, Culture, and Religion*; Professor of Theology, University of Chicago Divinity School.

Preface

*I want American history taught. Unless I'm in the book, you're
not in it either. History is not a procession of illustrious people.
It's about what happens to a people. Millions of anonymous
people is what history is about.*

—JAMES BALDWIN

Until now, no one-volume book has focused primarily on the rich religious
history of how Black churches emerged in the four metropolitan cities of
San Francisco, Oakland, Berkeley, and Richmond in California. To fill a
void that exists in Bay Area church history, this local history has been con-
solidated in one book; it is a story that had to be written and deserves to be
read. One of the most obvious questions that entered my mind was, Why
has little attention been paid to the rich religious experiences that comprise
the evolution of Black churches in the Bay Area?

*From Labor to Reward—Black Church Beginnings in San Francisco
Oakland, Berkeley and Richmond—1848–1972* constitutes a major contribution to the field of church history by tracing the growth of Black churches
in San Francisco, Oakland, Berkeley, and Richmond. Using sixty-two
churches and four timeframes, the Gold Rush (1849–1909), First Migration
(1910–1939), Second Great Migration (1940–1949), and the Civil Rights
Era (1950–1972), readers will travel back in time and experience the joys,
frustrations, and unity of Black people who sojourned from the Deep South
to the Bay Area and built a strong religious community as they struggled
against adversities of racism, housing discrimination, KKK threats of violence and death, and other sociopolitical barriers. The Black Church was the
center of the community providing spiritual and social support.

Using the biblical model of the early church, pioneer Black churches
shared their meager belongings, devoted themselves to fellowship, and were

filled with the Holy Spirit resulting in church planting and growth. Put another way, Howard Zinn reminds us in his groundbreaking book, *A Peoples
History of the United States*, that "ordinary people have made significant
contributions to history."

From Labor to Reward is a people's story addressed to all people who
desire to know about how Black churches emerged in the Bay Area. A dis-
tinctive feature of this book is that it uses local congregational records, oral
interviews, newspaper clippings, and other written sources. It should prove
invaluable to seminarians, professors, college and university students, clergy, and all others interested in the strengths and struggles of Black churches
in the Bay Area. Public Libraries, seminary libraries, the African American
Library and Museum, including the Smithsonian Institute will have a book
available to the public on church history that currently does not exist.

Readers will find a new liberating perspective on church history.
When pieces of history are missing, history remains incomplete; and this
book aims to close an existing gap in Black Church history.

I discovered in my research that history data pertaining to African
Americans are not always catalogued in one area because history is inter-
disciplinary. Some sources were found under geography, anthropology,
twentieth-century history, personal papers, and Black history, amongst others. What I did discover is that individual local congregation records, such
as church anniversary books, provide more accurate details of individual
church history.

Research went from work to "play"; it was like an "Easter-egg hunt"
unfolding and bringing to light what has been hidden. In some instances,
research led me to unexpected resources that proved to be invaluable. I
also used online databases, documents from archives in libraries, such as
microfilm, newspaper clippings, books, manuscripts, and other formats as
resources to place the missing pieces of history into their rightful chronological space. Most notably, the rich oral narratives that were provided in
face-to-face interviews captured the memories of living people.

This study goes beyond the growth of Black churches. Another dis-
tinctive feature is that the study interacts with the social conditions of Jim
Crow laws in California, racism, economics, and education by informing
readers about the social and political action that affected the quality of life
and living conditions of Black people.

In 1925, Delilah Beasley, became the first Black woman journalist
to write a regular column for a major metropolitan newspaper, *Oakland
Tribune*. Her column, *Activities Among Negroes*, captured local social and
special events, activities at local churches, as well as obituaries of notable people in the Bay Area. Her aim was to keep the Black community

informed about local events and to give white people a positive view of the
Black community. After Beasley's death in 1934, Lena Wysinger continued
the column through the 1940s. *Activities among Negroes* was a valuable
resource for this study.

As much as I wanted to include all Black churches in the selected timeframes, I was limited by space and available resource information; accord-
ingly, much Black history lingers outside of this story.

My interest in Black Church beginnings in the Bay Area was birthed
while studying for my Master of Divinity at the American Baptist Seminary
of the West in Berkeley, California.

In the spring of 2000, I took a course on African American religion at
the San Francisco Theological Seminary and Graduate Theological Union
Berkeley and became fascinated with the discipline of Black religion in
America from a social, cultural, and intellectual perspective—in particular,
the significance of the Black Church in the role of Black families, economics, and the "politics" of politics. Of interest is the fact that a vast number
of Black Southerners moved to the West for job opportunities as they fled
from oppressive economic conditions in search for a better life. Indeed it is
a story to be told and read.

Acknowledgments

It takes a village to write a book, and without village partners this book would not have been written. I am grateful and indebted to Reverend Dr. J. Alfred Smith Sr., Pastor Emeritus, Allen Temple Baptist Church Oakland, Ca and Professor Emeritus at American Baptist Seminary of the West, Berkeley for his words of encouragement to continue the journey of writing amidst days of feeling overwhelmed. Dr. Smith generously invested in my spiritual, academic theological growth and "pastored me through the process" with wise words of support and encouragement. He made spontaneous phone calls to pray and remind me to read Psalm 139:1–5. Malcolm Lowe, principal of *Yourtypetoo* consulting company was a great support with computer skills. To professors and friends I admire and who encouraged me in this endeavor, Dr. Dwight Hopkins, Professor of Theology at the University of Chicago, Dr. Linda E. Thomas, Professor of Theology and Anthropology, Lutheran School of Theology at Chicago, and Dr. James A. Noel, Professor of American Religion, San Francisco Theological Seminary, who introduced me to the love of Church history and was my academic advisor. A very special thanks to David Belcher, copy editor, WIPF & Stock Publications, for support in the editing process. Much appreciation to Calvin Jaffarain who typeset the manuscript and oversaw corrections.

The generous support of the staff at the African American Museum and Library (AAMLO). A special thank you to Dorothy Lazard, librarian, at the Oakland Public Library, Oakland History Room, and staff for providing guidance in researching historical files. My Allen Temple Baptist Church family spoke positive words of encouragement to keep writing. To my close friends and numerous relatives who reminded me to stay focused. I owe a debt of gratitude to my daughters, Valerie and Debra, and especially my grandchildren, Brandon, Brittany, Taylor, and Teralynn, for encouraging me and understanding that I was on a mission. Now unto God who charted the path ahead of me, I give thanks and glory.

Introduction

In this book, I attempt to thread together the history of the growth of Black churches in Oakland, Berkeley, Richmond, and San Francisco, California using three migration periods from 1849 to 1949 and the Civil Rights Movement from 1950 through 1972. When I speak about the Black Church, I use the term to identify the Christian religious location where Black people gather for worship. It has always been understood that the Black Church "is a generalized term for the collective identity of African American Christians in both academic and societal contexts."[1]

The Black Christians who formed the historic Black churches were seeking *freedom*. "During slavery it meant release from bondage; after emancipation it meant the right to be educated, to be employed, and to move about freely from place to place. In the twentieth century freedom means social, political, and economic justice."[2] In the twenty-first century, freedom means to be free from police brutality and the mass incarceration of Black males. The truths and rights sanctioned in the Declaration of Independence—life, liberty, and the pursuit of happiness—are denied Black Americans. Thus the quest for freedom continues.

The Gold Rush, First Migration, World War I, Great Migration, World War II, and the Civil Rights Era were the clusters that brought Blacks to California to improve living conditions, and to strive for racial justice. The emergence of Black churches in the Bay Area began with the Gold Rush of 1849 at Sutter's Mill near Coloma, California. The Emancipation Proclamation had not yet been signed and California was not admitted to the Union until September 9, 1850. The census count for Blacks indicated 962. The California Negro population doubled in the first three years of the gold rush. By 1852, two thousand Black men and women (about one percent of

1. Floyd-Thomas, and Floyd-Thomas. *Black Church Studies,* xxiv.
2. Lincoln and Mamiya, *The Black Church,* 4.

the population) were in California. Free or otherwise, Blacks lived under the constant threat of abuse, unwarranted arrest, and harassment.

The Gold Rush era was not an exodus of Blacks from the South, as the majority of Blacks were still in slavery. However there were a small number of Black men and a very few Black women who were "free"; they traveled by covered wagons and steamboats to mine the gold fields and start a new life. Slave masters looking to strike it rich brought their slaves with them from the South to work in the gold mines. California had been admitted to the Union as a free state on September 9, 1850, however slaves were still being auctioned for sale in Sacramento. This tension created the need for the California Supreme Court to enact a new law resulting in the Archy Lee fugitive slave case law. Black pioneers in the late 1800s left family and friends behind, arriving in California with only the clothes on their backs. They began the task of building a community with the church as the center. "The churches and schools of the California Black communities grew slowly in the decade of the 1850s; the first religious services that Black men attended in California were conducted by white men. It was not long before Blacks sought to organize their own independent churches in California."[3]

From the fragmentary materials on the first years of the 1850s, it is fairly certain that the first separate religious organization of Blacks in California, was the St. Andrew's African Methodist Episcopal Church in Sacramento founded by the Reverend Barney Fletcher who had gained his freedom in Maryland and then went to Sacramento, where he earned the money with which he purchased his wife and children.[4]

During the first migration period at the time of World War I, Blacks started a mass-exodus from the South to northern cities and the Far West in search of a better life. They came by Greyhound and Peerless buses, trunks of cars stuffed with their worldly goods, mattresses loaded on top of the car. Those that traveled by train also came with only suitcases and several boxes of fried chicken, with teacakes for desert. Everyone was looking for a brighter future in the "land of milk and honey." It did not take long for the new migrants to soon realize that the same forms of prejudice, Jim Crow and discrimination, were present in California. Hospitals did not accept Black patients, and Black children were barred from public schools.

To gain a sense of location, the San Francisco Bay Area, commonly known as the Bay Area is located in Northern California and consists of nine metropolitan counties. San Francisco, the only combined city-county in California was founded on June 29, 1776 located on the west side of San

3. Ibid., 158.
4. Lapp, *Blacks in Gold Rush California*, 22.

Francisco Bay. Oakland is not usually thought of as a Gold Rush town; yet it was the Gold Rush that brought the town into being following the establishment of San Francisco. Oakland is located in the East Bay, the county seat of Alameda County, and was incorporated on May 4, 1852. Oakland was selected as the western terminus of the Transcontinental Railroad in the twentieth century. Black pioneers moved to Oakland soon after the town was founded in 1852. William Walker Rich, originally from New York, arrived in Oakland in the early1850s and opened a restaurant on Main Street (now Broadway) near the estuary. The restaurant served clam chowder, and according to one account, when a customer ordered the house specialty, Rich would quickly step outside with a shovel, dig in the mudflats and return shortly with clams for the soup. Other Black pioneers also settled in the area west of what is now Lake Merritt and, according to the U.S. census, by 1860 there were twenty-three Blacks living in Oakland Township.

The City of Berkeley was incorporated in 1878 bordering Oakland to the north, as well as other small adjacent cities. Richmond is the only city of the four considered in this book that is located in Contra Costa County and was incorporated on August 7, 1905. Thus the East Bay was called the Contra Costa, meaning "the opposite shore" of San Francisco.

As Blacks moved in, the need for spiritual and social support became apparent. Bringing their culture, tradition and experiences from "home" in the South, Blacks began to build a vibrant church community. The concept of developing a Black Church in a Black community often started in private homes as prayer bands and Bible study using the living room as sacred space without the benefit of a preacher and absent of church constitutions, by-laws or membership requirements. Using the early church model, they shared their meager belongings, devoted themselves to fellowship, and were filled with the Holy Spirit. As more people joined, the group pooled their meager resources and rented space in storefronts; a phenomenon associated with Black churches. Other churches began when itinerant preachers conducted revivals in tents and a church was birthed from a revival.

The first recorded denomination in California was the African Methodist Episcopal Church, commonly referred to as AME. Secondly, Third Baptist Church was the first Baptist Church organized in the San Francisco Bay Area in 1852. The diversity of denominations expanded to AME Zion, Christian Methodist Episcopal Church, Pentecostal, Church of God in Christ, Presbyterian, and non-denominational.

With the founding of the church came the joy and pride of "naming the church." Churches were named after mountains in the Old Testament: Mt. Moriah, Mt. Sinai, Mt. Nebo, Mt. Hermon, Mt. Zion, Mt. Carmel, El Bethel, and so forth. Others used the New Testament such as First Corinthian

Baptist Church, The Church of Antioch; still other churches were named after the Saints such as St. John, St. Matthew, St. Paul, St. Luke, or St. Mark. Still
others were named after their founder, such as Allen Temple, McGlothen
Temple, Jones United Methodist, Taylor Memorial, Parks Chapel, Phillips
Temple, and Davis Chapel, to name a few, and this study profiles one church
named after a Black pioneer: Sojourner Truth Presbyterian Church. It was
also not uncommon for churches to be identified with street locations as
a means of avoiding conflicting names, 15th Street Church, 85th Avenue
Church, 32nd Street Church.

Black churches grew exponentially in the Bay Area due to the Second
Great Migration generated by World War II in the 1940s. With the increase
of migrants, the number of churches increased.

Sociologist, C. Eric Lincoln describes the importance of the Black
Church in this manner: "For Black people, the Black Church has always
been the social, cultural, political, location for the Black Community. It was
their school, their forum, the political arena, their social club, their art gal-
lery, their conservatory of music. It was lyceum and gymnasium as well as
sanctum sanctorum. Their religion was the peculiar sustaining force that
gave them the strength to endure when endurance gave no promise."

This study illustrates the context of the social phenomena that impacted the human condition of Black people in the Bay Area who struggled
to survive and build a strong religious community in the face of adversity.
Unlike many studies about the formulation of Black churches and the creation of Black communities using statistical data, and rigid social theory
frameworks of empirical evidence to interpret social phenomena, the point
of departure for this study uses human experiences, Black tradition and
takes into account the context and praxis of Black people who contributed
to history without the benefit of appearing in history books. In other words,
this study brings forth the "missing voices" of early pioneers, using their
experiences to give them a place in history. To that end, this book is written
from the view of people at the bottom; we are able to hear their voices as
they speak down the corridors of time. Like the followers of Jesus, these
ancestors faced great tribulation of distress, misery, affliction, and persecution, leaving a great legacy for future generations.

Part One, Gold Rush: 1849–1909, is the story of the Black experience
in early California, the continuation of slavery in "free California," the Archy Lee fugitive slave case, and other social conditions that were present.
Most notably, Black churches and a small Black community were established prior to the Proclamation Emancipation of 1863. The Elevator Publishing Company of San Francisco and Oakland was incorporated on June
12, 1888 as a newspaper for Blacks. Saint Andrews AME Church, started in

Sacramento, is the only church referenced outside of the Bay Area. The oral interview with Mary Thames, the great granddaughter of the founder of the first church, brought clarity to early church beginnings.

Part Two, The First Migration: 1910–1939, covers the period of World War I. This was the first era of the mass exodus of Blacks from the Deep South, creating a shift in the African American population to Northern cities and the Far West. The Bay Area was a major terminus point for Blacks. It was during this era that the first signs of separate communities for Blacks in the early 1900s with the establishment of Black churches of varying denominations: Baptist, African Methodist Episcopal, (AME), Christian Methodist Episcopal (CME), and Church of God in Christ (COGIC). At the same time, the women's movement contributed to building a strong Black community. Black women were active in the church and beyond forming social and literary clubs, institutions such as the Olds Folks Home, the Fannie Wall Home, and the Madame C. J. Walker home for homeless girls, to cite just a few examples of the many ways in which women contributed to racial uplift. The Black Women's Club movement had begun prior to this time frame and flourished during this period.

Additionally, the Watts Hospital in Oakland, founded by and for African Americans, and the Booker T. Washington Community Center (initially for Black soldiers) are a few of the many institutions that emerged.

The Universal Negro Improvement Association founded by Marcus Garvey, registered in the heart of the upcoming Black community in Oakland. Delilah Beasley, the first Black journalist to write a weekly newspaper column for *The Oakland Tribune* focused on local evens that shed positive light on Black people. When the Great Depression struck, Black churches became feeding stations for the poor. The Ku Klux Klan was openly organized in the Bay Area, wearing hoods and burning crosses with elected officials at the forefront.

Part Three, 1940–1949, focuses on the Great Migration and covers the time period with the continuation of the Black Church growth. Black communities emerged in the early 1940s bolstered by a growing economy resulting from shipyard dollars. As Black communities grew, more churches were added to the Bay Area. Oldtimers and newcomers clashed over social order. Black religious music was in transition; spirituals declined while gospel music increased. Jazz and blues artists flocked to the Bay Area creating a West Coast Harlem Renaissance. Shipyard money contributed to the increase of nightclubs such as Slim Jenkins and Minnie Lus. Following the postwar era, Black neighborhoods began to decline.

Part Four, 1950–1972, focuses on several postwar trends. Urban renewal that destroyed Black neighborhoods, civil rights, and the Black Power

movement came into existence. Urban renewal played a major role in that
Black churches were expanded beyond enclaves in the cities. Racial covenants were lifted, causing a shift in demographics. Oakland was the home
of the Black Panther movement in the late 1960s. The National Committee
of Black Clergymen, hosted by the Alamo Clergy and the Center for Urban
Black Studies met at the Claremont Hotel in 1969 in Berkeley to discuss how
the Black Church would respond to the new civil rights movement.

During the mid-1970s, gospel music took a new direction when two
brothers, Edwin and Walter Hawkins, gave birth to a genre of music called
contemporary gospel in the Ephesians Church of God in Christ, Berkeley.

Throughout this book, I use the terms slave, Negro, Colored, African
American, and Black interchangeably. History has taken many winding
roads for African Americans, thus the search for naming oneself has been
ongoing since arriving from Africa. Second, the term Black Church is used
to identify Black Christians who gather for worship at an identified location.

In summary, the past speaks to our present, the many Black pioneers
that labored in the vineyard to build a strong Black Church community in
the four metropolitan cities in the Bay Area is a message out of the people
to the people.

Part I—Gold Rush Migration Era 1848–1900

The Black Experience in Early California Antebellum Years—1815–1861

If our people are to fight their way out of bondage, we must arm them with the sword and the shield and the buckler of pride-belief in themselves and their possibilities based on a sure knowledge of the past.

—MARY MCLEOD BETHUNE

The Gold Rush attracted men from all walks of life who wanted to strike it rich in the golden state of California. Word spread rapidly that one could get "rich overnight." Men from all walks of life including farmers, slave owners, slaves, freed slaves and others simply picked up their meager belongings and headed West by horse or wagon train, determined to become wealthy. Among the blacks entering California were freed slaves, however the majority were slaves brought to California by their slave masters as property to prospect for gold in the mother lode country. For blacks, both freed slaves and slaves were accustomed to toiling from sun up to sun down. Thus sifting and picking for gold nuggets was far more appealing than picking cotton. Some of the slaves left families behind with the intent of buying their freedom. The spirit of the poor slaves was encouraged by the thought that eventually they would be reunited with their families and live with a sense of dignity and pride. The hope for freedom was the driving force that gave them determination to work.[1].

By 1850, a contentious battle over whether California would be admitted to the union as a slave state or free state had turned into a heated battle. The country was evenly divided into fifteen northerly free states and fifteen southerly slave states. A settlement agreement was finally reached in the Compromise of 1850 admitting California to the union as a free state on September 9, 1850. For slaves and freed slaves it was an answered prayer, but not for long. A backlash started amongst disgruntled supporters of slavery and slaveholders who had already brought their slaves to California and wanted to ensure that they could continue to retain their slaves as property. The practice of slavery was fully in place. One of the provisions considered would prevent both slaves and freed slaves from coming to California. Several years later, proslavery politicians and supporters of slavery were successful in introducing a bill known as the California Fugitive Slave Act. The Bill protected slave owners and made it illegal for slaves to run away from their slave masters.[2] The majority of slaves who could not read or write were not informed of the law and were left in the dark. By 1852 the number of slaves in California exceeded 2,200. The population growth along with activists who were becoming vocal about California being a free state was problematic for supporters of slavery. Legislators, mostly Democrats who supported slavery, used their legislative powers to manipulate revisions in the Fugitive Slave Law to protect slave owners. Slaves were not emancipated at the time California was admitted, leaving slave owners the right to retain their slaves as property.[3] The southern practice of slavery continued in California though the state was a free state.

In the meantime, the early black pioneers to California were caught in the snares of quasi-freedom for freed slaves and slaves who were residing in a non-slave state that practiced slavery. Indeed, California may have appeared to be the Promised Land for freedom, however, uncovered history revealed otherwise.

Negroes for Sale in "Free" California

California entered the union in September 9, 1850 as a free state, however, two years after its admission, an ad appeared in the San Francisco Herald newspaper June 1852: "NEGRO FOR SALE:—I will sale at public auction a

1. Fremont, *A Year of American Travel*, 114.
2. Beasley, *The Negro Trailblazers of California*, 43.
3. Ibid., 46.

Negro having agreed to said sale in preference to being sent home. I value him at $300 but if any or all of his abolition brethren wish to show that they have the first opportunity of releasing said Negro slave from bondage by calling on the subscriber at the Southern House previous to that time, and paying $100.00."[4]

Stephen Hill, a slave from Arkansas was brought to California by his slave owner, Wood Tucker prior to the Gold Rush. Tucker later returned to Arkansas and, according to Hill, had given him his freedom papers. Unexpectedly in August 1954, some men claiming to represent Tucker attempted to abduct him, claiming he was a fugitive slave. Hill's freedom papers were later found in his cabinet and eventually he was set free, but not without a fight. There were numerous cases that tested the Fugitive Slave Law, but none as well known as the Archy Lee case.[5]

Archy Lee

The Archy Lee fugitive slave trial was the most famous and celebrated fugitive slave case in California. Archy Lee was brought to California by his slave owner, Stovall. After living in California for some time, Archy Lee was hired out by Mr. Stovall. At some point the Stovall's wanted to return to Mississippi with Archy Lee against his will. Initially the court ruled in favor of Lee because Stovall was not considered a transient because of the length of time he had lived in California. The California Supreme Court ruled that the Fugitive Slave Law applied in the favor of slaveholders who considered California a temporary home and could then reclaim their slave as property. Stovall's attorneys argued that Stovall never intended to live in California though evidence suggest otherwise as he had also opened a school. Lee's freedom was revoked pending an appeal. Numerous people including white abolitionists came to the defense of Lee. Prominent San Francisco blacks Mammy Pleasant and George Washington Dennis helped to raise more than $50,000 for Lee's legal defense.[6] Several years later, the case was heard by Judge Robert Robinson on January 7, 1858. Lee was represented by the well-known antislavery lawyer Joseph W. Winans, Judge Robinson ruled in favor of Archy Lee to be a free man. Lee was later arrested on a warrant. Archy Lee was finally declared free April 4, 1858.[7]

---

4. *Democratic State Journal*, June 1852; Goode, *California's Black Pioneers.*

5. De Ferrari, *Gold Spring Diary of John Jolly*, 162–63.

6. Goode, *California's Black Pioneers*, 65.

7. Lapp, *Blacks in Gold Rush California*, 148.

There was much legal wrangling with regards to the case and the language of the Fugitive Slave Law. Stovall's attorneys argued that Lee was in violation of the 1850 National Fugitive Slave Law, and for a favorable verdict. The matter was brought before United States Commissioner William Penn Johnson who had jurisdiction over federal matters. Much to the surprise of the Stovall team, Colonel Baker of the US Commissioner's office ruled that Archy Lee had not crossed state lines, he was not a fugitive, and that his request for freedom came inside of California, therefore Mississippi slave laws did not apply in California.[8] The greatest evidence in favor of Lee was that Stovall had opened a school in California showing that he was not merely a transient but also had established a business.[9] In spite of California being admitted as a free state to the union, the footprints of slavery were deeply embedded in the practices of California.

California Colored Conventions—1855–1865

We know through painful experience that freedom is never voluntarily given by the oppressor, it must be demanded by the oppressed.

—MARTIN LUTHER KING JR.

The California Convention was part of a larger movement that had its roots in the New England states. Bishop T. M. D. Ward, Rev. Jeremiah Sanderson, Rev. J. J. Moore, Darius Stokes, Peter Lester, and others brought to California their previous abolitionist experiences from the Northeastern states and drew strength from their continued relationship with Frederick Douglass to start a similar movement in California. Delegates for the convention included ministers and others from Northern California who focused on racial uplift. The convention allowed the opportunity for the Colored people throughout the state to meet in a centralized location to compare notes, to discuss their conditions, and to propose resolutions for a change in California laws that were oppressive to black people with regards to testimony in court, owning land and property, education, and voting rights. The organizational structure of the convention was divided into sub-committees to discuss California statute laws. The conventions were not without disagreements amongst the delegates with regards to wording on proposals. The conventions were successful in obtaining signatures of white supporters.

8. *Chronicle*, Mar. 19, 20, 1858; *Herald*, Mar. 20, 1858; *Alta*, Mar. 20, 1858
9. *Alta*, April 15, 1858; *Chronicle*, April 7, 15, 1858

First Convention of Colored Citizens of the State of California

First Convention of Colored Citizens of the State of California was held in Sacramento at St. Andrews AME Church, Sacramento, in November 1855. Rev. Jeremiah Sanderson's opening words set the tone for the convention. In part he stated: "There is a deep interest in the work in which we are about to engage. We are scattered all over the state in small numbers, the laws scarcely recognize us; we are misunderstood, and misrepresented; it was needful that we should meet, communicate, and confer with each other upon some plan of representing our interest before the people."[10] Regardless of the offense, blacks were denied the right to testify in court against a white person: "*[A]nd persons having one-half or more of Negro blood, shall not be witnesses in an action or proceeding; to which a white person is a party.*"[11]

Discussion was often hotly debated as tempers flared on how the convention would frame its response to the California state legislature. In an emotional plea, J. H. Townsend, member of the State Executive Committee said in part:

> You have enacted a law, excluding our testimony in the Courts of justice of the State, in cases of proceedings wherein white persons are parties; thus openly encouraging and countenancing the vicious and dishonest to take advantage of us; a law, which while it does not advantage you, is a great wrong to us. At the same time, you freely admit the evidence of men in your midst who are ignorant of the first principles of our Government-who know not the alphabet. Many colored men, who have been educated in your first colleges, are not allowed to testify . . . People of California! We entreat you to repeal that unjust law.[12]

The arguments from the first convention were carried over to the next convention.

Second Convention

The Second Colored Convention convened December 9-12, 1856 in Sacramento. While the right to testify was testimony was still their main concern,

10. Proceedings from the *State Convention of the Colored People of California,* Sacramento, Ca., 1855, p. 5

11. California Supreme Court Section 394, dated 1862, 14th Section of the Act of April 16, 1850; italics in original.

12. Proceedings from the *First State Convention of the Colored People of California,* Sacramento, CA, 1855, p. 27

they also took up the cause for public education that excluded blacks. The summary of the California law in 1860 made it illegal for Blacks, Chinese, and Indians to attend public schools if white parents did not object.

Third Convention

The Third Colored Convention convened on October 13, 1857 at St. Cyprian's A.M.E. Church, San Francisco. Education and the right to testify, and the California poll tax, continued to be main focuses of the convention. Mifflin Gibbs and John Lester, delegates to the convention and store proprietors in San Francisco refused to pay poll taxes, which were a prerequisite to vote, yet they were discriminated against and denied the right to vote. Both Gibbs and Lester were served notice and, after refusing to pay the tax, goods were seized from their store.[13]

The second concern added the cause of the Homestead Law in California that was predatory toward blacks. Though it was legal to purchase land if a white person wanted to claim the land, the law protected the white man because a black could not testify against him.[14]

A summary of the murder of George W. Gordon, one of the leading delegates in the first two conventions as recorded by Delilah Beasley illustrate the unjust laws that violated black people in California.

> George W. Gordon sister had a millinery store in San Francisco. A White man robbed the store. Gordon's pursued him, shouting "Stop thief!" The next morning the thief came to the store and demanded an apology. Gordon was then pistol whipped and shot dead. The incident was witnessed by a fair complexion black man. His testimony was ruled out after an examination revealed his hair showed he had one-sixteenth drop of Negro blood. Mr. Fink, a white man, who owned the building of the businesses of the Gordons was also an eye witness. Had it not been for the testimony of Mr. Fink, a white man, the murderer would have been free because the testimony of blacks were not allowed in court.[15]

The Conventions provided opportunities in spaces of Black churches to raise critical concerns that affected the conditions of black people in California. They were the collective beginnings in California that forced onto

---

13. Bergman and Bergman, *The Chorological History of the Negro in America*, 213.
14. Beasley, *The Negro Trailblazers*, 60.
15. Ibid 54.

the center stage the paradox of California being a free state with oppressive laws against the state.

Black Church Beginnings

The emergence of both free black preachers and independent black Baptist congregations in the 1700s was a momentous achievement for the African slave community in America. It was the closest thing to revolutionary expression available to them.

—JAMES M. WASHINGTON

Introduction

Black church beginnings is deeply rooted in the context of slave religion that was practiced in hush harbors secretly by slaves in their quarters in the South. Religion gave the slaves hope in a dismal situation where they were treated inhumanly and considered chattel. The majority of blacks who came to California during the Gold Rush era in 1949, were accustomed to independent worship traditions. It was only natural that when blacks came to California, they did not leave behind their felt need to continue their religious styles of worship of coming together independently. As small black enclaves formed in the El Dorado Hills near the gold mines, the wheels of motion were beginning to turn to start a Black church near their community. When the time was ripe, the first Black church was birthed in California in 1850 in Sacramento, one year after the Gold Rush. The Black church is the only black-owned institution under one roof that served the black community for multiple purposes extending beyond religion. For instance, during the week, the church served as a schoolhouse, it was where politics were discussed, leaders emerged, where they taught themselves public speaking, how to debate issues. It was the place where marriages took place and the dead was buried. The Black church was the community and the community was the Black church, inseparable.

First Organized Black Church in California Saint Andrews African Methodist Church—Sacramento 1850

Though Sacramento is not located in the Bay Area, St. Andrews African Methodist Episcopal Church is the first known Black church to be organized in California in 1850, the same year California was admitted to the Union. Sacramento, the state capitol, was also located near the gold fields where a larger portion of Blacks resided. Saint Andrews was the host church for the first organized Colored Conventions. As so many early start-up churches, the home was the meeting place. A small band of believers gathered in the homes of would-be members. St. Andrews was organized in the home of Daniel Blue on I Street between 4th and 5th Streets. Initially the name of the church was Bethel AME Church and later changed to St. Andrews AME Church. The Reverend Barney Fletcher was called Reverend when the church was first organized, though he apparently was not fully ordained until later. The Reverend James Fitzgerald became the first official pastor serving from 1851–1852, followed by a series of pastors; the Reverend A. Giles served from 1852–1854. The Reverend George Fletcher served from 1853–1854. The Reverend Darius Stokes served from 1854–1856. An Elder, Thomas M D. Ward, who had strong ties as an abolitionist from back East, organized the first Sunday school and served briefly as the pastor from 1854–1856.[16]

By July 1851, this small congregation had collected $1,500 and owned a debt-free church. In 1851 the congregation was officially admitted into the denomination of the African Methodist Episcopal Church, establishing itself as the first African Methodist Episcopal Church on the Pacific Coast. The population growth for blacks in Sacramento was small, but large enough to start a church.

Mary Robinson Thames, an active member of St. Andrews, has deep family roots with the church. She is most proud that her relatives, Isaac and Elizabeth Thorn-Scott Flood, both started the first school for black children in Oakland. Most notably, her mother, Ethel Guinn, the great-great niece of Barney Fletcher, was one of the founding members of St. Andrews along with Daniel Blue. The East Lawn Cemetery in Sacramento honored Daniel Blue with a headstone acknowledging that his house served at the location for St. Andrews, and that it was the oldest African-American congregation on the Pacific Coast organized in 1850. The original site for St. Andrews was also designated as a historical institution by Sacramento County Historical

---

16. *Sacramento Historical Society Golden Notes* 11, no. 1 (1964) 26–27; and *Sacramento Bee*, November 11, 1950, 100th Anniversary.

Society on January 7, 1995. In the face of harsh discrimination, and with little resources, this small band of determined freed slaves were instrumental in starting the first Black church in California. The original 1850 wooden church building served as the meeting place for the First State Convention of the California Colored Citizens, which met November 20–22, 1855.[17]

Black Church Beginnings San Francisco

Regardless of denomination, when Negroes migrated from the South to the Pacific Coast, they needed a sacred space to keep in touch with God and each other.

San Francisco and Oakland became destination points for the first urban Black migrants. The 1880 census count shows San Francisco was the largest urban black population with 12,628, and Oakland 595. With San Francisco leading the population count for blacks coming to the Bay Area, it also became the first urban metropolitan city in the Bay Area where a Black church was organized.

Prior to the first institutionalized Black church in San Francisco, a few blacks attended the major white churches. By 1852, San Francisco had both black Methodist and Baptist churches.

St. Cyprian African Methodist Episcopal Church 1852

St. Cyprian African Methodist Episcopal Church was the first organized Black church in San Francisco (later renamed Bethel A.M.E. Church). It all started when two men, the Reverend Charles Stewart and Edward Gomez wanted a place to worship. A carpenter who was also a reverend built a small pulpit with sixteen benches and it was dedicated as the first African Methodist Church in San Francisco. The Reverend Joseph Thompson served as the first minister. With a business attitude, he ensured that Articles of Incorporation were drawn up for the church, securing the signature of the mayor, who pledged $100. The Reverend Thompson headed off to Sacramento and obtained the governor's signature and approval along with an additional $100 in gold. There is no evidence that the church expected such a great boost in money for their church. Perhaps prompted by the support of the mayor, the Reverend Thompson secured the governor's

17. Sacramento County Historical Society on January 7, 1995East Lawn Cemetery located in Sacramento, California. [N.p]; Sacramento Historical Society History of St. Andrews African Methodist Episcopal Church [n.d] [www.standrewsame.org/history accessed September 15, 2013

signature with a hefty sum of $100 in gold. With finances in hand to start a respectable church, the well-experienced and educated Reverend T. M. D. Ward was called from Philadelphia to be installed as the pastor along with the Reverend Darius Stokes who served as his assistant. Both men were abolitionists from the New England area with close ties to William L. Garrison. Two years after the church was organized on May 22, 1854, it served as the first school house for twenty-three Negro pupils in the basement of the church. At the time, children of Black, Mongolian or Indian descent were not allowed to attend schools with White children. The conditions for learning were less than adequate. In addition to the lack of heat, or proper ventilation, children ranging from elementary to high school age shared the same room with no books. Discrimination and segregation coupled with economic hardships made for dark days for these early pioneers. Nevertheless, the members were doing their best with their modest means. In spite of the situation, St. Cyprian Church was a spiritual, cultural, and educational beacon in the community. It was not until 1875 that the practice of segregated schools was eliminated. Though the early years proved to be unsettling as the church moved to numerous locations, Reverend T. M. D. Ward reorganized the church into a middle-class church without the shouting and frenzy of uncontrolled emotions. Being called middle-class was a status symbol that made the members feel proud of themselves, including those who were lower-class without middle-class income. Somehow, when they all came together, they were united as one. The congregation managed to raise $5,500 and relocated to a more prestigious location known as Grace (or Powell Street). With less than one hundred members, the congregation managed to become debt free in 1864, and started a rigorous campaign to renovate and remodel the church. William P. Powell Sr., a well-known abolitionist from New York, visited St. Cyprian and was impressed, commenting, "Well, I never! In all my travels saw the like-colored worshipers *rung* to church and *belled* to prayers."[18]

The Reverend Ward eventually left San Francisco in the South and was elevated to Bishop in 1868. By now St. Cyprian was well established. Some members of the AME Zion Church had joined St. Cyprian and, at some point, a power struggle ensued causing conflict that led to a church split. The majority of the members left and started another church, naming it Pilgrim AME Church. The Reverend Jeremiah Burke Sanderson, who had worked closely with the Reverend Ward as abolitionists in the New England area became the next pastor of Pilgrim AME and served as the schoolmaster.

18. Daniels, *Pioneer Urbanites*, pp 118, 119.

Union Bethel African Methodist Episcopal Church

In 1862, Little Pilgrim A.M. E. Church was renamed to Union Bethel African Methodist Episcopal Church and dedicated August 10, 1862. Union Bethel A.M.E. Church continued to grow, and the California Conference of the African Methodist Episcopal Church was held on April 6, 1865 at the Powell Street location. Not much is known about Union Bethel after its initial renaming. Bishop Ward returned to San Francisco and gave an impressive speech at Union Bethel titled "The Aspects, Prospects and Retrospect's of the Negro Race" on the occasion of the anniversary of the Emancipation Proclamation. Bishop T. M. D. Ward was one of the most celebrated race men during his time. He was called from labor to reward June 10, 1894, leaving an outstanding legacy as a race man during his time. Union Bethel suffered severe damage from the 1906 San Francisco earthquake. Fortunately, the church was renovated and held services ready for opening service only three months later, July 15, 1906, with the Reverend A. A. Burleigh serving as pastor. By now, the majority of the members had relocated to Oakland. Elias Hochstadter of San Francisco died April 8, 1890 and left a trust $100,000 in gold to establish a fund as an incentive for all Negro children of the public schools of San Francisco to achieve higher education. Between the years of 1906–1944, little written history is recorded. By the early 1940s, the Second Great Migration was in full bloom. On January 21, 1945 the Reverend C. D. Tolliver was installed as Pastor. With the influx of migrants, the church grew. After remaining on Powell Street for eighty-four years, the Reverend Tolliver led the church in relocating to 916 Laguna Street, and within six months the mortgage was burned and a new parsonage was purchased. After a while the church was renamed Bethel African Methodist Episcopal Church

Bethel African Methodist Episcopal Church

Fast forward to the years of 1968–1972:

> [U]nder the administration of Reverend J. Austell Hall, a new sanctuary and an education building were built. The church sponsored a federally funded housing unit; Freedom West. The Reverend Cecil Whitney Howard was assigned to Bethel and continued to build the church to involve all age groups in all aspects of the church's life. A new era was ushered in in 1992 when Reverend J. Edgar Boyd was assigned to Bethel in 1992. Among the many programs were the Endowment Fund, the

Allen Investment Club, the Allen Community Development Corporation and the Young African American Achievers Project. The Reverend Edgar Boyd was transferred to First AME Church, Los Angeles, leaving an impeccable record. [19]

Because of the itinerant process in the AME denomination, numerous ministers occupy the pulpits. Throughout the history of Bethel AME church, the pulpit has been graced by numerous influential social activists: Ida B. Wells, the Reverend Adam Clayton Powell Sr., W. E. Dubois, Paul Robertson, Mary McLeod Bethune, Booker T. Washington, Weldon Johnson, and others were among the many outstanding speakers who visited Bay Area Black churches and spoke on racism. One of the outstanding pioneer speakers to come to San Francisco was Bishop Benjamin W. Arnett, who had the occasion to visit Bethel A.M.E. church. *The San Francisco Chronicle* reported on September 12, 1900 that Bishop Arnett gave a stirring sermon/speech appealing to the Negroes to have racial pride, never being shameful of their color. In part he said: "You are probably not aware of the fact, but it is true, that the majority of mankind belongs to the darker races. It is no cause for shame that you are as God made you, and not white as some of your brothers. It is rather an honor . . . Be proud of the fact that you belong to your race. With the three books of power, the Bible, the spelling-book, and the bankbook, we will press forward and take our rightful place in the history of the world."[20]

Though Bishop Arnett did not serve in the ministry at Bethel A.M.E. Church, he left an indelible impression in San Francisco at the Bethel A.M.E. Church when he urged the hearers to work, fight and press on. Bishop Arnett was called from labor to reward in 1906.

First African Methodist Episcopal Zion Church—1852

John Jamison Moore was born a slave in 1818 in West Virginia. In August 1852, the Reverend Moore was living in San Francisco and founded the A.M.E. Zion Church in San Francisco located on Stockton Street between Broadway and Vallejo Streets and remained there until the 1906 earthquake destroyed the building. Early documentation of the church is scanty. The building had a value of around $4000, fifty pupils, and an extensive library for a small church. Reverend Moore served as chaplain at the first Colored

19. Bethel African Methodist Episcopal Church [n.d.] [n.pag]
20. *San Francisco Chronicle*, September 12, 1900

Convention of California, and was also one of the school organizers at St Cyprian before he founded the Zion AME Church.

In 1864, the church purchased property owned by Reverend Thomas Starr King Church and became known as the Star King Methodist (Zion) Church. In additional to meeting spiritual needs, Reverend Moore pointed the church toward the direction of social activism, education and political sustenance.[21]

Following the Reverend Moore's departure, a series of ministers pastored the church. Without leadership the church struggled for survival until 1918 when the Reverend J. J. Byers became pastor. The Reverend Byers had the awesome responsibility to repair whatever damage had been done during the struggling years and move forward in rebuilding the church.

Reverend Byers brought a leadership style that focused on social justice. He was known as a race man, social activist, and was one of the founders of the First Colored Convention of California and helped to establish the Booker T. Washington Community Center in San Francisco for teens and young adults. Byers's leadership style paid off, as the church moved into the category of a middle-class church. The Reverend Magruder succeeded the Reverend Byers after his departure in 1926. Byers, Magruder, and Dr. Frederick Haynes were pillars of strength in the community, laboring for social justice. Magruder remained until he was called from labor to reward in 1941.

During the Second Great Migration, the Reverend H. B. Gantt became the guiding force for integrating the two classes of people in the church: newcomers with the pioneers. He had to walk a tight rope to appease both groups. On one hand, the pioneers were considered the more refined middle-class group, showing less emotions. On the other hand, the migrants mostly belonged to the status of the lower-class group. They were prone to shouting all over the place because they were so happy to have made it to California.

A major shift occurred during the late 1940s, when the Fillmore district, where the church was located on Geary St. was designated for redevelopment. By the early to mid-60s, redevelopment had displaced the Black community leaving the ugly scars that impacted the community socially and economically. The Reverend Dr. Roy L. Bennett served from 1956 to 1965. During his tenure he had the responsibility of relocating the church.

21. Beasley, *The Negro Trail Blazers of California*, 160. A compilation of records from the California Archives in the Bancroft Library at the University of California, in Berkeley; and from the Diaries, Old Papers, and conversations of Old Pioneers in the State of California. It is a True Record of Facts, as they pertain to the history of the pioneer and present-day Negroes of California.

A new church building was erected in 1960 at 2159 Golden Gate Avenue in San Francisco.[22] ·

Third Baptist Church 1852

Third Baptist Church was first established under the name as the First Colored Baptist Church of San Francisco in August 1852 in the home of William and Eliza Davis on Kearney Street. Seven other devout followers were among the original organizers: Abraham Brown, Thomas Bundy, Thomas Davenport, Willie Denton, Harry Fields, George Lewis, and Fielding Spots.[23]

In 1854, the First Colored Baptist Church purchased the old First Baptist Church and moved it to a location on Dupont Street, between Greenwich and Filbert Streets. James W. Capen was the first Pastor, serving in an interim position from 1852 to 1856. In 1855, First Colored changed its name to Third Baptist Church and its legal name was not changed until 1908. Between 1852 and 1856, the church suffered greatly without a pastor—supply ministers, mostly white, conducted services in the homes of members. This arrangement changed in 1856 with the arrival of the first African-American Pastor, the Reverend Charles Satchell of Cincinnati, Ohio, a graduate of Oberlin College and a leader of the Abolitionist Movement, who pastored the church from 1856 to 1860. Shortly after Reverend Satchell's arrival, he came up with a creative way to increase membership by baptizing in the bay. Two years later, the church had lost all but thirty-one members due to blacks heading to British Columbia to strike it rich in the Fraser River Gold Rush. To make matters worse, the dynamic Reverend Satchell had also left.[24]

The gold-rush fever lasted only two years and, happily for the church, with the return of blacks, membership increased. A lot was purchased at Bush and Powell Streets from the sale of the building and a new church was dedicated March 14, 1869 under the leadership of the Reverend J. H. Kelly. Misfortune stalked the church once again when the 1906 earthquake destroyed the church leaving a vacant lot and very few members. The lot was eventually sold and a new church edifice was built for $49,000. Slowly, the church began to draw membership and officially changed its name in 1908 to reflect its emergence as the third communion of Baptists founded in San Francisco, and to attract members as a nonracial church.[25]

22. First African Methodist Episcopal Church, history document, www.firstamezionsf.org (accessed September 15, 2013).

23. *Third Baptist Church 150 Anniversary Book*, 2.

24. Lapp, *Blacks in Gold Rush California*, 161–62.

25. Third Baptist Church 150 *Historical Highlights* 150th Anniversary, p. 2. Many

It was not until the highly motivated and charismatic Dr. Frederick Douglas Haynes Sr. came to Third Baptist August 29, 1932 that the church began to have stability in leadership; he held the position as pastor for nearly four decades. Dr. Haynes Sr., an activist, led the church into the trenches of social justice and became a major voice for the black community. His no-nonsense style of not biting his tongue had a way of making city hall feel uneasy. While the Great Depression was having a negative effect overall in society, Tabitha Anderson, the first black female attorney to practice law in San Francisco and branch president of the NAACP, died unexpectedly; the funeral was hosted at Third Baptist with large numbers of friends paying tribute to one of the most outstanding young Negro women on the Pacific Coast.[26] Tensions between the races were high during the Great Migration Years. On May 23, 1940, the northern section of the California State Association of Colored Women sponsored a lively debate on how the freedom of the press was abusive and should be stopped. Mrs. Bertha Peoples, chairman of Ways and Means for the State, was in charge of the debate. At the conclusion of the debate, a social was held for the cast of *Show Boat*, which played at the Curran Theater during the week.[27]

With the Great Migration bringing thousands to the Bay Area, and the reputation that Dr. Haynes Sr. had earned as a voice crying in the wilderness, it was not surprising that the membership swelled to over twenty-five hundred. On October 21, 1952, the Reverend Haynes led the congregation from the Hyde and Clay Streets site to the new edifice at 1399 McAllister Street. In 1956, the youth building was erected.

The Reverend E. J. Magruder, Pastor of First AME Zion Church, the Reverend Jesse L. Boyd, Pastor of Bethel AME Church, the Reverend F. D. Haynes, Pastor, Third Baptist Church, the Reverend C. Jones Roberts, Pastor Emmanuel Gospel Mission, and the Reverend V. D. Jenkins were among the Ministerial Alliance, a coalition of prominent ministers in San Francisco who advocated for social justice and equality. Together, they sponsored a Negro Day program for July 25, 1940 at Treasure Island.[28]

In 1947, Dr. Haynes became the first African American to run for the Board of Supervisors. With all of his political clout and connections, he was

---

of the churches did not chronicle their history with specificity. When I went to the churches, I was given documents with no dates and no page numbers. For that reason, sources appear at times incomplete—unfortunately, when it comes to black history, much of it comes to us through oral narratives.

26. Wysinger, *Activities among Negroes*, July 21, 1935.

27. Lena Wysinger, *Oakland Tribune Activities Among Negroes*, June 2, 1940

28. Ibid, June 23, 1940

defeated. For eight years, Haynes served as president of the California State Baptist Convention and chairman of the National Baptist Convention.[29]

Under the Reverend Haynes Sr.'s, driving dedication to social justice, Third Baptist Church was the first West Coast religious institution in the black community to welcome to its podium after his split with the NAACP the great Dr. W.E.B. DuBois, on the occasion of celebrating his ninetieth birthday; moreover, the sanctuary of Third Baptist was made available to Dr. and Mrs. DuBois for lectures whenever they were in the area. Dr. Haynes was called from labor to reward in February 1971.[30]

The San Francisco Examiner recorded even the balcony was jammed with people at the home-going celebration; when Mahalia Jackson began singing. "I'll be listening for my name," the mostly middle-aged congregation urged her "come on, come on, sing out."

The Reverend Frederick Douglas Haynes Jr., son of Reverend Frederick Sr., succeeded his father as pastor on June 25, 1972. Following in his father's footsteps, however, with a mind of his own, Reverend Haynes Jr. established his ministry on three principles: 1) a learning church, 2) a stewardship church, and 3) an evangelical church. After serving only three short years as Pastor, Reverend Dr. Frederick Haynes Jr. was unexpectedly called from labor to reward on September 3, 1975, creating a serious void in the greater Bay Area.

A new era of leadership was ushered in on September 19, 1976, when Dr. Amos C. Brown, was installed as pastor of the church. Among the many dignitaries to attend the installation for Dr. Brown included the late Reverend Dr. Gardner C. Taylor (Concord Baptist Church, New York), who was the installation speaker. Other participants included Rev. Dr. J. Alfred Smith Sr. (Allen Temple Baptist Church), the Honorable Edmund G. Brown Jr. (Governor, State of California), the Honorable Congressman Phillip Burton, the late Honorable George R Moscone, to name a few.[31]

Dr. Brown has earned the distinction as a social justice activist preacher, scholar, theologian, and pastor. Dr. Brown's commitment to the spiritual, educational, and political dimensions of the gospel are reflected in his spirited Civil Rights activism. Two years after his installation, the church had a fully accredited summer school in 1978. Dr. Brown established an African Refugee Resource Center that has settled over two thousand five hundred refugees. Dr. Brown, a visionary with a bent toward social justice

29. Broussard *Black San Francisco* (Kansas: University Press, 1993), p 237

30. *Sun Reporter* Newspaper, Editorials A Tribute to Rev. F. D. Haynes March 6, 1971.

31. Installation Program, Reverend Amos Brown, September 19, 1976, Third Baptist Church. San Francisco. Third Baptist Church Brief History.

established the Charles Albert Tindley Academy of Music. Another first for Dr. Brown was the ordination of women to preach and to serve on the deacons' ministry (note not a deaconess). Third Baptist Church was granted historical landmark number 1010 by the California Historical Society at Grant and Greenwich Streets.[32] Dr. Brown serves as president of the San Francisco NAACP.

A glance backwards shows San Francisco was led by strong Black leaders who clearly understood the necessity for developing racial pride. With odds stacked against them, such as the denial of voting rights, public education, and racial discrimination, these early pioneer race leaders fought against racial injustices, race pride, and racial solidarity. Notably, prior to the Emancipation Proclamation, three black churches had been organized in the Bay Area, Bethel AME, First Zion AME, and Third Baptist.

Black Church Beginnings: Oakland

Oakland was incorporated on May 4, 1852, and, by 1860, the city was designated as the western terminal for the Transcontinental Railroad. Oakland was more attractive to Blacks than San Francisco because of employment opportunities. The income of blacks in the late 1800s brought the attention of the local newspaper with this headline:

> On October 10, 1889, the *Oakland Enquirer Newspaper* headline read: COLORED CITIZENS- about Five Hundred of Them in Oakland. An Estimate that they own $200,000 of Property— Their Religion and Social Affiliations. Oakland was a growing community for black people. The Colored people of Oakland, as a whole, are fairly progressive, some are very substantial citizens. It has been estimated that $200,000 worth of property in this city is held by colored men, which is a good showing. Colored people are naturally religious-far more in the average than white people . . . the majority belong to or attend some church. They have only one church of their own, the African Methodist Church on Fifteenth Street. A majority of the colored inhabitants of Oakland live in the Second, Fourth and Seventh wards. They have several fraternal and benevolent organizations, including a lodge of the United Order of Odd Fellows.[33]

According to the U. S. Census of 1860, Oakland's population was 1,543. It is unclear if blacks were part of the census count; if so, they accounted

32. Brown, *Third Baptist Church 150th Church Anniversary.*

33. *Oakland Enquirer* Newspaper October 10, 1889

for nearly one-third of the citizens. While it is not clear why the Enquirer headlined the income and census of Coloreds living in Oakland, it could have been a signal that a change was on the horizon. Shortly thereafter racial covenants restricting where blacks and Asians could live soon started to appear.

Blacks in Oakland figured prominently in the fine arts of music. Professor Elmer Keeton came to Oakland from St. Louis in 1922 and established music camps offering piano and voice lessons. Black churches often hosted concerts. Beasley wrote, "The colored citizens of Oakland can be justly proud of the fact Professor Keeton, a graduate of Northwestern University is a credit to their institution and to his race."[34] Individual churches would render special Christmas programs such as "The Nativity at First AME" and a sacred cantata given by the Golden Gate Choral Club at Market Street Seventh Day Adventist Church.

First African Methodist Episcopal Church

> The First African Methodist Episcopal Church was the first Black Church established in Oakland in 1858. Isaac and Elizabeth Flood, John and Hettie Peterson, William Harper, and others came together to form the first all-black church, an African Methodist Episcopal mission in Oakland. The Flood's had connections with the first black church established in Sacramento; St. Andrews A.M.E. Church. The church was formally designated a mission since it had no pastor and met in the homes of members on a rotating basis; at times itinerant pastors would preside over the services.[35]

FAME was the only Black church in Oakland organized prior to the signing of the Emancipation Proclamation.

In 1862, the Reverend Barney Fletcher, one of the founders of the St. Andrews AME Church in Sacramento in 1850 presided as minister of the Oakland A. M. E. Mission Church less than a year. Following Reverend Fletcher's short term, Abraham Gross became the preacher at the Oakland A.M.E. Mission. His objective was to transform the mission into a full-fledged church. Due to its rapid growth, the location soon became inadequate and the Carpenter School House, Oakland's first school building was purchased and the church was relocated to West and 7th Streets, where it became known as the Shiloh A. M. E. Church. In 1862, the Reverend

34. Delilah Beasley, "Activities among Negroes," *Oakland Tribune*, May 11, 1924
35. Hausler, *Blacks in Oakland*, 8.

Abraham Gross became the pastor of the Shiloh A. M. E. Church. According to church historian Eleanora Amos, in 1863, the same year that the Proclamation Emancipation was signed, the mission officially became a church and received the name Shiloh. John Lane served as the first pastor of the Shiloh church. For a period of sixteen years, the church was conducted by laymen and local preachers. The Reverend Jeremiah Sanderson, an abolitionist from the New England area wasted no time utilizing his activism skills when he moved to California. He was one of the delegates for the First Colored Convention of California, worked fiercely to desegregate schools in California and served as pastor for a brief period. His untimely death occurred in 1875 while returning home from a prayer meeting and was struck by a train. Mary Sanderson Grasses was the first public school teacher in Oakland.

After the death of the Reverend Sanderson, the Reverend James Grisby came from the Midwest to become the pastor. Under the Reverend Grisby's able leadership, the church expanded and moved to the building located on 15th Street between Market and West Streets and was dedicated in March 1884. The church became known as the Fifteenth Street Church because of its location. Extensive remodeling was completed under the leadership of the Reverend O. E. Jones.

The Reverend O. E. Jones was a dynamic leader. It was not unusual for congregations in Oakland and San Francisco to fiercely recruit the Reverend Jones to their churches. The Reverend Jones was educated at Wilberforce University for a teaching career, taught public school in Kentucky, and attended Payne Theological Seminary at Wilberforce where he later taught theology. Coming to Oakland's Frist A. M. E. Church on 15th Street, he soon proved himself to be an eloquent preacher. The Reverend Jones served 1900–1910. In 1915, the First A. M. E. Church conducted revival services after heartily advertising the appearance of the Reverend Lena Mason of Philadelphia as the Greatest Woman Evangelist.[36] First A. M. E. emphasized family consciousness by hosting a Father and Son Day on November 16, 1915, with special short talks. An appeal was presented on behalf of Meharry Medical College and hospital by Dr. Jones, a local physician.[37] FAME was a leading church in many areas of the community. The colored Masonic lodges and chapters of the Eastbay cities met at FAME to become incorporated and build a Masonic Temple for the race in Oakland.[38]

36. McBroome, *Parallel Communities,* 37.

37. Delilah Beasley, Activities among Negroes, *Oakland Tribune,* Nov. 22, 1924.

38. Ibid., December 23, 1925.

In 1949, which marked the beginning of the Progressive Regime, the Reverend Dr. H. Solomon Hill was among the ministers who served and contributed to the wide popularity of the church. Under his leadership and forward thinking, the Reverend Hill was instrumental in moving the congregation to its present location at 37th Street and Telegraph Avenue, Oakland. A series of ministers followed the Reverend Hill including the Reverend Frederick O. Murph who served from 1986–1996.

On Sunday October 5, 1996, a new era was ushered in with the appointment of the Reverend Dr. Harold R. Mayberry. His motto was: "God is Our Father, Christ is our Redeemer, and Man is our Brother," initiating a program that encouraged men to serve as priest, provider, and protector of the church, home, and community. Dr. Mayberry wasted no time in reestablishing First African Methodist Episcopal Church as a church for the community. Numerous outreach ministries serving the community include Adopt-a-Family, Single & Couples' Ministry, Health Ministry, Commission on Social Action, a Tutorial program, among many others. Dr. Mayberry's political involvement has established FAME as a meeting place for politicians and community leaders.[39] Dr. Harold Mayberry is one of the leading social justice pastors in the Bay Area.[40]

Beth Eden Baptist Church

The second Black church to emerge in Oakland started as a prayer band in the home of Henry and Sarah Homager at 763 7th Street, Oakland on February 17, 1889. One year later, the Reverend Washington Gray became the first pastor. The Reverend Gray had a down-home southern style of preaching that attracted a few members from FAME to join Beth Eden. The Reverend Gray's strong personality led to disagreements and he left to start a new church named Ebenezer Missionary Baptist Church that lasted from 1890 to 1894 On October 15, 1891, Beth Eden Baptist Church incorporated in Alameda County when it filed its Articles of Incorporation with the State of California. Oakland's population swelled from 1,543 in 1860 to 48,682 in 1890. In that same year the church became a part of the Central Baptist Association as the church experienced rapid growth. The Reverend Robert Alexander McGuinn served briefly followed by the Reverend James L. Allen (later founded the Allen Temple Baptist Church). The Reverend Allen came from El Paso, Texas and remained pastor of Beth Eden for six years until he

39. Oakland Public Library, History Room, *First A. M.E. Church History 140*[th] *Year Anniversary 1858–1998.*

40. Ibid.

relocated to Oregon. Following the Reverend James L. Allen, the Reverends John W. Dwelle, John Allen, and J. A. Dennis all served for brief periods of time. The Reverend Dennis resigned after serving one year to become the pastor of North Oakland Baptist Church.[41] Beth Eden earned its reputation as the "Mother Church" because the Reverends Allen and Dennis both founded other black Baptist churches in Oakland.

In 1921, after a vigorous pastoral search, the Reverend J. P. Hubbard (Mt. Zion Baptist Church, Clarksburg, West Virginia), was appointed pastor and the church soon expanded into a middle-class status church. The Great Depression left the members struggling to survive as a church family. Beth Eden became a feeding location to help give people food and shelter, with the women playing a significant role. Beasley reported on the celebration of Beth Eden purchasing a new and elegant church home, under the leadership of Pastor Hubbard.[42] In 1899, women of Beth Eden founded the Fanny Jackson Coppin Club, also known as the Mother Club of the black women's club movement in the state. The women were not just socialites, they helped to build a strong community. The club raised building funds, organized musical and literary programs, and performed a variety of service projects.[43] To further the growth of the church, in 1925, the Young Women's Progressive Club was organized to lend assistance to the church.

As the church continued to grow, a new church site was secured in August 1925 at 10th & Magnolia Streets, the present home location for Beth Eden. In 1935, a parsonage was purchased and the upper floor of the church was converted into two apartments. Members who needed living quarters could seek aid in the church-owned property on 14th Street in Oakland. In a similar manner, young women were welcomed to the Beth Eden Women's Mission Home on Adeline Street. On April 21, 1940, Wysinger reported in *Negroes in the News* that the National Baptist Convention, Inc., Dr. L. K. Williams arrived in Metropolitan Oakland Wednesday evening for a weekend conclave. More than fifty race leaders came from every part of the United States, Africa, and the Bahamas. After a sightseeing trip around the Bay Area, Wednesday night, hundreds of church people and friends met at the Beth Eden Baptist Church, led by the Reverend J. P. Hubbard. The objective of the convention is to encourage Christian activities and to extend the mortgage burning campaign of the National Baptist Convention USA, Inc., which was celebrating its sixtieth anniversary, September 4–8, 1940 in Birmingham, Alabama.

41. Beth Eden Baptist Church Centennial 1990 p 48
42. Delilah Beasley, "Activities among Negroes," *Oakland Tribune*, March 1, 1925.
43. Crouchett et al., *Visions toward Tomorrow*, 14.

By 1945, the population in Oakland had climbed to 400,935. The Reverend Hubbard left an indelible impression on the community and church before being called from labor to reward in 1955, after serving thirty-four years. In 1956 the Reverend Alvin Chester Dones was called as pastor. At the time, the Reverend Dones was sixty-three years old. Some members of the pulpit selection committee believed the Reverend Dones was too old to pastor and filed a lawsuit attempting to stop his installation. The Alameda County Superior Court ruled that the Reverend Dones could be pastor. Some disgruntled members of the pulpit selection were not pleased with the ruling and left the church to form the Church of the Good Shepherd in North Oakland. Beth Eden continued to prosper as debts were paid, and church plant improvements were accomplished. The most noteworthy accomplishment during that time was the formation of the Beth Eden Housing Corporation. The Reverend Dones retired in 1971.[44]

A new era was ushered in when the Reverend Dr. Gillette O. James, who had served as Assistant Pastor for about a year, accepted the call as pastor in March 1971. Under Dr. James's leadership, Beth Eden continued to be a stalwart church of the community. In 1982, a new sanctuary was built costing two million dollars. Various women within the Beth Eden church family took the lead and were instrumental in the church's summer lunch program that serves the needs of children and youth in the area. Beth Eden had also contributed money to a mission church in Antigua, West Indies. Beth Eden has been widely known for involving women in various community leadership roles. Women took the lead in developing women's clubs and were very involved in community development surrounded around social, economic, and political concerns.[45]

On April 13, 2000, the Honorable Congresswoman Barbara Lee in the House of Representatives honored Beth Eden Baptist Church in its 110th Anniversary, saying, "For more than a century, Beth Eden has been a West Oakland landmark of faith, activity and commitment to building a stronger community."[46]

Downs Memorial Methodist Episcopal Church

Downs Memorial Methodist Episcopal Church grew out of the Golden Gate Methodist Episcopal Church Oakland in 1890 at the corner of 59th

44. *Beth Eden Baptist Church Centennial History Book*, 51.

45. Ibid., 51.

46. Honorable Barbara Lee of California, in the House of Representatives, Congressional Record—Extensions of Remarks E562, April 13, 2000.

and Gaskill Streets under the direction of Dr. E. R. Dill and ministered by the Reverend Frank Baker. With the influx of thousands of Blacks migrating from the South to the Bay Area in the 1940s, Whites were leaving the city and abandoning their churches. In 1946, Golden Gate Methodist Episcopal Church, originally a White church, closed due to declining membership after almost sixty years. With the increase of blacks coming to the Bay Area, the Reverend Warren was certain that Golden Gate Methodist would be a wonderful site for a church to house the new immigrants. He petitioned Bishop James Baker to re-open Golden Gate Methodist Episcopal Church. As a result, the Reverend John Doggett, a civil rights activist was appointed Pastor and served from 1942 to 1949. In 1948, the church was renamed Downs Memorial Methodist Church in memory of Dr. Karl Downs, a young black Methodist minister who served as the pastor of Scotts Methodist Church in Pasadena, California and was known for being outspoken as an activist, and for his work in reconciliation between the races. Following the Reverend Doggett, the Revered Roy C. Nichols was appointed pastor by the bishop in May 1949.[47]

The Reverend Nichols was the right person for the time when the Bay Area was shifting in political climate. The Reverend Nichols was well educated with degrees from Lincoln University in Pennsylvania and a full scholarship to attend the Pacific School of Religion in Berkeley. Before his assignment at Downs, he was asked to start a church in South Berkeley. The rapid growth of the church placed extra demands on Pastor Nichols; he dropped out of school for three years and eventually received his Master's of Divinity in 1947. In the meantime he married Dr. Ruth Richardson, a podiatrist, and together they had two children. Emphasis is placed on Dr. Roy Nichols mainly because so much of the history of the church was recorded during his era.

Two years later Nichols was given command of Downs Memorial Church, originally an all-white pastorate strangled by a changing neighborhood with only eighteen members. In addition to the demand of being a pastor, Nichols was deeply involved in local politics and the greater community. He chaired the education committee of the Berkeley chapter of the National Association for the Advancement of Colored People and became president of the Berkeley School Board in the early 1960s. He ran for Berkeley City Council and lost. Two years later he was elected to the Berkeley Board of Education and, in 1963, was elected its president.[48] During Nichols

47. Downs Memorial United Methodist Church, http://downsmumc.org/About.html (accessed Jan. 11, 2014).

48. *Oakland Tribune* Newspaper July, 1964.

era as pastor, the church was the host to numerous NAACP meetings and community forums. Reverend Nichols was articulate and commanded the attention of civic leaders while numerous pastors in the area also looked to him for advice and direction.

Sunday, July 5, 1964 ended the era for Roy Nichols as pastor of Downs after twenty-three years. The Reverend Nichols was called to Salem United Methodist Church, New York, and the first African American elected Bishop in the United Methodist Church. He was called from labor to reward October 9, 2002.[49]

The Reverend Amos Cambric Jr. served as pastor from 1964 to 1967. Under his leadership the Gospel Choir was organized, and the Mrs. Marion Downs (widow of Karl Downs) appeared twice in concert. The Reverend Cambric worked tirelessly on the War on Poverty Program as Oakland had been declared a depressed area eligible for government funding. The Reverend Cambric was transferred and the Reverend Charles H. Belcher was appointed from 1967 to 1971. During this period, the Black Panther Party was organized and the Civil Rights Movement was impacting the entire United States. At the 1968 Conference in Dallas, Texas, Downs Memorial Methodist Episcopal Church was renamed Downs Memorial United Methodist Church to conform to the uniting of the Methodist Church and the Evangelical United Brethren Church. The church was successful in paying off the mortgage in 1971.

Following the Reverend Belcher, the Reverend Charles H. Lee Sr. was appointed to Downs from 1971 to 1987. During November 9–11, 1980, the congregation celebrated the completion of Phase Two and Three of the Expansion and Development program. Significant during this period was the ordination of the Reverend Dorothy Williams as the first black woman pastor in the California Nevada Annual Conference. The Reverend Williams served as associate pastor of Downs from 1982 to 1985. The Reverend Douglass E. Fitch Sr. was appointed to Downs from 1987 to 1999. Under his leadership Downs experienced tremendous growth. Alma Berry accepted her call into ministry and was ordained a deacon in 1992. The Reverend Berry was later ordained as a minister and appointed as pastor of Ridge Point United Methodist Church in San Francisco.

The Reverend Kelvin Sauls served as pastor from 1999 to 2006. Under his dynamic leadership, the church continued to grow and was involved in local, national and international ministries. Much of the Reverend Saul's drive and compassion for the outcast and oppressed has roots in his experiences growing up in Johannesburg and participating in the student

49. "Bishop Nichols Remembered," *Berkeley Daily Planet*, October 18, 2002.

movement against the nation's policy of racial segregation. Sauls said, "Fighting for accessibility to quality education is what got me up every day." During the spring of 2003, senior affordable housing was built in partnership with Downs Community Development Corporation. The housing was named for the long time pastor, Bishop Roy C. Nichols.[50]

The Reverend Lorraine McNeal was appointed to Downs in 2006 as the first woman to become Senior Pastor of the church. This was a time of great change and transition. Today Downs continues to work in collaboration with sister Methodist Churches in the areas of leadership development and spiritual formation. Downs Memorial Methodist Church continues to be a beacon of light in the local community and beyond.[51]

Greater Cooper A. M. E. Zion Church, Oakland

The first African Methodist Episcopal Zion Church in Oakland was established circa 1897–1899 in a vacant storehouse for three dollars a month rent as a mission. Founding members W. C. Morrison, George Watkins, Mrs. Tobe Williams, and Mrs. Elizabeth Kyles served on the committee to locate a facility that was on Campbell Street in Oakland. The building fund raising efforts fell short of money and members of the A. M. E. Zion Church, along with Mr. Ezekiel Cooper of the A. M. E. Zion church, loaned them the balance to purchase the church. With no regular pastor, local ministers were invited to minister. The church moved to different locations, because the stores where they met were always being sold out from under them.

In 1900, Bishop Walters appointed the Reverend C. B. T. Moore as the first pastor. His tenure was brief because of poor health. After Moore left, in 1902, former pastor of Beth Eden the Reverend S. W. Hawkins was appointed pastor and remained until June 1904.[52] In the meanwhile the loan to the Coopers was still outstanding. In lieu of the loan being paid off, Mr. Cooper requested that the church carry his last name. The church was renamed Cooper AME Zion Church.

Cooper AME Zion served as a meeting place for numerous organizations including the Oakland NAACP, which held its annual meeting at Zion and encouraged the attendees to subscribe to *Crisis* Magazine, the official magazine for the NAACP founded by W. E. DuBois in 1910. The church also hosted the Attucks Club's twelfth anniversary on June 9, 1935. Pastor

50. Downs Memorial Methodist Episcopal Church History Anniversary.

51. Ibid.

52. Souvenir Program Golden Anniversary History of the Greater Cooper A.M.E. Zion Church, p. 1.

Lankford gave a speech titled "Negroes as I Have Known Them." [53] It was not unusual for the church and organizations that believed in fighting all kinds of segregation to band together for racial pride discussions. Cooper was growing in size just before the Great Depression, and so the church sold its Campbell Street location to a Baptist Congregation and Cooper A.M.E. Zion relocated to a church on Union Street, between 8th and 9th streets in Oakland. The Union Street church was almost three times as large as the Campbell Street location.

During the war years, the population for Blacks tripled in size, resulting in a housing shortage. To accommodate housing needs, the Federal Housing Authority condemned portions of West Oakland, including the Cooper A.M.E. Zion Church on Union Street and paid the congregation a sum of $17,000. The Members purchased a building at 1420 Myrtle Street and paid for it in full. With the remaining funds, the congregation purchased property at 1925, 1927, and 1929 Filbert Street and assumed a mortgage for the balance. Shortly thereafter, the sanctuary was badly damaged by fire of incendiary origin. After much hard work, the sanctuary was restored to its original beauty.[54]

In 1944, Bishop Brown appointed the Reverend G. Linwood Fauntleroy as Pastor of Cooper A.M.E. Zion Church. Much joy was felt, for here we had finally secured the man that was much needed on the Coast: he was young, energetic, extremely talented in music, and had a family who shared with him his musical abilities. Through the Reverend Fauntleroy's musical leadership, Cooper created musical programs that attracted migrants. The Reverend Fauntleroy transformed Cooper from a staid, sleep church into a vital, growing institution. The church was completely renovated including a lounge, new furniture, five hundred new chairs, a new Hammond organ, and amplified chimes including sound system—all paid in full. Under the Reverend Fauntleroy's superb direction as a director and arranger of music the Cathedral Choir was organized, and has reached such prominence that the Choir is rated among the best in the State of California. Dozens of concerns given here and throughout the Bay Area have drawn thousands of music lovers, who are interested in the higher type of church music, and its efforts have been responsible for several thousands of dollars raised for the church. The church has grown, to become one of the most benevolent churches in the East Bay area. Following the Reverend Fauntleroy, a number

53. Beasley, "Activities among Negroes," *Oakland Tribune*, December 2, 1923.
54. Wysinger "Activities Among Negroes," *Oakland Tribune*, April 14, 1940.

of ministers pastored Cooper. The Reverend Mark A. Thomas assumed the position of pastor in 2012.[55]

North Oakland Baptist Church

In 1904, North Oakland Baptist Church was organized in the home of Mr. and Mrs. Richard Clark Brother on Myrtle Street, Oakland. The church was first known as Richard Clark Memorial and later North Oakland Church of Christ before it was finally named North Oakland Missionary Baptist Church. With the increase of membership, the Clarks donated a lot to build the first church. The Reverend James A. Dennis who previously served as pastor of Beth Eden Baptist Church was called to be the first pastor of North Oakland. Under his leadership, the first church building was completed on 29th Street, and was known as the North Oakland Church of Christ. The Reverend Dennis served from 1905 to 1908 followed by the Reverends C. X. Laws, Davis, and Brown.

In 1913, the Reverend Dr. G. C. Coleman of Washington D.C. was elected pastor of North Oakland Church. Dr. Coleman was educated, and his presence brought dignity to the church and greater community. Dr. Coleman fit the definition of what was known as a race man throughout the Black community. "If a man fights for his race, if he seems to be all for the race, if he is fearless in his approach to white people, he becomes a race hero."[56] As a result, race men and women from around the country were often guest speakers at North Oakland.

Dr. Coleman organized The National Baptist Association of Northern California with five churches in its membership. Its first annual financial report was $54.00; at the fifth annual session it was $700. The Association was known distinctively for conducting church affairs and controlling its church property. On October 18, 1922, at the North Oakland Baptist Church,

Dr. Coleman gave a speech titled "What We Stand for" to the Negro Baptist Association of Northern California:

> When white Baptists say, Let me help you, and I will help you, but you must give the title of your property over to me to safe-guard and hold it for you, the time has come for me to say no. For to give over the control of our Church property is to confess our weakness and ignorance of self-control. We lose our right for self-government, the sovereignty of the church dies, our

55. Greater Cooper AME Zion History Book.
56. St. Drake and Cayton, *Black Metropolis*, 395.

religious freedom is gone, and the help that we might get from
Heaven's God is thrown away . . . Our white brethren should
not get angry with us because we take God's word as meaning
something to us. I am not against our white friends helping, but
when their help ties my hands and disrupts my Christian work
and thwarts my ideals, I would rather not have their help.[57]

The thrust of Dr. Coleman's speech was to convey a message to not give
up control of the church. Dr. Coleman was also a supporter of women. "Dr.
Coleman supported the recognition of women in the church by declaring
the third Sunday in January 1914 as the first Women's Day by taking the
precedence that had been established by Nannie Helen Burroughs. Burroughs had presented the idea of Women's Day, whereby women would lead
and speak in worship service as a national event."[58] The Women's Day effort
proved profitable, raising large sums of money as membership continued
to grow.

In 1925, the church was destroyed by a fire. However, the determined
members rebounded and built a $50,000 educational building. The Rever-
end Walter F. Watkins, pastor of Berkeley Baptist Church, commented, "I
found that the Reverend Coleman had done more for his race in Oakland
than all of the Negro preachers put together . . . He was the cause of the City
of Oakland having Colored firemen, and all of the Colored men that hold
political jobs are here by the request of this great preacher."[59] In 1938, Dr.
Coleman's health began to fail, and Dr. A.O. Bell was appointed the assistant
pastor. Dr. Coleman went from labor to reward August 10, 1942. Frederick
Morrow, coordinator of branches of the National Association for Advancement of Colored People was the invited guest speaker, Sunday March 9,
1941 at 11:00 a.m. The twenty-eight-year-old coordinator said in part: "It is
discouraging to me, a young man (yet in some ways) to see us succumbing
to streamline methods in the church that is like a Frigidaire. I am glad to get
here to see that in this community you have ignored streamlined processes
and are acting and being yourselves. It is the best and safest way to live.
Morrow used as his text, I Corinthians 13:1–2. He referred to the method
in which the Negro was treated and continued, 'No place in the world wants
us. Twenty years ago it might have been possible to go to Brazil. Today, since
the Nazis have got into South America, it is just as tolerant as Georgia or
Mississippi. America is the only land we know. We were born here and we

57. Watkins, *They Cry of the West.*

58. Taylor, *Pastoral Leadership Training & Mentoring,* 58.

59. Watkins, *The Cry of the West,* 9.

helped to build it; whether anyone likes it or not. We are here to stay. We must make up our minds to that one fact."[60]

The church continued its growth under the leadership of Dr. Bell. North Oakland Baptist Church had always been a spiritual church, but when the Reverend Bell came with his magnanimous personality, the eyes of Oakland and California were upon the church. Choirs were reorganized, including the Women's Chorus being renamed the Inspirational Chorus and a junior choir was implemented. In 1951 the Reverend A. O. Bell observed his Golden Jubilee. A week's program was held commemorating his accomplishments. North Oakland continued to progress; ground breaking ceremonies for a new church were held July 5, 1959 at 3:00 p.m., and the new church with a seating capacity of 942 was completed and dedicated in May 1960. As the church grew, the Reverend Dr. Bell appointed the Reverend C. B. Murray in 1960 as his assistant to help with the growing responsibilities of the church. Due to failing health, the Reverend Bell resigned and the Reverend Claude B. Murray was called in 1967 to pastor the church and Bell became was named Pastor Emeritus. The Reverend Bell went from labor to reward in 1973.

Numerous local and international ministries and missions were formed under the Reverend Murray's leadership including the "The Voice of Africa," Wigfall Mission in Haiti, and the Lampkins Mission in Liberia, Africa. The Reverend Murray also served as the first vice moderator of the St. John Missionary Baptist Association of California, including parts of Nevada and internationally in Africa. The Reverend Claude B. Murray was called from labor to reward in 1982. The Reverend Sylvester Rutledge, a member since 1964, came up through the ranks of Deacon and was ordained into ministry in 1968 and was called to serve as senior after the death of Reverend Murray.[61]

Early Pioneers—Education for Blacks—Separate *BUT NOT* Equal

Plessy v. Ferguson, a United States Supreme Court case in 1896 upheld the rights of states to pass laws allowing racial segregation in public and private schools including restaurants, restrooms, and public transportation. In San Francisco, St. Cyprian AME Church was the first location that organized a school for black children in the basement.[62] Second-rate school facilities for black children, funded by local government and paid in part by taxes

60. Wysinger, "Activities among Negroes," *Oakland Tribune,* March 16, 1941.

61. North Oakland Baptist Church 1989 Anniversary Book.

62. De Graaf et al., *Seeking El Dorado,* 109.

levied on black parents, irritated them. It was clear that separate was never equal. The law provided for separate schools where there were ten or more black school-age children and for the admission of the black children to the white-enrolled schools if there were fewer than ten and if local whites did not object. Black parents fought hard for the right to have equal education for their children.

Across the Bay in Oakland, separate but not equal schools for black children were no better. According to Beasley, one of the early founders of First African Methodist Episcopal Church, Mrs. Elizabeth Thorn Scott-Flood, opened a private school for colored children circa 1857 in the old carpenter school house that was abandoned by whites for being inadequate whites for schooling.[63] Ten years later, the first public colored school in Oakland was taught by Miss Mary J. Sanderson, daughter of the Reverend Jeremiah Sanderson, near 10th Ave. and E. 11th Streets in 1867. Black families began to move out of the immediate area and relocate where work was available. As a result, the school closed in 1872 when enrollment fell below the required number of ten.[64] The Colored Convention of California had fought hard to end the discriminatory law preventing their children from being educated.

The first opportunity for a court case surfaced in San Francisco in 1874 by the parents of Mary Frances Ward, a young Black girl who was denied the opportunity to attend a school close to their home. Mary Frances was denied admittance by the principal, Noah Flood, on the grounds that there was a colored school. The California State Supreme Court ruled that Ward's rights were not violated because there was an all-black school available to her. The San Francisco Board of Education finally voted to end segregation in public schools for blacks in 1875 after a committee of the Board recommended that colored children be allowed to attend any public school and that separate schools be abolished.[65] In the pioneer years, it was the Black church that provided educational opportunities for black children. It was not until 1954 when the landmark case *Brown v. Board of Education*, in which the United States Supreme Court overturned the Plessy *v. Ferguson*

---

63. Bagwell, *Oakland The Story of a City*, 81.

64. Beasley, *Negro Trail Blazers of California*, 178.

65. Lapp, *Afro-Americans in California*, 21–23. See also Broussard, *Black San Francisco*, 19, quoting "Testimony of Mary Francis Ward," papers, California Historical Society, San Francisco; and the speech from Hon J. F. Cowdery of San Francisco; *Dwinelle's Argument on the Rights of Negroes in California to the Supreme Court of California, on the Rights of Colored Children to be admitted to the public schools,* California Historical Society, San Francisco; *Pacific Appeal,* January 9, August 7, and July 10, 1875; and De Graff et al., *Seeking El Dorado*, 110.

decision of 1896 which allowed state-sponsored segregation. It was the activism of the Black Church that served as the center for the black community, providing educational opportunities that otherwise were not available to black children. The Black Church remained consistently involved in the struggle for freedom.

Home for Aged and Infirm Colored People, Oakland 1892

The Home for the Aged and Infirm Colored People was founded by Mrs. Emma Scott, along with a generous donation by white businessman George Montgomery circa September 1892 in response to Colored people being refused convalescence care by white establishments. The first location was near Mills College on a hillside at 5245 Harrison Avenue (now Underwood Street). The cornerstone was laid by members of the District Grand Lodge No. 32 of the Grand United Lodge of Odd Fellows. Representatives from other social organizations and members of various churches were present for the grand opening.

With the exception of two men, William Storey and William Purnell, one of Oakland's first black doctors, the first Board of Directors was comprised almost entirely of Black women who were active in the California Black club movement and held women leadership roles in their respective churches. The Home charged a lifetime membership of $500 and was self-supporting. Black churches, social clubs, and societies contributed financially while private individuals supplied towels, pillows, and linen for the guests. Mr. Alvin Coffey, a former slave who had worked as a digger during the gold rush, became the first patient or, as some would say, inmate. His savings allowed him to donate money to fund his care. The Board of Directors established elaborate Articles of Incorporation. The governing Board of Directors had professional guidelines, with standing committees, the order of business, how funds would be maintained in the bank, an auditing system, as well as annual reports.

The Constitution, Article XVIII, read that inmates were required to pay $600 in advance and placed on probation for three months to determine if they qualified as a permanent residence.[66] The majority of old and infirmed Colored people were already experiencing rejection from the stigma of being poor and were not financially qualified to receive the much-needed care the home provided. In many cases they did not have family members to care for them because they also were experiencing rejection. As

66. Home for Aged and Infirm Colored People Constitution African American Library Museum Reference Archives.

a consequence of not having enough income from residences, by 1916 the Board of Directors had to admit with embarrassment they were experiencing financial difficulties and on the brink of closure. Letters of appeal were sent to friends of the home and other supporters asking for donations of supplies and money.[67] Matters worsened during the Great Depression years with fewer donations from the public. The Social Security Act of 1935 that was designed to help the elderly had a negative impact on the majority of Colored people because it excluded farming and domestic workers, which are the categories in which most colored workers were employed. With little income and few government subsidies, the Home was closed. On May 2, 1940, the Superior court of Alameda County dissolved the Home for the Aged and Infirm Colored People.[68] The Home for the Aged and Infirmed is another strident example of how early black pioneers blended their religious and secular involvement for racial uplift.

Reverend Isaac Flood, Pastor First African Methodist
Episcopal Church, Oakland circa 1858

67. African American Museum and Library at Oakland, California Reference History Room file, Home for Aged and Infirm.

68. African American Museum and Library at Oakland, documents from the Superior Court, State of California, Alameda County No. 157315 dated May 2, 1940, Oakland California.

Beth Eden Baptist Church Oakland circa late 1800

Reverend Samuel W. Hawkins, Pastor, Beth Eden
Baptist Church, Oakland 1908-1920

Reverend Dr. J Hubbard, Pastor, Beth Eden Baptist Church Oakland

Reverend John Henry Moore, Founder, Mt Zion Missionary
Baptist Church Oakland circa 1901

Reverend Dr. George C. Coleman, Pastor, North Oakland Baptist Church

Mrs. Mary B. Sanderson, teacher with Oakland Brooklyn
Colored School Students circa 1870

First African Methodist Episcopal Church, Choir Oakland

Fannie Wall Children's Home Oakland

Hettie B. Tilghhman, President, California Federted
Colored Women's Clubs circa 1925

Part II—First Great Migration, 1910–1939

We Shall Rise Up and Walk

It was a decision Negroes made to leave the South, not an historical imperative . . . this decision must have been preceded by some kind of psychological shift; a reinterpretation by the Negro of his role in this country.

—LeRoi Jones

The continued Jim Crow laws, lynching, and other social conflicts combined with opportunities for economic growth led to estimates that ranged from 500,000 to over a million African Americans including women and children leaving the South. The years between 1910 and 1930 were the beginning of a major demographic and cultural shift and a new era of African Americans leaving the South and migrating to Northern and Western states.

Amazingly, the migration was not a concerted effort with an announcement to move; it simply happened and was not noticed until years later starting with World War II. Quietly and with great courage, blacks packed their belongings, and the exodus began. Lincoln and Mamiya concluded that among the major causes for black migration were the mechanization of southern agriculture, the boll weevil attacks on the cotton crops, the lynching and violence of a rigid system of Jim Crow segregation, the long-term decline of sharecropping and individual farm ownership, and the need for cheap labor in northern factories and industries.[1]

---

1. Lincoln and Mamiya, *The Black Church in the African American Experience*, 95.

Emancipation may have ended legal slavery, but at the same time, it was the beginning of a new type of slavery: one without chains. As blacks migrants attempted to settle into a new lifestyle, it did not take long to understand that industrialized cities in the North and West were fraught with many of the hardships they had encountered in the South: hostility, restricted codes, broken families, unemployment, low wages, and an inner sadness.

The First Migration was not only a shift in black southerners leaving the South but it was also a cultural shift that changed the landscape of the Bay Area when a significant number of blacks came to California. Life was not easy as they struggled for economic survival.

While the Pacific Coast appeared to be the freest part of free America, at the turn of the century, little did Blacks in the South Dixie know that black westerners were beginning to worry about the southernization of the West [2] John Pittman, founder of *The San Francisco Spokesman*, and a University of California Berkeley graduate, recorded in 1921 that residential segregation is as real in California as in Mississippi.[3]

By 1900 over one thousand African Americans lived in Oakland. This population tripled by 1910, and by 1920 there were over six thousand blacks in Oakland. Migrants to the East Bay during the mid-nineteenth century came from the cotton belt of Texas and Oklahoma looking for work first in the cotton centers of Southern California and then drifting to the north.[4]

Only 1,654 blacks lived in San Francisco at the turn of the century, a decline of 10.4 percent from the previous census. Oakland almost doubled its black population between 1890 and 1900 and was considered more hospitable to blacks seeking industrial employment. By the year 1900, the black population of Oakland had swelled to more than one thousand from just under six hundred residents in 1880. The next ten years, 1900–1910, Oakland almost tripled its black population.[5] The great earthquake of 1906 that virtually destroyed major parts of San Francisco causing development in the East Bay to accelerate as many businesses and families moved from San Francisco to Oakland. Between the two cities of San Francisco and Oakland, eight black churches had been established. By this time, the black business district had begun to take shape along 7th Street in West Oakland. The first

2. Ibid., 36–37.

3. Broussard, *Black San Francisco the Struggle for Racial Equality in the West*, 33. Recorded by Broussard in telephone interview with Tarea Hall Pittman, September 16, 1997, Berkeley, California.

4. McBroome, *Parallel Communities African Americans in California's East Bay*, 31.

5. Broussard, *Black San Francisco: The Struggle for Racial Equality in the West*, 21–22.

black-owned real estate agency in Oakland, the Pacific Coast Real Estate and Employment Company, was a response to the urgent need for housing among blacks after the 1906 earthquake and the difficulty of getting white realtors to serve black clients. By 1910, approximately two hundred of Oakland's 3,055 black residents owned their own homes in the West Oakland area. By 1930, the number would be seven hundred, but blacks could no longer buy anywhere they wished.[6]

The Politics of Containment—Racial Covenants in the Early 1900s

They've got covenants restricting me—hemmed in—Can't breathe free

—LANGSTON HUGHES

With the population explosion during the First Migration, the black population grew, but the housing availability for blacks remained confined to restricted areas. Black churches were clustered in black neighborhoods because boundaries were established to keep blacks segregated to limited geographical areas known as their neighborhoods. Even when blacks moved into segregated neighborhoods, landlords raised rents as families doubled up just to keep a roof over their head. Legalized racial covenants were put into home deeds restricting Asians and blacks from moving into white neighborhoods. A restrictive covenant was jargon added to the title of a piece of real estate, dictating that the property could only be sold or rented by whites. The restrictions were not always hidden in fine print, but were obvious advertised as an attraction to promote certain neighborhoods. A typical covenant contained something like the following: "At no time shall said premises or any part thereof or any building erected thereon be sold, occupied, let or leased, or given to any one of any race other than the Caucasian, except that this covenant shall not prevent occupancy by domestic servants of a different race domiciled with an owner."[7]

Threats against black homebuyers were obvious. In 1923, E. A. Daly, a black newspaper publisher and real-estate agent in Oakland, recalled,

> Mr. Burt Powell . . . bought a house on Manila Avenue, Oakland. "We had to protect him for three or four weeks because the white people wanted to kill him because he moved in a white

6. Crouchett et al., *Visions toward Tomorrow*, 18–22.
7. Flamming, 69.

district. So we worked for him to watch over hm for a period of twenty-four hours for about three months." There was another on Genoa Street in the 5700 block. They put up a new house there and a Negro moved in. The white people tried to run this colored man out and we had to watch over him for about a month to keep the white people from molesting him.[8]

War was openly declared especially against blacks to keep them ghettoized in a "tender box" that eventually would result in blight and poverty. Noticeably were the railroad tracks, and eventually freeways that were physical barriers to the legal barriers, all designed to contain the Negro.

The *Oakland Enquirer* newspaper ran a front page ad on October 8, 1910: "North Oakland Residents War against the Negro—Fears wholesale invasion of blacks—Santa Fe and Power Residents lay blame to real estate dealers."

> War against the Negro as a prospective neighbor was started last night by the Santa Fe Improvement Association of North Oakland, one of the largest improvement clubs in the city, which met to combat what they assert is an attempt of the colored people to move from West Oakland into the fashionable North Oakland sections and passed resolutions asking that no land in their district be sold to the Negroes. There is an attempt on the part of the colored man to leave West Oakland and locate in the different residential districts of this city at the first time through the efforts of several unscrupulous real estate agents who is attempting to locate in several portions of North Oakland. You cannot mix the white and colored races in a desirable residential community and our object is to notify the colored man is not wanted.[9]

Restricted racial covenants designed to keep blacks and Asians in restricted areas was pervasive in the Bay Area. In Oakland, whites formed neighborhood improvement associations primarily for the purpose of keeping blacks out of their neighborhoods. They lobbied for local zoning restrictions to close hotels and rooming houses that attracted African Americans and for public investments to keep property values up by creating economic barriers against black buyers. They organized boycotts against realtors who sold to African Americans or against other businesses that catered to them. As the new middle class began to grow in Oakland, the housing restricted

8. Rhomberg, *No There Race, Class, and Political Community in Oakland,* 52.

9. *Oakland Enquirer* October 8, 1910 located in Oakland Public Library Blacks in History.

covenants also grew. Promoters of the Maxwell Park district at fifty-fifth Avenue, Oakland, bluntly stated, "No member of the African or Asiatic races will be permitted to hold title or rental."[10] Similar restrictions applied in the Lakeshore Highlands District: "No person of African, Japanese, Chinese, or of any Mongolian descent, shall be allowed to purchase, own or lease said property or any part thereof except in the capacity of domestic servants of the occupant thereof."[11] Similar restrictions were in force in San Francisco, Berkeley and Richmond. One white San Franciscan echoing the sentiment of the Daughters of the American Revolution admitted, "I wouldn't even want Marion Anderson as a neighbor."[12]

The San Francisco Chronicle ran this headline: "Willie Mays [Giants baseball player] is refused S.F. home—Negro." Mays offered $37,500 cash for the home that had views of the Pacific. A neighbor who lived a few doors away told reporters, "I happen to have a few pieces of property in this area, and I stand to lose a lot, if colored people move in." Only after Mayor Christopher stepped in was Mays allowed to purchase the home.[13]

As early as 1909, in the city of Richmond, CA, developers were inserting restrictive covenants into deeds of sale. A real estate brochure advertising a new housing development in south Richmond alluded to racial exclusiveness, invoking images of "savages running wild in central Africa."[14] It was not until the 1960s during the era of the Civil Rights Movement that racial covenants were eased. Assemblyman William Byron Rumford, Berkeley, introduced the California Fair Housing Act in 1963, known as the Rumford Fair Housing Act, which said property owners and landlords could no longer refuse to rent or sale their property to people of color. In 1968, the Fair Housing Act, Title VIII of the Civil Rights Act of 1968, outlawed refusal to sell or rent to any person because of race, religion, sex, color, or national origin.

10. Rhomberg, *No There Race, Class, and Political Community in Oakland*, 52.

11. Bagwell, *Oakland, The Story of a City*, 205.

12. Broussard, *Black San Francisco*, 173.

13. Taylor, *In Search of the Racial Frontier*, 289; Goode *California's Black Pioneers*, 147.

14. Moore, *To Place Our Deeds*, 23.

We Come to Bear Witness—Black Churches Continued to Grow

The fear that had shackled us all across the years left us suddenly when we were in that church together.

—RALPH ABERNATHY

During the early decades of the twentieth century, black church growth spread within West Oakland and to other parts of Oakland.

In the years that followed, that number began to increase because of the great migration of blacks coming from the south. An African American business district had begun to take shape along 7th Street, serving the "stratified complex, and rich" community that blossomed there.[15]

The migration of blacks leaving the South created "the Negro market." Both white and Negro merchants, as well as the Negro consumer, became increasingly conscious of the purchasing power as several hundred thousand people solidly massed in one compact community.[16] By the year 1900, the Black population of Oakland had swelled to more than one thousand from just under six hundred residents in 1880. Three black churches existed, and a Black business district had started to develop on 7th Street creating business opportunities and a Black market customer base that occupied the West Oakland area.[17] The 1906 earthquake did significant damage to structures in San Francisco, and as a result a major demographic shift resulted in blacks moving to Oakland creating a severe housing shortage.

The quake had destroyed churches and buildings in both cities. As a result church attendance increased as well as neighborhoods becoming overcrowded because blacks were not allowed to move beyond designated boundaries. In spite of segregation, poor people, working- and middle-class people, and the educated and prosperous all lived together, creating a viable network of support.

St Augustine's Episcopal Church

In 1910, the Negro Episcopalians in the Bay Area were scattered, attending white Episcopal churches. In 1910, the Reverend E. F. Gee, Rector of St. John's Church located at 8th and Grove Streets, Oakland, worked with the

15. Crouchett et al., *Visions toward Tomorrow*, 15.

16. Drake and Cayton, *Black Metropolis A Study of Negro Life in a Northern City*, 434.

17. Hausler, *Blacks in Oakland*, 43, 44.

few Negro members of his congregation to form the nucleus of a mission. The Rt. Reverend William Ford Nichols, Bishop, preached at a meeting of Negro Episcopalians assembled from the entire Bay Area. On the last Sunday in July 1910, St. Augustine's was formally established as a mission of the St. John's Parish. Services were held regularly thereafter at 6:00 p.m. on Sundays. Members were excited as they organized the St. Monica's Guild to assist the needy and to support the church. On August 4, 1911, the Reverend David R. Wallace was called from Chicago to serve as assistant to the bishop and provide leadership to the church. During his tenure the church flourished, a building fund was established, and Sunday School as well as the Men's Club was organized. In 1913, Archdeacon Emery assumed oversight of St. Augustine's and it became a diocesan mission. Shortly thereafter a cottage and a lot were purchased for $3,000 and the mission officially became the St. Augustine's Episcopal Church, holding its first service on May 4, 1913.

Lena Wysinger, who wrote a column for the *Oakland Tribune* called "Negroes and Their Activities," recognized the works of St. Augustine and wrote on July 7, 1940 that the church would celebrate their thirtieth anniversary and that the founder, the Reverend Gee, would be the celebrated speaker on July 28th. The Reverend Lewis Austin Baskervill served from October 1, 1946 until 1961 followed by the Reverend Richard Younge who was called in December 1961 and served as parish priest until 1966 when he left to serve as Chaplain at San Jose State College During the next year, the Vestry and lay leaders of the congregation ministered to the spiritual and material needs of the parish while the entire membership prayerfully considered the role of the church during the social climate of the 1960s that included the Civil Rights Movement and the Black Panthers. With profound insight motivated by a genuine desire to expand its Christian witness, St. Augustine decided that its ministry should emphasize innovative community involvement. The Reverend Earl A. Neil was rooted in social justice issues before being called to St. Augustine in December 1967. It was not long before St. Augustine turned its gaze on community needs and became less shy about celebration its African-American heritage. Within two short years, Reverend Neil's ministry included the Black Panther Party.

The First Great Migration—World War I: 1914–1918

The Great Migration and World War I had a significant impact on the Bay Area when thousands of African Americans departed the Deep South and headed for the Pacific Coast. Economic conditions in the South brought on by a severe drought then heavy rains and the boll weevil infestation destroyed the cotton crops. Since the majority of work by Blacks was farm labor, they had little opportunity to work and survive. Social conditions of Jim Crow laws, including lynching, made the South an unbearable place to live. With very few clothes, blacks began to leave the rural South for urban areas in the North, Midwest, and the Far West. Wherever they went, it did not take long for the same tensions that Negroes experienced in the South to become their realties throughout the United States.[18]

The 1920 census reports 5,489 black residents in Oakland's population of 216,265. Oakland's roster of black churches had grown from three in 1900 to ten in 1915. Between 1915 and 1930, Berkeley and Richmond also witnessed the founding of black churches. Black churches were the one-stop location where blacks came together to be nurtured and to build relationships and communities. Problem solving, socializing, and being informed about political conditions usually occurred in the black church.

Black Churches served as the meeting location for the NAACP to conduct membership drives. W. E. DuBois encouraged San Francisco Negroes to combine the NAACP branch offices in Northern California because of the numbers. As a result, the NAACP authorized a Northern California branch in 1915, with its headquarters in Oakland. It embraced the cities of San Francisco, Oakland, and Berkeley along with Alameda County.[19]

The NAACP also sought to establish a reputation as a racial watchdog agency, monitoring local businessmen and the press to make certain they did not malign blacks in their advertising or in their reporting of racial issues. The branch also took a keen interest in the plight of the Scottsboro Boys, who were imprisoned after allegedly raping two white women in Alabama. The branch sent small monetary contributions to the Scottsboro Defense Committee and held several meetings to inform the public about the status of these young men. The State Federation of Colored Women's Clubs sent $10 and the Oakland's black community established an East Bay Scottsboro Defense League. The interest of both San Francisco and Oakland's black community in national affairs illustrates a strong racial consciousness.[20]

In the meantime, blacks were showing their strength economically. On May 15, 1928, ten Black men applied for and were granted the right to incorporate and have a credit union. In part: "We, the undersigned citizens and residents of the State of California, do by these presence hereby voluntarily associate ourselves together for the purpose of incorporating a credit

18. Henri, *Black Migration Movement North*, 52.

19. Broussard, *Black San Francisco*, 76; DuBois, "Colored California's," 192–96.

20. Ibid., 82– 83; Executive Board Minutes, "San Francisco Branch, NAACP, Minutes, June 11, July 30, 1923, San Francisco Branch NAACP, Stewart-Flippin papers; Albert Morton to Mary White Ovington July 24, 1933, SFBF, NAACP Papers.

union under the laws of the State of California. The name of said corporation shall be "The Ethiopia Credit Union." With the exception of two of the members, all lived in West Oakland.[21]

Berkeley Middle Class, Moderately Speaking

At the turn of the century, Berkeley's Black population was approximately sixty-six. Black residents were spread throughout the city and not confined to one area like in Oakland. The first black church in Berkeley was established in 1919. Berkeley was considered by many to be more middle- to upper-class than West Oakland. The literacy rate was high among black residents; the majority could read and write. Most of the school-age children were also enrolled in classes because school segregation had been abolished.[22] Black doctors, aspiring lawyers, educators, and other civic leaders clustered in Berkeley because of U. C. Berkeley and because racial hostility was not as pervasive there. These individuals are not wealthy compared to the same level as whites, but they have more than average education and usually are well known as race leaders.[23]

Black students were regularly enrolling in degree programs at the University of California by the 1920s. Alexander Dumas Jones of San Francisco was the first black to enroll at the University of California Berkeley in 1881 followed by Charles Edward Carpenter as the first Black graduate in 1905, and Vivian Rogers was the first black female to graduate in 1909.

Walter Arthur Gordon, the son of a Pullman porter and grandson of slaves was the first African American to receive a Juris Doctorate from U. C. Berkeley's Boat Hall in 1922. He was a star player for the Cal Bears. Gordon was also the founder of the Alpha Phi Alpha fraternity.[24] By no means were black students free from racial hostility. Gordon was not allowed to stay in the same quarters as his white counterparts. Black sororities and fraternities provided a cultural setting for Black students who were not welcomed in all areas of social life at Cal Berkeley. One of the roles of the sororities and fraternities was to assist in housing for students the university rented to whites only. Individual families and local Black churches provided support to these

21. Articles of Incorporation of The Ethiopia Credit Union filed with the Department of the State of California Corporation Number 129242, dated May 15,1928 located in the Oakland Public Library History Room.

22. Gretchen Lemke, Afro-Americans in Berkeley 1859-1987 (Oakland, Ca. East Bay Negro Historical Society), unpublished manuscript, 1987, U. C. Berkeley, p. 11.

23. St Drake and Cayton, *Black Metropolis*, 527.

24. Crouchett *Visions toward Tomorrow*, 26; McBroome *Parallel Communities*, 59.

students. Vivian Osborne, a local graduate from Berkeley High School in 1914, applied to U. C. Berkeley with excellent academic records, but was required to take *four* entrance exams. Osborne founded U. C. Berkeley sorority chapter Delta Sigma Theta Sorority and the undergraduate Kappa Chapter, the first black sorority on a college campus in the western part of the country. Sometime in 1929, after graduation and marrying, Vivian Osborne Marsh organized Omega Sigma Alumna chapter so that Bay Area women could continue their involvement in Delta after leaving college. William Byron Rumford was an outstanding student at U. C. Berkeley who parked cars in San Francisco's Roof Garden Club to pay for his education. After graduating in 1931, Rumford opened up his own pharmacy in Berkeley and became a successful politician and assemblyman for the 17th District of Berkeley. He is most remembered for authoring the Fair Housing Bill and the Fair Employment Acts in California.[25]

Ida Louise Jackson, a pioneering black woman graduated in 1922 with a Bachelor of Arts Degree and a Master's Degree both from U. C. Berkeley, became the first black public school teacher in California. Ruth Acty became the first black teacher in the Berkeley School District.[26] Tarea Hall Pittman enrolled in U. C. Berkeley in 1923 at a time when on-campus housing was closed to Black students. After graduation, she helped to organize West Coast branches of the National Negro Congress. She was a civil rights worker who fought to desegregate the Oakland Fire Department and during the early 60s she served as Director of the West Coast Region of the NAACP.[27] The fact that the students were admitted to the University did not exclude the continued practice of hostility brought on by environmental racism.

Had it not been for Black churches such as McGee Avenue Baptist Church, North Oakland Baptist, FAME, and Beth Eden providing watch care (a tradition among black churches where students are adopted into families who provide spiritual and moral support) no doubt some of the students would not have excelled. Often operating in the background, the Black Church was a major source of support to the students.

McGee Avenue Baptist Church, Berkeley, 1918

Reverend Silas Lincoln Tillman organized a small mission of believers at 1934 Bonita Avenue, Berkeley, in 1918 to serve as a place of worship for

25. McBroome, *Parallel Communities*, 60.

26. DeGraaf et al., *Seeking El Dorado African Americans in California*, 223.

27. Crouchett *Visions Toward Tomorrow* p 26

the rapid growing population. Starting as a mission, it was later named Mt. Pleasant Baptist Church. The growth of the mission blossomed into a church. To assist with the early organizing, a group of ministers consisting of Dr. J. M. Riddle, Field Secretary of the General Baptist Association. the Reverend J. A. Dennis, pastor of Third Baptist Church of San Francisco, the Reverend S. W. Hawkins, pastor of Beth Eden Baptist Church, Oakland, and the Reverend J. A. Allen, Minister of the 85th Avenue Baptist Church, Oakland, came together to officially organize Mt Pleasant into a church The Reverend Tillman served as the first pastor and superintendent of its church school. Women played a supporting role to keep the church going as sexism did not allow women to hold pastoral positions in the church. Miss Josephine Phillips served as the church school secretary and Miss Coretta Robinson served as President for the Baptist Young Peoples Union department; Miss Carrie Franklin served as the first church clerk; Mrs. S. P. Malcolm became the first president of the Missionary Society and Mrs. Pricilla McDowell Roberts organized the first church choir.[28]

In 1935, the Reverend James Dee Wilson accepted the call to be pastor of Mt. Pleasant Baptist Church. The Reverend Wilson, a strong spiritual and civic leader, was also an activist for racial equality that extended into the community. With the onset of WWII and the Great Migration, the membership grew to the point that they needed a larger meeting place. In 1944, the church relocated to the corner of McGee and Stuart Streets in Berkeley and renamed the church McGee Avenue Baptist Church to reflect its location. Shortly after, a new sanctuary, a social hall, a modern kitchen hall and seventeen classrooms were built. The Pittsburg Courier reported that, "under his successful guidance, the church has grown in membership and programs and has a fine attendance of young people from the community at large."[29] The Reverend Wilson was called from labor to reward on September 16, 1949 after serving fourteen years, leaving an impressible mark on the community. Following the Reverend Wilson was the well-prepared Reverend Wadie H. Sypert, who had served as the Assistant Pastor. He was a well-educated, former school teacher and principal. The Reverend Sypert led the church into expanding its community outreach and exhausting its debt when the church expanded. The Reverend Sypert retired in 1971 and assumed the title of Pastor Emeritus. On October 1, 1971, the Reverend James H. Stewart was elected Pastor and provided extraordinary leadership by expanding church programs, remodeling the aging facilities, and acquiring additional properties, including making a donation of $20,000

28. McGee Avenue Baptist Church Anniversary Book 1918–1933.

29. *The Pittsburgh Courier*, 1940, p. 22.

for famine relief in Haiti. The Reverend Stewart was a pioneer in many areas of ministry, but none was more important to him than his commitment to women in ministry. He was the first pastor to ordain women as clergy and deacons.

After faithful service for twenty-one years, the Reverend Stewart retired in 1992. Following the Reverend Stewart the Reverend D. Mark Wilson was installed as pastor. Dr. Wilson was a dynamic preacher, accomplished musician, social activist, and served as an adjunct professor at the Graduate Theological Union in Berkeley. Dr. Wilson believed in the inclusive radical love of Jesus Christ who embraced all people regardless of sexual preference. He established ministries that included a computer center, a prison and domestic violence ministries, and an HIV/Aids ministry. After eleven and one half years, the Reverend Wilson resigned to pursue a full-time professorship role at the Pacific School of Religion, Berkeley. On March 26, 2006, the Reverend Michael A. Smith, who had grown up in the church from childhood, was called to pastor McGee by a near unanimous vote. The Reverend Smith extended the ministries of McGee beyond its walls and deeper into the community. With the onset of young black men being at risk, he founded a program to help at-risk fathers who needed support to help them develop parenting skills. The FAITH academy (Fathers Acting in Togetherness & Hope) extended itself beyond the church and out into the community. The Reverend Smith continued the tradition of ordaining and training women for ministry as clergy and deacons.[30]

North Richmond Baptist Church, 1919

The North Richmond Missionary Baptist Church (NRMBC) was the first Black Baptist church in Contra Costa County, becoming the most prestigious of Richmond's pre-war churches. The Reverend Doctor G. C. Coleman, Pastor of the North Oakland Baptist Church, became inspired with the vision of a church for the Negroes of Richmond. He met with a group of faithful Christians in the home of Mr. and Mrs. Willie Miles on Alamo Avenue in North Richmond in 1919 where the first worship services were held.[31] Community people were attracted to the church and membership grew. Information is scanty regarding the first location of the church where the cornerstone was laid in 1921. The Reverend Henry Holmes of Berkeley was the first appointed pastor. He served without a salary, and the small collection that was taken up was given back to the church by the Reverend

30. McGee Avenue Baptist Church Anniversary Book 1918-1933.

31. Moore, *To Place Our Deeds*, 27.

Holmes. The Reverend Holmes wanted North Richmond to be a part of an organized denomination, so he represented North Richmond in October 1922 at the third session of the Negro Baptist Missionary Associates with $3 while the Sunday school department gave $2, and the church body represented with $5.[32] Although the Reverend Holmes was ambitious, the congregation was dissatisfied with his preaching as he lacked that old time "fire" in his sermons that would invoke emotions of shouting and making a joyful noise unto the Lord. Under pressure the Reverend Holmes resigned in 1925.[33]

In 1931, the field missionary Reverend John Henry Moore recommended the Reverend F. W. Watkins to serve as a part-time pastor of North Richmond while he was also serving as part time pastor of Star Bethel of Oakland and New Hope Baptist Church in Sacramento. The Reverend Watkins had the kind of "fire" that caused the congregation to jump around and shout.[34] During the Great Depression and World War II, the church suffered economic setbacks, but it did not stop the women in the church from coming together with food drives, and sponsoring a "clean clothes closet" to help the needy.[35]

The congregation grew to over nine hundred members with seven choirs, an active Baptist Training Union (BTU), a Sunday School enrollment that numbered over three hundred, and the Women's Missionary Union and Brotherhood ministries were active including youth and young adults departments. By now, North Richmond had become one of the leading churches in the Bay Area, especially in Richmond. The Reverend Watkins was underpaid even with small raises. However his service remained dedicated. After moving into a new church facility equipped with a kitchen, a dining/social hall, a library, and classrooms, shortly thereafter, the Reverend Watkins was called from labor to reward on August 26, 1966.[36]

The Reverend Charles W. Newsome was prepared to take the mantle having served as an assistant pastor at the church and was easily elected as Pastor on June 18, 1967. Under the Reverend Newsome's leadership, North Richmond continued its strong affiliations with the St. John District Baptist

32. North Richmond Missionary Baptist Church 90th Anniversary History Book, unpublished, April 8, 2009..

33. Moore, *To Place Our Deeds*, 28. Slocum, interview; Freeman and Griffin, interview.

34. Moore, *To Place Our Deeds*, 28; North Richmond Missionary Baptist Church 90th Anniversary History Book, unpublished, April 8, 2009.

35. Moore, *To Place Our Deeds*, 38.

36. North Richmond Missionary Baptist Church 90th Anniversary History Book, unpublished, April 8, 2009.

Association, the California Baptist Association, and the National Baptist Association. The Reverend Newsome proved to be a visionary leader with a keen sense of civic responsibility, community involvement, and outreach to members of the congregation. On December 4, 1977, the Reverend Newsome led the march into the new church and a mortgage-burning ceremony was held earlier than most expected.[37]

The Honorable George Miller, Congressman for the Richmond area, honored Reverend Newsome on the occasion of his retirement and recognized the eighty-fifth anniversary of North Richmond on May 12, 2004. Congressman Miller referred to the Reverend Miller as his friend and a colleague in the shared struggles on behalf of the people in Richmond.[38]

The Reverend Newsome retired in 2004 and became Pastor Emeritus.

In 2004, the Reverend Dana Keith Mitchell Sr. became the interim pastor and was elected senior pastor in July 2005. Under Reverend Mitchell's leadership, the church continued to be involved in community activities and a strong commitment to teaching God's word. Reverend Mitchell helped the church with a new budget system and established financial goals for the church.[39]

Race Men Fighting Racism—Not in Our Backyard

When the NAACP was organized in 1909, it immediately established partnership with the Black Church in the struggle for social justice. Notably, W. E. DuBois was among the founders of the organization. In 1913, DuBois was touring the Bay Area and was instrumental in bringing Bay Area race leaders together in establishing a Northern California branch of the NAACP in Oakland. Not too long after the Northern Branch was established, it faced its first major battle against the film *The Birth of a Nation*.[40]

Walter A. Butler, president of the northern California NAACP sent a letter of protest to Oakland Mayor E. K. Mott on May of 1915, two years before the film was shown in San Francisco, stating the film not "only maligns the Colored People but is immoral in its teachings and likely to lead the people to race hatred resulting in mob violence." Mott declined to ban the film in Oakland because that would just increase its power and popularity; managers would promote it in San Francisco as the film that was suppressed

37. Ibid., 3.

38. *United States Congressional Record* 150, no. 68 (May 15, 2004) E863.

39. North Richmond Missionary Baptist Church 90th Anniversary History Book, unpublished, April 8, 2009.

40. Broussard, *Black San Francisco*, 76.

in Oakland, he said, producing "a thousand times more publicity than if permitted to run its course." Butler also wrote Governor Hiram A. Johnson that the full board of California's NAACP was protesting publicity posters using the governor's name to promote the film, and reminding him that *The Birth of a Nation* (also known as the Klansman), however glorious and spectacular, is a justification of lynching that promotes racial hatred.[41] Governor Johnson refused to withdraw his support for the film. The Directors of the Northern California Branch of the National Association for the Advancement of Colored People in its membership, held a meeting in Oakland, May 3rd for the purpose of continuing its efforts to stop the production of the play in Oakland (Letter Oakland History room).[42] It was not until 1921 that the State of California banned *The Birth of a Nation* from circulation.

A Nation within a Nation—The Women Were There

I felt so tall within, I felt the power of a nation within me

—SOJOURNER TRUTH

The truth worth of a race must be measured by the character of its womanhood

—MARY MCLEOD BETHUNE

History has not always recorded the contributions that women made in society, especially Black women who have the triple jeopardy of racism, classism, and sexism. There is evidence to suggest that the church did not view women as equals with men, even though many were well educated with degrees. Though the odds were against them for full participation, nevertheless whether frustrated or not, they found their self-worth as contributors in society through their combined efforts to lift the race through works of charity, being outspoken and advocating for racial equality. With segregation as much a part of the fabric in California as it was in southern states, women formed various clubs to fight against racism. Migrant Black women used their innate skills and cultural traditions that were developed in their roles as mothers, church women, wives, and community organizers to work collectively together for racial uplift. The National Association of Colored Women was established in 1896. Its inaugural meeting included

41. Primary source Letter to Mott from Butler, May 4, 1915, located in Oakland History Room Library in Files "Blacks in Oakland," Part II.

42. Ibid.

seventy-three delegates representing eighty-two clubs from fifty cities in the state. The prime mover of the Colored Women's Club was Eliza Warner of Los Angeles who traveled up the coast to Oakland, where she met with other race women in the Bay Area to establish a Colored Women's club. The meeting took place at Oakland's 15th Street FAME Church, later renamed First African Methodist Episcopal Church. For about two years, the CWC operated independently of the members of a state federation. Local clubs pursed separate aims but joined together in annual conventions to elect statewide officers.[43] In addition to women meeting at the First African Methodist Episcopal Church, the Mother Club of the Black Women's Club Movement was founded in 1899 by members of Beth Eden Baptist Church in order to provide hospitality to blacks visiting the East Bay. Taking as its motto, "Not failure, but low aim is crime," the Fanny Jackson Coppin Club organized musical and literary programs and study and undertook a variety of service projects. The stated objective of this club was to develop musical and literary inclinations of its members and work for the interests and uplift of humanity. The women of the Coppin Club undertook an ambitious project, the construction and operation of the Home for Aged and Infirm Colored People, which opened in East Oakland on August 22, 1899. Under the leadership of Mrs. Emma Scott, the project won the support from blacks as well as whites.

Women, some White, who belonged to local churches in the East Bay, helped to establish the Chlora Hayes Sledge Club in 1919, named in honor of Chlora Hayes Sledge, who was an activist for racial uplift. She served on the Board of Directors of Oakland's Fanny Wall Home for Colored Orphans and presided over the California Association of Colored Women in the 1920s, pursuing an array of health, educational, and political goals.[44]

Similarly, the Richmond Self Improvement Club, supported by the black church in the East Bay, represented Richmond at the National Association of Colored women's (NACW) fifteenth biennial convention held in Oakland in 1926. Among the agenda items was establishing a national educational scholarship for black women and passing anti-lynching legislation.[45] Across the Bay the Philomath Club in San Francisco, a branch of the California Federation of Women's Clubs were holding debates on race questions and whether the color line exist in women's clubs. The *Pacific Appeal* regularly covered the debates and reported on their front page: "[T]he

43. Flamming, *Bound for Freedom*, 137. Donald Hausler, "Blacks in Oakland," unpublished manuscript, Oakland History Room 974.66, vols. 1, 2 and 3, p. 15.

44. Lawrence B. De Graaf p 218

45. Moore, *To Place Our Deeds*, 30-31.

affirmative contended that colored women should not be permitted to join the federation, upon the ground that they were not of sufficiently high standard to affiliate with the white sex."[46] Another popular club in San Francisco known as the Booker T. Washington Community Center, was organized by ministers and women in the early 1900s to support the social and educational needs of the black community. The center also served as a forum for racial issues where the NAACP held some of its meetings. At some point, the center was strapped due to financial problems; the women were successful in raising over $2000 to keep the center alive.[47] The State Federation of Colored Women's Club's Irene Bell Ruggles and other members founded the Madame C. J. Walker Home for Motherless Girls. The home provided shelter, recreation, and companionship for a limited number of Black women in San Francisco during the early 1900s.[48] Sue Baily Thurman, wife of Howard Thurman, along with Frances B. Glover and Anna Magruder, wife of Reverend E. J. Magruder of First AME Zion Church, were among the many black women who were leaders in the church and the community. At the urging of Mary McLeod Bethune, Thurman organized a local chapter of the National Council of Negro Women in 1945.[49]

Racism, segregation, and discrimination caused separate branches of both the YWCA and YMCA to be created for Black people. In 1920, members from local churches including Mrs. Willie Henry, Melba Stafford and Hettie B. Tilghman, Mary Albrier, and Delilah Beasley organized the Linden Center Young Women's Christian Association including religious vocational training and cultural programs.[50] R. D. DeFrantz, the National Secretary from New York, was invited as principal speaker. He praised the Y and stated, "I read an article which classed Oakland Negroes as one of the three cities having the highest literacy in the United States."[51]

The local Linden branch operated as a segregated institution until 1944, when the national policy integrated the local branch into the main body of the Y. W. C. A. In 1960, the building was demolished to make room for the Acorn housing project. The high point of the clubs' booster role

46. McBroome, *Parallel Communities*, 35, quoting from *San Francisco Pacific Coast Appeal*, 7 December 1901, p. 1. The debates often centered on the subject of whether colored women's clubs should be permitted to integrate with white women's clubs.

47. *History of the Booker T. Washington Center* 1920-1970 n.p as cited in Broussard pp 90,91

48. Iantha Villa Mays *History of the California Association of Colored Women's Clubs*, 1908-1955 (Oakland, Ca. East Bay Negro Historical Society, n.d) .

49. Broussard, *Black San Francisco*, 187.

50. De Graaf et al., *Seeking El Dorado*, 216.

51. Wysinger, "Activities among Negroes," *Oakland Tribune*, June 23, 1935.

came in 1926 when the northern federation hosted the fifteenth biennial national convention of the National Association of Colored Women's Club at the Oakland auditorium. So intrigued, black club women from Chicago chartered seven Pullman cars to attend the convention.[52]

By 1913, there were clubs scattered throughout the Bay Area founded by black women: in San Francisco, Sacramento, San Jose, Stockton, and Oakland.

The advocacy of Black women in establishing organizations to benefit the community figured prominently in the church where many of the clubs were organized. The church, community, and women clubs depended on each other for racial solidarity as they shared common sentiments with regards to fighting against structures of discrimination. In Beasley's column on May 4, 1930, she wrote about the National Observance of Better Homes in America and what it meant to Negro citizens. Women who were activists in the community put the program together. One speech drew the attention of Father David R. Wallace, pastor of St. Augustine who reminded the audience not to lose focus: better houses do not mean better homes. The Negro is interested in all that goes to make up a better American life while focusing on material and financial need of the community.

Allen Temple Baptist Church 1919

The Reverend James Lewis Allen, born in slavery July 12, 1853 to David and Mary Allen of Leasburgh, Loundon County, Virginia, was the founder of Allen Temple Baptist church in 1919. Reverend Allen began his ministry at the age of sixteen with his first assignment in Clarksville, Texas where he served as a schoolteacher and minister before moving to El Paso, Texas. From El Paso, the Reverend Allen, a seminary-trained minister, having graduated from Maryland Seminary and Howard University, was called to pastor Beth Eden Baptist Church, Oakland, from 1895 to 1901. After serving six years, the Reverend Allen relocated to Oregon. In 1917, and two years later after returning to Oakland, the American Baptist Churches sent the Reverend Allen to East Oakland to start a church.

One year after Reverend Allen founded Allen Temple Baptist Church the 1920 census count reported 5,489 black residents in Oakland and nine black churches with the majority of them clustered in West Oakland. Allen Temple was the first black church known to be founded in East Oakland by a black man. Rev. Dr. J. Alfred Smith Sr., records the following from the *Western Appeal*, a black newspaper dated April 1, 1927: "The church started

52 l Crouchett, *Visions toward Tomorrow*, 26.

in a little hall on E. 14th Street and Seminary Avenue with an oil heater and a few borrowed chairs, with still fewer members, during the years that tried man's souls-when conditions were such that only a man who was really interested in the morals of a community, the training of youth, the satisfaction of a desire on the part of worshippers for a place to assemble, and whose heart and soul were sincere and filled with an ambition to help suffering humanity."[53]

The church relocated to a house on 85th Avenue at A Street and, as was the custom of so many churches, it became known by its location: the 85th Avenue Baptist church. Records were lost during the infancy years, thus little is known about the details of members and officers.[54]

After retirement, Reverend Allen maintained his residence on Tyler Street, Berkeley. Allen was called from labor to reward November 6, 1940, at the age of eighty-eight years and three months.

Impressive funeral services for the Reverend Allen were held at Beth Eden Baptist Church. The body lay in state in the church during the morning. Reverend J. D. Wilson, pastor of Mt. Pleasant Baptist Church (later known as McGee Avenue), officiated and was assisted by a score of ministers who eulogized his useful and Christian life. The mass of floral designs and scores of telegrams, letters, and cards of sympathy revealed the esteem in which the aged minister was held. The Reverend Allen was known nationally he held charges and supplied pulpits all over the state for more than forty-five years.[55] The Evergreen Cemetery, Oakland, records the Reverend Allen's burial date, November 9, 1940.

Following the Reverend Allen, there was a series of pastoral changes. The Reverend James Dee Wilson served for one year, 1926. According to the McGee Avenue Church history records, the Reverend James Dee Wilson became pastor of McGee Avenue Baptist Church in 1935. The Reverend Wilson was called from labor to reward, September 16, 1949. Dr. Reed H. Thomas served as pastor from 1927 to 1929. A gospel of black liberation was threaded into the various ministries. No doubt the Reverend Thomas was influenced by the Marcus Garvey movement that had established a United Negro Improvement Association (UNIA) chapter on 8th Street in Oakland, in what was called the Liberty Hall, in response to the Ku Klux Klan (KKK) having headquarters in Oakland and targeting mostly blacks in the community. Prior to the Reverend Thomas's resignation in 1929, he encouraged

---

53. Smith Sr, *Thus Far by Faith*, 17.

54. Ibid.

55. Wysinger, *Oakland Tribune Negro Affair*, November 17, 1940.

the church to change the name of the church from the 85th Avenue Baptist Church to the Allen Temple Baptist Church in honor of its founder.[56]

The mantle of leadership was passed to G. W. Wildy who entered the Berkeley Baptist Divinity School where he received a certificate in ministry; shortly thereafter he was installed as the third pastor of Allen Temple Baptist Church.[57] The Reverend Wildy served as pastor from 1929 to 1950. At the beginning of his ministry, the Great Depression hit the nation hard. Resources were scarce and money was scarcer. Not only were families struggling but the church was struggling as well. Allen Temple was among other churches that fed the hungry and clothed the naked. The Reverend Wildy had his sights on having a church school as he forged ahead to fight against illiteracy while strengthening young people. On February 18, 1940, a new facility was dedicated in honor of Pastor G. J. Wildy.

World War II brought hundreds of thousands of black migrants from the South seeking improved economic opportunities and escaping the oppression of discrimination. West Oakland continued to be the enclave for the black community, businesses, and black churches. To attract new members to his struggling congregation, Pastor Wildy advertised in black newspapers, telling them about Allen Temple Baptist Church. Slowly, as membership gradually grew, Allen Temple began to establish a reputation as a gathering place where community leaders and other pastors came to discuss important issues impacting the black communities. Though Pastor Wildy was effective, disharmony settled into the environment of the church causing the Reverend Wildy to resign. He preached his farewell sermon February 1950 and later organized the Cosmopolitan Baptist Church with a few of the Allen Temple members.[58] The Reverend Wildy was called from labor to reward, February 15, 1993. Augustus L. Carpenter, a seasoned man of age and wisdom was elected pastor of Allen in the spring of 1950. Not only did he have the task of pastoral leadership, he had to walk a delicate line in bringing healing and reconciliation to the congregation. TheReverend Carpenter proved to be exactly what the church needed at that time. On September 29, 1950, the first deacons of Allen Temple were ordained by the Reverend Carpenter. The Reverend Carpenter soon found his role as pastor expanding beyond the stained glass windows. The Reverend Carpenter responded to the needs of the community and the NAACP to help fight racism and housing discrimination.[59] Following the postwar years during the

56. Ibid., 26.
57. Ibid., 27.
58. Smith Sr., *Thus Far By Faith*, 36.
59. Ibid., 42, 43.

early 50s, West Oakland took a downward spiral for black West Oaklanders causing many of them to relocate to East Oakland: racial covenants were slowly being lifted, West Oakland was being destroyed by the urban renewal and interstate highway programs. The Bay Area Rapid Transit District was building overhead tracks directly down 7th Street—the area became blighted and the white flight to suburbia was well underway. With the increase of blacks in East Oakland, membership at Allen Temple began to grow significantly. By now the church was doing a better job of keeping records and publishing Sunday bulletins with the help of Mrs. Marie F. Johnson and Mr. Lee Conroe.[60] While it is not clear exactly why the Reverend Carpenter reluctantly submitted his letter of resignation January 8, 1958, he continued to be a guest preacher at local churches. He was called from labor to reward, January 9, 1961, in Oakland.[61]

Six months after the resignation of Pastor Carpenter, the Reverend Charles Christopher Bailey became the next pastor serving from 1958 to 1969. At the age of twenty-four, the Reverend Bailey had received his doctorate in Political Science from Lincoln University, San Francisco. Pastor Bailey had a style of organizational leadership. He established regular office hours, improved the accounting and record keeping, and established a Board of Christian Education. The forward-thinking leadership style of Pastor Bailey signaled the beginning of a significant change in the image of Allen Temple. He soon realigned Allen Temple with churches that were associated with the American Baptist Churches. Uniquely, Allen Temple was the first of the Black churches to move into an all-White association by integrating with the American Baptists in Northern California. Pastor Bailey's progressive leadership style was highly appealing to middle-class Blacks, many of whom were businessmen and -women in the community that helped to reshape the church. Ministries and boards within the church were active in raising funds for a new expanded sanctuary.[62]

The women's club movement undoubtedly was the driving force in thrusting women to the forefront as leaders in civic and religious organizations. Dr. Bailey was not afraid to have women assume leadership roles as they were key in the life of the church. Sister Albertine Shelton of the Women's Missionary Society was the first President of the Business and Professional Women, who took on the responsibility to raise substantial monies to help young people in the church who were college bound. Mrs. Arville

60. Ibid., 44.
61. Ibid., 46.
62. Ibid., 49.

Gilmore became the church representative with the Oakland Council of Churches. Dr. Bailey resigned in 1968, leaving a great legacy.

A New Era

A new era was ushered in with the installation of the Reverend Dr. Smith Sr. on February 21, 1971, Dr. J. Alfred Smith Sr., along with his wife Joanna Goodwin Smith and their five children, were active church members. By the start of the 1970s, the Civil Rights Movement was ending and the Black Panther Party was in its infancy stage, still struggling for its true identity. Oakland was making national and international news as a revolutionary city in revolutionary change.

Allen Temple was located behind the Black Panther East Oakland Headquarters at the corner of 85th Avenue and East 14th Street; Dr. Smith Sr., affectionally called J. Alfred, did not alienate himself or Allen Temple from the Panther Party. Dr. Smith recognized that there was a need for a healthy rapport for the Panthers and the Black Church to coexist in harmony as they shared many common goals for the black community, namely, education, justice, peace, decent housing, employment, and destiny over the Black Community. The membership rolls grew to include political leaders, educators, doctors, lawyers, and working people joined Allen Temple in great numbers, working to strengthen the church and the community. It was not unusual that national elected officials as well as great theologians such as Dr. Howard Thurman, Dr. James Cone, Dr. Renita Weems, Bishop Desmond Tutu, and Allan Boesak (both from South Africa), Dr. Gardner C. Taylor, Drs. Henry and Ella Mitchell, and Presidents of the Progressive National Baptist Convention, were among the many that graced the pulpit.

Dr. Smith Sr.'s philosophy was a simple statement: "In order to get to the sweet by and by, you, you have to deal with the nasty now and now"— translated that meant, "Get out of the rocking chair of lazy religion," don't be a spectator, become a participator. Dr. Smith Sr., along with the leaders of the church, led marches, and took evangelism to the streets. As Allen Temple grew, a new sanctuary was built and two Sunday worship services were established.

In the late 1970s and through the 1980s East Oakland was undergoing a major demographic shift as Hispanics began to populate the area. In 1988, the Reverend Ruben Hurtado was guided to Allen Temple Baptist Church. Through the encouragement of the Reverend Gloria Aguilar and Deacon Armando Aguilar, a strong spiritual husband and wife team, the Reverend Rueben Hurtado became pastor of Iglesia Bautista de Allen Temple, a new Allen ministry branch to meet the needs of the growing Hispanic community.

In 1997, Dr. Smith Sr., along with other Christian leaders, brainstormed his vision to start a Christian educational institute that would focus on educating women and men for responsible Christian leadership in the church and society. The Leadership Institute has grown to become a liberal arts institution offering programs in Christian ministry, prophetic justice, biblical studies, and liberation theology. Dr. Smith Sr. served as Chancellor and Dr. L. P. Lewis was appointed Dean, followed by Dr. Jesse Perry serving as Dean. In 2012, the Reverend Dr. Brenda Guess was appointed Chancellor and Dean. In 2001, co-pastor Dr. Smith Jr. resigned to start a ministry in Nevada. He later became pastor of Antioch Baptist Church, San Jose. In 2009 Dr. Smith Jr. was elected pastor of Allen Temple after his father retired.

Millennium Era

The Reverend Dr. J. Alfred Smith Jr., was installed as the Senior Pastor at Allen Temple on March 15, 2009 coming from the Antioch Baptist Church, San Jose, where he served for almost six years. Dr. J. Alfred Smith Jr. has been a prophetic voice and continues the legacy he helped start as an activist for social, economic, and political justice when he was the assistant pastor and co-pastor.

The church reached a new milestone when Dr. Smith chose the highly gifted and talented Reverend Doctor Jacqueline Thompson to serve as the assistant pastor of the church. Dr. Thompson is a gifted prolific preacher. Together this team works to reframe and retool the future of the church to be inclusive of the millennium age.

Parks Chapel AME Church, Oakland 1919

Parks Chapel African Methodist Episcopal Church was organized as a mission in September 1919 by the Reverend J. M. Brown, the previous pastor of the First African Methodist Church in Oakland. From a mission, Parks became known as the Centennial Methodist Church and later renamed Parks Chapel AME in honor of the late Rt. Reverend H. B. Parks. Charter members included Mary Wilson, Samuella Baker, M. F. Baker, Victoria McCoy, B. F. Fuller, R. M. Marshall, Maggie Marshall, and Ruth Wilson-Larche. The first location for worship was in the American Trust Company building at 7th and Henry Streets in West Oakland and later relocated to

9th and Chester Streets with an upper and lower sanctuary including dining hall and kitchen. During the Great Depression Parks Chapel suffered
financially; however, the church managed to recover and carry on the strong
tradition of an AME Church.[63]

From 1926 to 1956, the church was served by a number of pastors.
In 1952, Parks Chapels membership outgrew its location at 9th and Chester Streets and through financing relocated to 724 14th Street, Oakland in
1953. Under the leadership of the Reverend M. L. Simmons, Parks Chapel
relocated to 476 34th Street when racial covenants were lifted allowing them
to leave the predominately black area of West Oakland. Membership had
grown significantly by 1969 during the post-war era. A number of ministers
succeeded the Reverend Simmons, but when the Reverend Booker T. Guyton
Sr. was appointed Pastor in 1986 his vision and goals that focused on family
unity and community solidarity was like a magnet that attracted churches,
including the nearby Summit Hospital to partnership with the church to
serve an underserved community. Several years later, in October 1989, Parks
Chapel suffered severe damage by the Loma Prieta earthquake that destroyed
the sanctuary. The Reverend Guyton earned a reputation as a great pastor
and leader. As a result of his good works, in 1996, he was elevated to the
position of Presiding Elder for the Oakland / San Jose District supervising
other pastors. Following the Reverend Guyton Reverend Andrew Simpson
Jr. was assigned and led the church further into the community with a program aimed at youth and young adult. The Reverend Simpson served until
he was reassigned in 1999. Following Simpson, the Reverend Dr. Donna E.
Allen, was assigned. Her vision was to grow the church through conversion,
deliverance and strengthening. Membership and ministries grew including
the expansion of global ministries. In 2004, a strong husband and wife team,
the Reverend Dr. Tyrone Hicks and the Reverend Phyllis Hicks, received the
assignment for the Reverend Benjamin Hollins and his wife, the Reverend
Annette Hollins, were appointed to Parks in 2007. This dynamic team went
beyond the normal to reach the youth and young adults and church membership once again began to flourish. With the itinerant process that moves
ministers to different churches, the Rt. Reverend Bishop Theodore Kirkland
Sr. was assigned to the Fifth Episcopal District in 2008 for the western region.
He reassigned a number of pastors to other churches. One year later he appointed the Reverend E. Teresa Nelson as pastor of Parks Chapel who brings
a new vision. Her motto, "Where there is no vision, the people will perish,"
along with her gifted preaching, is springing new life into the church.[64]

63. Parks Chapel AME Church History unpublished

64. Parks Chapel AME Church History http:/www.parkschapelame.org/about-us.
html

The 1920s—Tragedy and Laughter

Liberate the minds of men and ultimately you will liberate the
bodies of men.

—Marcus Garvey

Universal Negro Improvement Association (UNIA), 1920

The Universal Negro Improvement Association, known as the UNIA, was first founded by Marcus Garvey in 1914 in Jamaica, New York with its objective being to educate Blacks about self pride. Garvey used the Bible often, quoting Psalm 68:31, "Princes shall come out of Egypt." His motto was "One God! One Aim! One Destiny! Let Justice be Done to all mankind." The seeds of the Garvey Movement were planted after Garvey read and was greatly influenced by Booker T. Washington's *Up from Slavery*. What Garvey drew from the readings was that blacks needed to first improve themselves, form their own government, and not depend on America's government for anything.[65] Garvey's movement also focused on sending six million Black Americans to Africa. The Garvey movement spread to the Pacific Coast with UNIA branches in San Francisco, Oakland, and Los Angeles. The Oakland branch no. 188 was charted circa December 1920, leading San Francisco with more followers. Within five years the branch bought the building at 1483–85 8th Street, Oakland, and renamed it Liberty Hall. Membership had grown to more than five hundred as a result of WWI that brought migrants from the South. The members converted the ground floor into an auditorium where self-pride was the topic of meetings. With a renovated building there was a grand opening and dedication on Sunday, March 11, 1928. News of UNIA meetings, including ladies day, Garvey Day, etc., was regularly reported in various newspapers.[66] One of its strongest opponents was W. E. B. DuBois and the two groups were openly at odds with each other. The black leaders in San Francisco considered the Garvey Movement a scheme devised to prey on the uneducated, whereas the NAACP felt the Garveyism movement impacted its growth. On the one hand the Garvey movement was recruiting at the grass roots level, and on the other hand the NAACP

65. Edmund David Cronon *Black Moses* (Milwaukee: The University of Wisconsin Press, 1969) pp 16, 18

66. United States Department of the Interior National Park Service, National Register of Historic Places Section 8, Oakland District p 8.2

focused more on legal battles. In each case the two groups were fighting for racial equality with opposing approaches.[67]

A major recruiting strategy that the Garvey movement used in Oakland was to employ local prominent pastors, many of them leaders in the community who could persuade entire congregations to join the UNIA. The chaplain, the Reverend R. W. Clarke, is credited with being the founder. According to local newspapers during the early 1900s, other ministers who were Garveyites included: the Reverend J. E. Fletcher, the Reverend Dr. J. J. Byers, Pastor of Cooper's AME Zion, the Reverend J. E. Parham of Philips Chapel, Berkeley, the Reverend F. W. Haynes, the Reverend Father David Richard Wallace of St. Augustine Mission, Oakland, the Reverend J. Wesley Thomas, Taylor Memorial, and the Reverend Coleman, Pastor of North Oakland Baptist Church.[68]

Beth Eden Baptist Church opened its doors to host a lecture by Captain E. L. Gaines of New York City. Captain Gaines, a minister of Legion for the UNIA, spoke on the objects and aims of the UNIA. Oakland residents were responsive to the self-help philosophy of the UNIA and turned out in large numbers on June 4-5, 1922 when Marcus Garvey spoke there as part of his California tour. At his first speech, there were six detectives from the Department of Justice's Bureau of Investigation in the audience. Asked by his Oakland promoters whether Garvey wanted them removed, Garvey declined and went on with his speech. Denouncing white racism and supremacy in the United States, Garvey stressed the need for unity among colored races. Among the supporters of the Garvey Movement included race women Delilah Beasley, black reporter for the *Oakland Daily Tribune*, and Frances Albrier, a Black Cross Nurse and Vice-President of the Women's Auxiliary in 1923.[69]

Heavily influenced by the growth of the Garvey Movement in the Bay Area, Black newspapers such as the *California Voice* and the *Pacific Appeal* became staunch advocates of black self-help programs. On July 31, 1931, a fire severely damaged the roof and second floor of Liberty Hall. Although Oakland Branch No. 188 continued to meet, the fire seems to mark the end of the UNIA's efforts to organize the black community in the East Bay. The significance of Liberty Hall continued after the UNIA dwindled when it became the location for Father Divine's Peace Mission Father Divine, a self-proclaimed spiritual leader according to the July 1936 edition of the

67. Broussard p 86

68. Franklin Moore *The Universal Negro Improvement Association in Oakland* p 5 . Unpublished b located in the Oakland Library History Room,

69. McBroome, 56

New Day newspaper based in New York listing twenty-eight branches of the Peace Mission in California, with one in Oakland at the Liberty Hall address. [70]

The Oakland Peace Mission is best remembered by Depression era residents of West Oakland for the sumptuous banquets that were served in the annex for only a few pennies a person. In addition to the banquet hall and offices, Peace Mission facilities included a dormitory and a furniture repair shop. The movement began to decline after the start of World War II.

The significance of Liberty Hall is that it was the locus of two different international mass movements with zealous leaders fighting in their own ways to gain economic, social, and civil rights for black people everywhere. Most noteworthy is that Liberty Hall was owned by the local chapters of the UNIA and the Father Divine Mission. The Liberty Hall stands as an important symbol of two strong revolutionary and charismatic movements, planting the early seeds of Oakland becoming known as a revolutionary city.[71]

Ku Klux Klan—Organized Bigotry

The Ku Klux Klan resurfaced in 1915, but was not restricted to southern states. The First Migration was well under way when thousands of blacks and whites left the South headed for northern and western states seeking better jobs and improved lifestyle as a result of WWI.[72] The Bay Area was especially attractive to members of the Klan as well as black migrants as it was becoming an industrial region because of work in the shipyards. On one hand blacks were seeking freedom from the oppressive South, and on the other hand Klan members saw a double opportunity not only to find work but also to expand its racist hatred toward blacks and its propaganda especially toward Catholics in other areas. The Klan hid behind the shield of religion, purporting to be a fundamentalist conservative group committed to defending morality, yet members used violence and intimidation threats. The Klan was especially appealing to like-minded white people who were seeking companionship with others who embraced its ideology. The prominence of the Klan meant that "membership in the Klan became quite

70. National Park Service, National Register of Historic Places Section 8, Oakland District p 8.2

71. Oakland Museum History Room – File Oakland Districts: West Oakland United States Department of the Interior National Park Service National Register of Historic Places Registration Form Section Number 8, p 8.4.

72. Seymour Martin Lipset and Earl Raab *The Politics of Unreason Right-Wing Extremism in America 1790-1970* (New York: Harper & Row, Publishers 1973) p 117

a status symbol."[73] Klan leaders did not hesitate to brag about the fact that law enforcement officers and ministers had joined their order.

The presence of the Klan infiltrated into the government, including shipyards, unions, and dominated private businesses. They were a menace to groups such as the NAACP and other race organizations that were fighting for justice in the Bay Area. Unlike the South, there is very little evidence to suggest that the Klan openly attacked Bay Area black churches with cross burnings, bombings, and other tactics of intimidation, yet strong evidence support that racism was largely perpetrated by members of the Klan.

When *The Birth of a Nation* movie came out in 1915 portraying white supremacy with Ku Klux Klan men wearing white hoods and riding horses with white hoods, the movie reinforced existing hatred toward blacks. One of the scenes in the movie was a cross burning on the lawn of a black family, obviously promoting racial pride of white supremacy while maligning black men in particular as savages and raping white women. The controversial movie was a national box-office seller fueling hatred.

By 1921, there were enough Klansmen in the East Bay to open a downtown office in Oakland in August 1921 and, within six months, Ku Klux Klan No. 9 had received its formal charter in January 1922.[74] After opening its office the Klan wasted no time in initiating and recruiting additional members. On the night of May 5, 1922, a crowd of some fifteen hundred men wearing white robes and masks gathered silently in a valley in the hills above Oakland, California. Rows of parked cars lined the nearby road and two searchlights beamed across the sky as a fiery cross burned behind an altar draped with the American flag. At a given signal, five hundred more unmasked men marched four abreast toward the altar to take their oaths and be initiated into the order of the Knights of the Ku Klux Klan.[75]

Two weeks later, the May 26, 1922 *Oakland Tribune* edition reported that the Oakland City Council proposed a ban on Klansmen wearing their masks and gowns in outdoor ceremonies, subjecting violators to arrest and a misdemeanor criminal charge with a fine not to exceed $500.

The threat of violating the law had little effect on the Klan openly continuing its activities. By 1924, the Oakland Klan alone enrolled at least two thousand members, including such prominent and ordinary citizens as Protestant clergy, small businessmen, professionals, managers, and

73. Alexander, *The Ku Klux Klan in the Southwest*, 246.

74. *San Francisco Chronicle*, August 12, 1921; March 4, 12, 1922; May 11, 15, 1922.

75 Rhomberg, *No There There*, 1; *Oakland Post-Enquirer*, May 6, 1922; *San Francisco Examiner*, May 7, 1922.

salesmen, public employees and public officials, including the son of a U.S. Congressman.[76]

Within two years after the initiation in the Oakland Hills, on Saturday, March 8, 1924, the monster naturalization ceremony by Oakland Klan No. 9, Realm of California, was held at the Oakland Auditorium.

> Approximately fifteen thousand Klansmen and Klanswomen occupied the main section of the Oakland auditorium and five thousand spectators filled the balcony. It is estimated that five thousand Klansmen appeared in full regalia. More than one thousand aliens were naturalized in the Invisible Empire, Knights of the Ku Klux Klan. In addition the vast throng who gained admittance, it is conservatively estimated that fifteen thousand people milled around the door and refused to disperse until they heard the speaker. The speaker prefaced his remarks with his definition of the Klan which he characterized as "White, Anglo-Saxon, Protestant, patriotic fraternity." He declared the order was an instrument for upholding justice and the law. Separation of church, and state and the un-contaminated public schools are two of the principles which he particularly emphasized.

Surprisingly, not all deeds were bad deeds; the *Oakland Tribune* dated December 24, 1922, recorded: "K.K.K. Give Shoes to Orphan Children—Six men wearing the regalia of the Ku Klux Klan drove up in an automobile to the Fred Finch Orphanage yesterday afternoon, and presented 37 of the children with a pair of shoes each. The children were delighted with their gifts and the hood visitors drove off without waiting to be thanked."

The growth of the Klan was unstoppable as they continued recruitment efforts. In May 1925, a charter was granted to Oakland Klan No. 9 Auditorium to witness the swearing in of five hundred members joining the national order.[77] By now the Klan had leaders being elected to city and county governmental positions. The most successful Klan politicians were Burton F. Becker, chief of police in Piedmont, an elite suburban enclave of Oakland, and William Parker. Becker was later elected Sheriff of Alameda County in 1926. In 1930, after years of investigation by Alameda County District Attorney Earl Warren, Becker was tried and convicted on corrup-

---

76. Knights of the Klu Klux Klan, Inc., v. Leon Francis et al., case file no. 81245, Civil Division, California Superior Court, Alameda county, 1925; *Oakland Tribune*, August 24, 1925. 132 The Imperial Knight-Hawk published from the Imperial Palace, Atlanta, Georgia, Knights of the Ku Klux Klan Vol II, No. 1, April 16, 1924.

77. *Oakland Tribune*, August 24, 1925.

tion charges, removed from office, and sent to prison.[78] In its continuing efforts to expand the membership of the Oakland Klan, members advertised in the *Oakland Tribune*, June 26, 1930:

> All Native Born Protestant Americans are invited to join the Ku Klux Klan. This All American organization is now conducting a vigorous drive for fifty thousand new members. The Ku Klux Klan calls for men-men who believe in God and the Constitution of the United States. The Ku Klux Klan wants every American citizen to have a job and a home. The Ku Klux Klan seeks men who have the courage to aid in enforcing the law. The Ku Klux Klan knows that America must rule Crime or Crime will rule America. Address J.R.B., P.O. Box 833, Oakland.

Although the Klan's activities declined after WWII, there was evidence they were still active. Many of the Klan members did not fear retaliation by the law as they were employed as law enforcement officers and some appointed and or elected judges. Headlines in the *San Francisco Chronicle*, December 4, 1946 read: "Klan threaten to lynch Negro whose home burned." The article continued with: "The Ku Klux Klan served notice on San Mateo County yesterday that it is on the march. As their first victim, they selected John T. Walker, 22 year old Negro war veteran whose unfurnished home near Redwood City was burned to the ground. They told him to get out or be hung on a fiery cross."

The exact causes for the Klan's decline can be attributed to a number of factors: internal fighting, corruption, leaders being incarcerated, efforts of the NAACP, and losing its power to control the government.

Watts Hospital: First Black Hospital in Oakland, 1926

When Dr. William Watts, a graduate of Meharry Medical College in Nashville, Tennessee, settled in Oakland, he was disturbed to see that blacks were refused proper medical care by both private and county hospitals. Black physicians were not allowed to treat their patients in hospitals and, if they were seen at all, they had to be turned over to a white physician. The hospital in Alameda County refused to admit black women into the training program. In 1926, Dr. Watts was motivated to open the first black hospital in West Oakland at 3437 Harlan Street.

78. Warren, *The Memoirs of Earl Warren*, 99–100, cited by Rhomberg, *No There There*, 61.

Beasley wrote that the opening of the hospital made history, being the first of its kind in the Bay Area. It is not known how funds were obtained to secure a building, hospital equipment, and twenty-two beds.[79] The hospital also served as a sanitarium and a training school for black nurses. The hospital measured twenty-five feet wide by one hundred and ten feet long and constructed of concrete. Dr. Watts maintained an office nearby at 1191 36th Street Oakland. He specialized in surgery and the treatment of female diseases. Dr. Watts penned a column, "How to Keep Well," for the *Western Times*.[80] With the Great Depression on the horizon, the hospital closed after a year. The pioneering efforts of Dr. William Watts are worth remembering. An extensive ledger containing patient names is maintained in the African American Library in Oakland.[81] Highland Hospital eventually integrated the nurses training program in 1928, eliminating the need for a separate African-American hospital.

Let the Church Roll on

Taylor Memorial Methodist Episcopal Church: Oakland, California, 1920

Taylor Memorial Methodist Episcopal Church started out as the Bishop Jones Literary Society and grew into a mission of the Methodist Church in 1921 by twenty-two founding members. The group initially met in the Community House at 8th and Chestnut Streets, Oakland, circa March 1921. At some point, the group decided they wanted to organize a Methodist Episcopal Church in Oakland. President D. L. Jones connected the group to the Reverend H. E. Milnes the Methodist Episcopal District Superintendent. Word spread to Mayor Taylor of Alameda, California who gave an unspecified generous donation to erect the first building for the church and requested that the church be named in memory of his father, the late Bishop William Taylor; the members agreed to change the name to Taylor Memorial. The first Christian meeting was held in 1921 with Superintendent Milnes in charge, and pulpit ministers were supplied to pastor the church. Taylor Memorial was chartered on October 29, 1921 and with sufficient finances the church secured property at 12th & Magnolia Streets with the Reverend Albert Scott, serving as the first pastor. The Reverend Scott was proud of

79. Delilah Beasley, *Oakland Tribune*, March 26,1926.

80. Donald Hausler *Blacks in Oakland 1852–1987*, Oakland Public Library History Room, Oakland, 1987.

81. African American Museum, Oakland, California; and Oakland Public Library, History of William M.Watts.

the church and wanted the community to participate in his installation and inspect the building. The reception was well attended by both white and Negro people and, with a steady growth, the church prospered both in terms of finances and membership. After the Reverend Scott left, the Reverends George Carter and John Wesley Thomas served for brief periods.[82]

From 1928 to 1940, the Reverend H. T. S. Johnson, the son of slave parents on a plantation, served as the fourth pastor for twelve years. The Reverend Johnson was a visionary leader and the church became involved in community activities and civil rights issues. By 1940, the membership had grown from one hundred and fifty members to 1,008 members. The Reverend Johnson was at the forefront in leading the fight locally for equality of job opportunities as bus drivers, toll collectors, and other positions including educators long before the formal protests of the 1960 Civil Rights Movements.[83]

Delilah Beasley recorded in her weekly column in the *Oakland Tribune*, December 21, 1933 that

> one of the most valuable and far reaching actions taken by an inter-racial organization in Northern California was the Eastbay Ministerial Fellowship in their regular session . . . Reverend H. T. S. Johnson, Pastor, Taylor Memorial Methodist Church declared that lynching orgies are a sad commentary on Christianity in America. He pointed out that Christianity is now on trial and declared that there is a possibility that young people of the Negro race may turn to communism in preference to Christianity.

Johnson appealed to all white ministers to voice their convictions in the matter of race prejudices and lynching not alone out of justice to the Negro race, but also to save Christianity that will correspond to Race-Relations Sunday approved annually by the Federal Council of Churches of Christ in America that observes the second Sunday in February where white and black races exchange pulpits in an effort to create better race relations.[84]

82. Beasley, "Activities among Negroes," *Oakland Tribune*, September 23, 1923.

83. Taylor Memorial Methodist Episcopal Church Historical Facts, unpublished.

84. Beasley, "Activities among Negroes," *Oakland Tribune*, December 21, 1933. In the same article Dr. Rudolph I. Coffee, former rabbi of Temple Sinai, lauded the Negro preachers and reminded the ministers that five hundred and sixty thousand Jews are now suffering persecution in Germany. Hitler is the most dangerous man in the world today, Coffee stated. "Hitler is no messiah, he is a mad man. If Hitlerism spreads throughout America, Christianity is doomed. Hitlerism is already in the East and just today, I saw a Nazi emblem in an Oakland Window."

The Reverend Johnson labored tirelessly in the community by speaking out against racial injustices. He was called from labor to reward on September 5, 1962.

The Reverend Dr. Charles L. Warren served as pastor of Taylor from 1941 to 1958. He was well educated, including receiving a Doctor of Divinity from Houston-Tilloston and Gammon Theological seminaries. Under Dr. Warren's leadership, a new sanctuary was completely rebuilt, with a dedication service and mortgage burning November 28, 1954. A new educational building was added and later renamed The Charles L. Warren Educational Building. Taylor Memorial was one of the well-attended churches and was a magnet for community discussions and out of town speakers. Dr. Warren was later called to go to New York City in 1958, to serve as minister of Saint Mark's Methodist Church. Dr. Warren held the position as Executive Director of the Council of Churches of Greater Washington headquartered in Washington, D.C.[85] The Reverend Dr. Warren was called from labor to reward October 1971.

The Reverend Dr. Robert D. Hill served from 1958 to 1966. Under Dr. Hill's skilled, leadership, a financial drive was successfully initiated to begin the expansion and new building construction for the members and community of Taylor Church. Dr. Hill served in many capacities in the church and in the community. In 1966, he was appointed to the office of District Superintendent of the Golden Gate District and served until 1972. The church grew from nine hundred and thirty members to 1,403 members. With the increase of membership, the church needed additional space. Dr. Hill helped to raise $75,000 toward the building goal. In 1966, Dr. Hill was appointed to he office of District Superintendent of the Golden Gate District. Following Dr. Hill, the Reverend Thomas P. Grissom Jr. served as pastor for six years. The Reverend Grissom, a well-educated man, held degrees from Clark and Gammon Seminary, Atlanta, and studied at Atlanta University, Columbia University, New York, and San Francisco Theological Seminary. Taylor Memorial continued to have a strong presence in the community and plans were drawn up for a new multipurpose facility. The Taylor complex was completed in 1976 and used consistently by community groups for conferences, weddings, banquets, and civic activities. Dr. Hill was called from labor to reward on January 14, 1987.

The Reverend Warner Harrison Brown Jr. served as the ninth pastor from 1987 to 1998. His leadership in the church and community were outstanding. He received his BA degree in sociology with an emphasis in criminology from the University of Maryland, College Park, a Masters of

---

85. Taylor Memorial Methodist Episcopal Church Historical Facts, unpublished.

Divinity from Wesley Theological Seminary, Washington D.C., the Reverend Brown initiated many new and innovative programs under the slogan "Catch the Spirit." He received numerous honors and accolades during his tenure. The Reverend Brown was recognized as an outstanding leader. Dr. Brown served until 1998. In 2000, he was elevated to Bishop of the United Methodist Church and assigned to the Denver Episcopal Area of the Western Jurisdictional Conference and later reassigned to lead the California-Nevada Conference.

The Reverend Lorraine McNeal made history as the first female associate pastor of Taylor, serving from 1995 to 2003. Reverend McNeal was educated and raised in Oakland. She brought a strong background in human relations and the growth of Taylor Memorial continued under her leadership. In 2003, the Reverend McNeal was appointed as Senior Pastor, Downs Memorial United Methodist Church, and Oakland.

The Reverend Ronald Edward Swisher was born in Oakland, graduated from the University of San Francisco, and attended seminary at the Pacific School of Religion in Berkeley. Reverend Swisher served as Taylor's tenth Senior Pastor from 1998 to 2010. On July 10, 2010, the Reverend Andrea Davidson made history when she was appointed as the first female senior pastor of Taylor Memorial. She continues to carrying on the traditions of Taylor with community involvement as well as bringing a vitalization of involving the youth in the church.

New Hope Baptist Church Oakland 1921

The New Hope Baptist Church was organized in 1921 at the Carpenters Union Hall located at 761 12th Street, Oakland, by the Reverend Samuel W. Hawkins, former pastor of Beth Eden Baptist Church. The First Migration brought a stream of Black immigrants from the South, and the need for churches grew. The church raised $3,000 and purchased the edifice of the Christian Advent Congregation Church at 933 33rd Street, Oakland, California. The site was later purchased for $3,500 by the Alameda County Board of Education for a new Junior High School in the community, later named Hoover Junior High. After serving as pastor for five years, in 1926 the Reverend James E. Moore became the second pastor. The church was severely damaged by fire, forcing New Hope to return to Carpenter's Union Hall for worship services. Later, the church purchased a lot located at 915 37th Street for $2,000. With monies on hand and lumber salvaged from the burned church, New Hope erected its first sanctuary.

In 1930, the Reverend Moore resigned, having served as pastor for four years. In 1930, the Reverend H. R. Smith became New Hope's third pastor. He served for fifteen years before resigning in 1945.

In March of 1945, Reverend Huey W. Watson, former pastor of the Greater Ludlen Chapel Baptist Church of Monroe, Louisiana became New Hope's fourth pastor. Pastor Watson was a dynamic and influential leader; people flocked to the church, and it was not long thereafter that membership had grown to more than one thousand. The church raised a little more than $125,000 and purchased a lot on the corner of 36th and Market Streets for the sum of $4,500. The Groundbreaking Ceremony took place on January 18, 1947, and the late Reverend Frederick Haynes Sr., Pastor of the Third Baptist Church of San Francisco, California, delivered the ceremonial message. Six months later, on July 7, 1947, the New Hope Church began a building project to accommodate the ever-increasing growth of the membership. Approximately nine months later, the church relocated. The occasion was joyous as they marched on Sunday, April 18, 1948, from 915 37th Street to 892 36th Street. A few short months later, Attorney George Vaughn laid the cornerstone for the new location on October 10, 1948.

After fourteen years of service, Pastor Watson resigned in 1959. The Reverend Watson later organized and built the Bethany Baptist Church located at 5400 Adeline Street, Oakland, California. On August 15, 1960, the Reverend James T. McCullum Sr., former Pastor of Steele Memorial Baptist Church, Little Rock, Arkansas, became New Hope's fifth pastor in its long notable history. Under the leadership of Pastor McCullum, membership grew and the church edifice was remodeled in 1972 to expand the pulpit, choir stand—restrooms, an elevator, a baptistery, and complete kitchen were also added. To better serve the growing congregation, New Hope purchased its first two mini-buses for a new venture, the Community Bus Ministry.

As the years passed, New Hope continued to grow prodigiously. During 1980–1981, the church paid off all of its properties ahead of schedule. In 1986, the proud members purchased beautiful pews. To bring church affairs into modern existence, computers were purchased to store and maintain records. Additional properties were purchased on 37th Street to provide additional parking for an increasing membership. Due to failing health, the Reverend James T. McCullum retired as pastor in June 1992 having served as pastor for thirty-two years. The Reverend McCullum was called from labor to reward, circa January 1994.

In February 1994, the Reverend Hubert L. Garnett, former pastor of Tabernacle of Faith Baptist Church of San Francisco, became New Hope's sixth pastor. Under the leadership of Pastor Garnett, church membership grew. In 1998, the church was refurbished with new carpeting, flooring, lighting, and balcony seating. New chairs were purchased for the lower auditorium.

In 2002, an elevator was added to the church and restrooms were remodeled to make the church accessible to handicapped persons. Pastor Garnett resigned circa July 2011.

On October 20, 2012, Bishop Sean F. Teal became the seventh pastor.[86]

Mount Zion Missionary Baptist Church: Oakland, 1922

The Reverend John Henry Moore founded the Mount Zion Missionary Baptist Church in 1922 and remained pastor through 1929 without receiving a salary. On October 18, 1922, Mount Zion became a member of the Negro Baptist Association of Northern California, currently known as St. John Missionary Baptist Association. Representation fees were $5 for the church and $3 for Sunday School. Approximately one year later, the church relocated to the corner of 8th and Chester Streets, Oakland. The names and the number of original members are not known. What is known is that the finances were meager. Members sold quilt raffles and trips around the world and held apron socials, fish fries, and gumbo dinners to help finance the expenses for the church. The Southern Pacific Railway was not far away and proved to be a great place to lure customers for the delicious meals. The late deacon L. R. McCowan sold dinners to his coworkers at the Southern Pacific Yards. Prescott school teaches were regular supporters including Oakland's first black Public School teacher, Ida Louise Jackson. With little funds and much faith, Mt. Zion once again relocated to 895 Campbell Street, Oakland, where the first property was purchased. Tithing was not part of the weekly offering, thus group captains collected $35 weekly dues and $10 in pastor's aid.

The Reverend William Clark was elected as pastor in 1935 and served until 1950. The church was forced to move as a result of the population increase brought on by migrants coming from the South during WWII. The building was purchased by the City of Oakland to build government housing for the war workers. In 1941 the church was creative in fundraising, selling spades for $25 to anyone who wanted to participate in the groundbreaking service for a new church location at 1712 12th Street. The Reverend Clark established the William Clark Church Universal Theological Seminary. The Reverend B. S. Peebles served as the first Dean. The Reverend Otis D. Banks Sr. served as President of the church seminary, which was open to all men

86. http://www.nhbcoakland.com/history.html (accessed October 16, 2013). All historical facts obtained from the North Oakland Baptist Church unpublished historical anniversary book.

and women who desired to study for Christian service. A host of ministers served as associate ministers under the Reverend Clark's leadership, including the Reverend W. A. Holly who succeeded the Reverend Clark after he was called from labor to reward circa 1950. In May 22, 1950, Associate Minister W. A. Holly was installed as pastor at the 1203 Willow Street location. The Reverend Holly was a dynamic spiritual leader and involved himself in the growth of the church. He was daunting in introducing new changes and procedures to the church. The church grew financially and purchased adjacent lots. Additional remodeling to the church included a library, a ladies lounge, a nursery and educational facilities. In 1955, the Reverend Holly guided the church into establishing the Mt. Zion Evangelical School, with the Reverend Nathaniel Linzie as Dean. The school was well attended by local church leaders who desired to gain additional biblical knowledge. In 1961, the Youth Council was organized to focus on young persons between the ages of fifteen to twenty-nine years. In 1962, the Board of Christian Education was organized with the Reverend Nathaniel Linzie serving as Dean followed by the Reverend Marvin Peoples and the Reverend W. O. Mouton. Dr. Marvin Peoples later united with the Allen Temple Baptist Church where he served as the chair of the Board of Christian Education before he was called to be pastor of Liberty Hill Missionary Baptist Church, Berkeley.

Reverend Holly eventually left Mt. Zion and was elected the first pastor of the Foothill Missionary Baptist Church followed by the Reverend T. J. Prince who served briefly from 1972 to 1974. Under his leadership a transportation ministry was initiated with three mini buses to transport members. The Reverend Henry L. Hudson followed the Reverend Prince and was installed as pastor in October 1975. The Reverend R. T. George delivered the installation message, "God's Servant in the Field of Labor," and the Reverend Dr. Alvin C. Dones, who had served as interim pastor, gave the charge to the church where members vowed not to cause disturbances in the church. The Reverend Hudson voluntarily retired in 1989 and the respected title of Pastor Emeritus was bestowed upon him.

In 1988, the Reverend Frank Grimsley united with Mt. Zion and served as an associate minister. He was innovative as a visionary leader that involved the church in community projects. In 1989, the Reverend Cornelius L. Seibert Jr. was voted as pastor of Mt. Zion having previously served on the ministerial staff. Pastor Seibert served as Secretary of Baptist Ministers Union, Vice Moderator at Large for St. John District Association, and as Assistant Dean of St. John Congress on Christian Education. In August 1999, at the tender age of 29, the Reverend Brian D. Hunter was called to pastor the historic Mt Zion Missionary Baptist Church. After seven years as pastor, and with the Reverend Dr. M. T. Thompson retiring from the Berkeley Mt.

Zion Baptist Church (no connection), the Reverend Hunter was installed as the senior pastor of the Berkeley Mt Zion Missionary Baptist church. Other ministers who were considered sons of Mt. Zion went on to become founders and pastors of local churches: The Reverend G. H. Hudson became pastor of Star Bethel Baptist Church in 1939 and served for twenty-two years. The late Reverend G. G. Griffin organized and became pastor of Macedonia Baptist Church of North Richmond in 1940 and also organized the Solid Rock Baptist Church, Oakland, on September 15, 1943. The Reverend I. H. Lewis became pastor of Harmony Baptist Church in 1941, serving for many years.

The Reverend Herbert Guice received his license to preach under the Reverend William Clark and later founded the Bethel Missionary Baptist Church. The late Reverend Arthur Williams joined Mt. Zion in 1943, was ordained by the Reverend W. A. Holly in the 1950s, and became pastor of Sweet Home Baptist Church for twenty-one years.[87]

Market Street Seventh Day Adventist Church

The roots of the Market Street Seventh Day Adventist church go back to November 1923, when Lourainne Vanderberb Mitchell, Marie Kisack, and Gertrude Drake, three pioneering women, had an idea to establish a Black Seventh-Day Adventist Church in West Oakland where the majority of the black population resided. These three women were pioneers in that it as unusual for women to establish a church. Together, the women petitioned the president of the Northern California Conference, G. A. Roberts, to organize the black members in the Oakland area. Previous attempts to organize this work had been denied by the Northern California Conference. The NCC granted their request, and the journey began under the direction of Pastor Owen A. Troy Sr. on April 2, 1924, assisted by Dr. V. C. Hamilton, a layman in the Adventist work. During its formative years the church met in the Peralta Hall near 11th and Castro Streets and was known as the Second Oakland Church of Seventh-Day Adventist. The church later relocated to 25th Street & Telegraph Ave. and again relocated to 34th and Market Streets in 1924 purchasing a building for $8,000 and renamed the church to Market Street Seventh Day Adventist Church to reflect its location. Membership continued to grow during the post WWII years and the Market Street Seventh Day Adventist became recognized as the mother church among Seventh Day Adventist churches. The church also started the Golden Gate Academy, an elementary and high school on property owned by the church on Alcatraz

87. Mt Zion Missionary Baptist Church, unpublished history facts written by Thelma King, Church Historian, Emeritus.

Avenue, Berkeley, in 1923. Over the years, the church has been pastored by
a number of ministers. The ministry outreach of the church includes health
seminars, health fairs, cooking classes, distribution of Thanksgiving food
baskets to needy families in the community, and providing food boxes for
the homeless and needy as well as clothing and basic care packages. In 2006,
the Market Street Church was granted permission to begin the process of
building a new facility and relocating to the Golden Gate Academy site on
Mountain Blvd in Oakland. As the Market Street Church continues to grow
and expand the boundaries of outreach, the church continues to pursue the
development of a new church that will help the church to serve the needs of
the congregation and the community.[88]

Beebe Memorial Christian Methodist Episcopal Cathedral

By the late nineteenth century in Oakland, African Americans could choose
among three major African Methodist denominations: African Methodist Episcopal Church (AME), African Methodist Episcopal Zion Church
(AMEZ), or the Colored Methodist Episcopal Church (CME.)

Beebe Memorial CME came into existence in January 1925 when
a small group of Christians gathered in the home of Mr. and Mrs. Jerry
Wayner (Catherine Scott) to launch the first CME Mission Church in Oakland. Along with the Wayners were Bishop Charles H. Philips, Presiding
Elder, W. B. Butler and the Reverend Floyd Haynes, and others. The Reverend Haynes was assigned to pastor the new mission for two years. During
his brief tenure the infant congregation purchased a small building on 37th
Street in Oakland.

At the end of two years, the Reverend Haynes was transferred and the
small congregation dwindled even further. For three years, a succession of
local preachers served the mission, including the Reverends R. Ruffins, G.
Lollar, and C. H. Houston. Between 1932 and 1941, the struggle for Beebe,
also known as the little church under the palms, struggled to stay alive. With
a small membership, Beatrice Russell expressed, "We prayed and prayed for
that little church but we didn't grow, we just carried on."[89] At some point
during the early years, the church was rented to a local Baptist church as the
congregation was too small to support it. Between 1925 and 1946, fourteen
pastors served the small congregation. In 1932, the Reverend J. G. Collins, a
noted CME evangelist from Louisiana, was assigned to lead the congregation.

88. Market Street Seventh Day Adventist Church 90th Anniversary Book 2013,
unpublished.

89. Bebe Memorial C.M.E. Cathedral Church History, 1958, p. 14.

He revived the congregation and set out to launch an extensive evangelistic campaign. In the tradition of Methodist itineracy, the Reverend Collins was transferred, leaving the church with only interim pastors, and once again membership declined. After a brief search, the Reverend E. C. Washington was later installed as pastor. It was not until the 1940s when thousands of migrants flooded the East Bay from the South seeking employment at the shipyards and looking for a new church home. Beebe was on the rebound with standing-room only. It is not known when the Reverend Washington was transferred. Several pastors followed after the Reverend Washington. Reverend Lindsey Rucker was appointed pastor, and the church purchased a larger property at 598 31st Street, Oakland, at the cost of $55,000, a considerable sum of money. Through various church activities the congregation raised $25,000, but they still needed $30,000 more to complete the transaction. Lending agencies were not readily accommodating church groups at that time, especially black church groups. Time was against them, for they had only thirty days to raise the balance of the money. Not knowing where the needed funds would come from, the congregation proceeded with faith and prayer and the answer came through the former pastor, the Reverend E. C. Washington, and President of the Bay Cities Political Club. The Reverend Washington had a banker friend who gave a $30,000 loan to the congregation. The property on 31st Street was finally purchased, and on December 7, 1947, the Reverend L. S. White, successor to the Reverend Rucker, led the congregation into their new sanctuary. In its new location Beebe's growth was steady, reaching a total of twelve hundred members by the end of 1950.

During Reverend White's tenure the church was officially renamed from the First CME Mission Church to Beebe Memorial Christian Methodist Episcopal Church, in tribute to Joseph Andrew Beebe, the 4th Bishop of the Christian Methodist Episcopal Church (formally Colored Methodist Episcopal Church South). The Reverend White was succeeded by the Reverend Lane C. Cleaves in 1950. The Reverend Cleaves, a noted scholar, proved himself an able administrator. The indebtedness he inherited, which was $2,000 on the church building and $14,000 on the parsonage, was liquidated during his two-year tenure. In 1952, ill health forced the premature retirement of Reverend Cleaves and he was succeeded by Reverend Robert C. Thomas, a supply pastor who completed the 1952–1953 conference year. In 1954, the Reverend Melvin J. Bell, a transferee from the Louisiana Conference noted for his preaching and who appealed to both old and young, was assigned to Beebe. The Reverend Bell reorganized the youth department, increasing its membership in excess of fifty voices in the youth choir alone. Under Reverend Bell's leadership, income properties adjacent to the church were purchased, a transaction that proved invaluable when the State of California proposed a series of freeways, one of which would require the demolition of the church building and adjacent properties. Once again the congregation was faced with the task of relocating and a building fund was initiated during the Reverend Bell's last years as pastor. Beebe was one of the many black institutions that felt the sting of the destruction of the Black community during the 1950s redevelopment period.

In 1958, the Reverend S. R. H. Banks succeeded Reverend Bell who passed away suddenly within the first year. In November, 1958 Reverend John H. Dorn was assigned to complete the Reverend Bank's unexpired term. The Reverend Dorn immediately set out to purchase a new church site at 3900 Telegraph Avenue, Oakland, at the cost of $195,000. In 1963, the Reverend Dorn was transferred to Los Angeles and was succeeded by the Reverend Robert C. Thomas. The congregation continued the building plans, and on December 9, 1963, the building contract was awarded to the Camping Construction Company. The theater building that stood on the land at 3900 Telegraph Ave. was demolished and ground breaking soon started for a new church. Following the Annual Conference in circa 1965, the Reverend Thomas withdrew from the CME fellowship and was succeeded by the Reverend Lewis S. White who came in at a time Beebe was experiencing difficulties. The Reverend White encouraged the church to continue with their building plans, which would exceed one million dollars. On April 17, 1966, the congregation gathered at 598 31st Street where they had worship and began the grand march to the new church location at 3900 Telegraph Ave. Three months later, a service of concentration was held on Sunday, July 31, 1966 for the new $1.1 million Bebee Memorial Christian Methodist Episcopal Church.[90] The Rt. Reverend Walter H. Amos of Detroit, Presiding Bishop of the 9th Episcopal District to which the Oakland congregation is related, officiated. The Reverend Dr. Herbert Guice, Pastor, Bethel Missionary Baptist Church, along with the congregation and choir participated in a special 3:00 p.m. service. The main sanctuary had a seating capacity of fifteen hundred with a balcony that was filled to capacity. The new church included a pastor's study, bishop's office, associate minister's office, stewards and trustees' room, choir room, ushers' room, first aid, and two lounges with an adjoining twenty-two room educational facility and chapel. The celebration was a star during a turbulent time for Oakland when the Black Panthers were being organized.[91]

90. *Oakland Tribune*, July 28, 1966.

91. Beebe Memorial Christian Methodist Episcopal Cathedral information gathered from Beebe Church history, http://experiencebmc.org , and the *Oakland Tribune*, July 28, 1966.

The Dawning of a New Day

In 2003, Reverend Dr. Charley Hames Jr. was appointed by Bishop Henry M. Williamson Sr. to serve as pastor of the historic Beebe Memorial Cathedral. Dr. Hames brought a dynamic leadership that attracts young adults. Under Dr. Hames's leadership, the church has grown to more than twenty-five hundred members with two Sunday worship experiences making it one of the premier houses of worship in the San Francisco Bay Area. Dr. Hames has been named Pastor of the Year by the CME 9th Episcopal District with outreach ministries that focus on the whole family. In addition to revitalizing its witness, the church has opened its doors to many community and non-profit organizations in the Bay Area along with a television and radio ministry.

The Memorial Tabernacle Church, 1925

The Memorial Tabernacle (Christ Holy Sanctified Church), Oakland, was founded in 1925 by Bishop Judge and Sarah King. The First Christ Holy Sanctified Church in Oakland was located in a two-story house on 7th Street, the heart of the business district for blacks in West Oakland. Seventh Street was culturally rich, diverse, and had a colorful social nightlife. Visitors from other parts of the country often frequented the popular nightclubs and bars located on the 7th Street strip where well-known jazz musicians and blues singers performed. Bishop Judge and Sarah King considered the area a rich harvest for ministry and winning souls for Christ. They preached on street corners, in front of bars, and invited people into their homes. The church grew rapidly as one of the great Pentecostal churches in the Bay Area where well-known revivalists and evangelists came to conduct revival services at the church.

The congregation later moved to a larger building at 1711 7th Street. Bishop Judge King was called from labor to reward in 1945. His son, Bishop Ulysses S. King Sr. succeeded as pastor. Bishop Ulysses King was a progressive thinker, spiritual leader, church administrator, organizer, and an anointed preacher and musician. His vision for the church included community involvement. Bishop King had a strong belief that the doctrine of holiness and sanctification could be taught in other communities of faith without fear or prejudice. Bishop King joined the Center for Urban Black Studies in Berkeley, California, and later received an Honorary Doctor of Divinity degree from the same institution.

In 1960, the U. S. Postal Service purchased several blocks of land and property on 7th Street to build a Main Post Office. It was also during this time that The Bay Area Rapid Transit District was clearing houses and business for the mass transportation system by uprooting the Black business community on 7th Street in Oakland. The train tracks were built above ground rather than underground and forced West Oakland homeowners to sell at below market prices. The Seventh Street Mission, along with numerous black businesses and other churches were forced out; it was the beginning of the ending of a strong black community. Bishop King, Mother M. K. Williams, and Deacon Tommy Thomas looked at several churches for sale and purchased a building form the Evangelical & Reformed Church, 5801 Racine Street in North Oakland, where blacks were slowly being allowed to reside following WWII.

For over sixty years, Bishop Ulysses King, was the lead minister of the church. He preached throughout the United States and served the church and the people of God throughout the United States in varying denominations and even established a church in Uyo, Nigeria, May 12, 1976. On July 5, 1985, Bishop Ulysses S. King Sr. was called from labor to reward. The Reverend Stephen King was elected to succeed Bishop Ulysses King Sr. The church continues to stand as a beacon of light in the community.[92]

McGlothen Temple Church of God in Christ, 1925

The early beginnings of the Richmond Community Church of God in Christ in Richmond, California started in 1925 in the home of Mr. and Mrs. Willie (Annie E.) Miles on Alamo Street, Richmond. Services were held in homes until the church was formally organized with the help of Elder S. W. Harrison who served as pastor for several years. After his resignation, Elder F.E. Fears was appointed Pastor and served for several years.

For a number of years the church was unstable because of the number of ministers coming and going. In 1941, a powerhouse by the name of Bishop G. W. "Dad" McGlothen was appointed pastor. Bishop McGlothen raised enough funds to start a major building project for the church, which was completed in March 1946. The church was dedicated and renamed McGlothen Temple Church of God in Christ in honor of Bishop G. W. McGlothen.

McGlothen Temple gained notoriety as the church home of Doctor Mattie "Mom" McGlothen. She achieved the highest position in the Church of God in Christ Women's Department, when she was appointed National and International Supervisor of Women of the Churches of God in Christ,

92. http://www.mtchurch.org/mission.shtml (accessed September 20, 2013).

Incorporated. Bishop McGlothen served as Pastor until he was called from labor to reward circa 1964. Bishop Davis succeeded him that same year.

Bishop Clarence J. Davis was very active in the vineyard. He was known and respected locally and nationally prior to his appointment as pastor having served as Jurisdictional Prelate of California Northwest Ecclesiastical Jurisdiction, Assistant to Bishop Mathis, Area Superintendent, District Superintendent for the Richmond District, and Chairman of the California Northwest and Church of God in Christ National Women's Finance Departments.

In 1986, Bishop Davis was called from labor to reward having served faithfully. He was succeeded by Administrative Assistant John Jennings in 1987. He was a hard, dedicated, faithful worker. He serves as the Senior Administrative Assistant to Bishop W. W. Hamilton and is the founder and Superintendent of the Greater Richmond District. Dr. Jennings also served as the Chairman of the California Northwest State Finance Department. From humble beginnings as the Richmond Community Church of God in Christ the leadership set goals to build the church's membership and fulfill the spiritual needs of both members and community. A building has been dedicated and named The Bishop Clarence James Davis Educational Building and the Doctor Mattie McGlothen Library/Museum. McGlothen Temple Church established itself as the mother church of Richmond, when it opened doors for worship during the First Migration in the early 1920s.[93] McGlothen Temple was a far cry from a quiet-worship-style church. Tambourines, piano playing that could not be distinguished from juke joints, along with shouting and frenzy, drew young people to the church.[94]

Memorial Tabernacle and McGlothen both started in 1925. Like many other churches, these two storefront churches were constructed much like the newcomers homes—with few resources and much ingenuity. Often a small congregation pooled their money and rented a store or some other retail structure. Others met in private homes or held tent services. Wherever they met, it did not matter, once the music started and the Holy Ghost experience fell upon the worshipers, there emerged what W. E. B. Dubois described as the frenzy of explosive emotions coupled with shouting, speaking in tongues, arms waving, laughing, and crying.[95] The emotionally charged worship style and exuberant gospel music of the newcomers' churches reflected a cumulative expression of the African-American urban experience yet retained the traditional values of black folk life as it has evolved

93. McGlothen Temple Church of God In Christ History.

94. Moore, *To Place our Deeds*, 28.

95. DuBois, *The Souls of Black Folk*, 136.

since slave days.[96] Though most high-class people were not members of Holy-Ghost-style churches because they did not reflect their middle class upbringing, when they did visit most felt an experience that was missing in their cold and unemotional churches. Some even called the high-class churches refrigerator churches, because they were so cold.

The Great Depression—The Neck Bone Years

There are no good times to be black in America, but some times are worse than others.

—David Bradley

On Black Tuesday, October 29, 1929, the stock-market crash triggered the Great Depression. In 1930, 50 percent of African Americans were unemployed. The Wall Street Stock market crashed and hundreds of thousands of people lost their jobs and homes. The Bay Area was not spared from the economic plight that brought on the Depression. White people were only too glad to get jobs that were once considered colored and below their standard and even demanded that blacks be fired if it meant a white man was out of work.[97] Not surprisingly, somehow, the food assistance programs seemed to run out of assistance when the blacks finally inched their way to the front of the line. John Hope Franklin commented that in starvation there was discrimination, for in few places was relief administered on the basis of equality. Some religious and charitable organizations excluded Negroes from the soup kitchens, which they operated to relieve the suffering.[98] The Great Depression was hard on single, divorced, or widowed women, but it hit black women even harder. Black women found themselves out of work as white women took over jobs such as domestics, waitresses, cooks, nurses, and maids. Black beauticians and barbers were not hit as hard because whites were unable to provide black hair care as well as cosmetics. Since white people did almost all of the hiring in the United States, it went without saying that they would not offer the better jobs to black people, much less place them as bosses over whites. Even those African Americans with college degrees found most avenues of employment blocked.[99]

---

96. Moore, *To Place Our Deeds*, 141.
97. Goode, *California's Black Pioneers*, 132, 133.
98. Franklin, *From Slavery to Freedom*, 496.
99. Flamming, *Bound for Freedom*, 70.

Churches were not exempt from feeling the effects of a devasting downturn. Choices had to be made by members whether to give offerings to the church or keep a roof over the family's head. At the same time, somehow, some of the more prominent Black churches provided assistance to members and nonmembers. The North Richmond Missionary Baptist Church held canned food drives and sponsored a clean clothes closet for needy residents. One woman commented, "We like to help people, we prepared big pots of beans and fed all the people who were hungry, and there were a lot of hungry people." One old timer recalls, "Some of us sleep on the church floor with our handmade quilts from home."[100] Along with black churches, the YWCA provided food, clothing, sleeping space, and job referrals. Religious institutions continued their programs, doing the best they could to help with unemployment and other cultural functions during the neck bone years.

The Great Depression was a giant step backward for San Francisco blacks. These were the most difficult years economically. Never before in San Francisco's history had so many Blacks from all classes been either unemployed or chronically underemployed.[101] William Pittman, a prominent black dentist, could not support his family, so he worked as a chauffeur temporarily, earning only $80 a month. Pittman's wife, Tarea Hall Pittman, a 1925 University of California graduate, worked in a cannery until her position was terminated.[102]

On the national front, Franklin D. Roosevelt was elected president in the midst of the Great Depression based on his promise to bring a New Deal that would bring relief by way of governmental programs that would provide governmental assistance using the three R's: relief, recovery, and reform. In fact Roosevelt used as his campaign theme song, "Happy Days Are Here Again," signaling a new beginning. However, the New Deal was often seen as a raw deal for Blacks who continued to suffer from racism and discrimination that put them at the bottom of receiving governmental assistance. Governmental assistance programs, dubbed the alphabet programs, such as the Works Progress Administration, better known as the WPA, Federal Works Agency, known as the FWA, and the Social Security Administration, known as the SSA, proved to bring minimal improvement for blacks. The trickle-down effect was minimal for Blacks.

Some blacks felt the WPA was the most important to them. One Negro preacher told his flock, "Let Jesus lead you and Roosevelt feed you."[103]

100. Moore, *To Place Our Deeds*, 38.

101. Broussard, *Black San Francisco*, 113.

102. Ibid., 118.

103. St. Clair Drake and Cayton, *Black Metropolis*, 1:354.

Following the Great Depression Blacks continued to suffer economically mostly in housing and jobs. With the advent of WWII following the Great Depression, in some ways it signaled a new beginning for blacks who sojourned to the West Coast in search of job opportunities in the shipyards.

Bethlehem Lutheran Church, Oakland

From very humble beginning in 1929 two sets of sisters, Mrs. Adelia Pollard, Mrs. Bessie Wilcox, and Mrs. Marylese Golphin, and the second set, Mrs. Effie Reed and Mrs. Alberta Johnson, along with their families and a few friends, came to California from Louisiana like so many other migrants in search of a better life. After settling in West Oakland, they wanted to have a black Lutheran Church for Black people in West Oakland. Like so many other start-up churches, the old Carpenters Hall on 7th Street in West Oakland became their first meeting place. This small group of Christians became known as the Lutheran Witnesses of West Oakland. They cooked dinners to raise funds to maintain the church. During the early years, part-time pastors connected with the Lutheran Church-Missouri Synod through the Synodical Conference Missionary Board. The first part-time pastor was Reverend John McDavid, a Black Lutheran pastor who made monthly trips from Los Angeles to provide moral and spiritual support. The exact time that Pastor McDavid served is unknown; however, Pastor Otto Theiss, Professor at Concordia College in Oakland, succeeded him and served for almost ten years. During Pastor Theiss's tenure, the church received a grant of $3,000 from the Synodical Conference Missionary Board and used $2,700 to purchase a building at 16th and Magnolia Streets Oakland for a place to call their own. After Pastor Thesis left, Pastor A. H. Wessling served for almost five years. By this time, the membership had increased and the church needed a full-time pastor. The Reverend Charles Cline was commissioned by the Synodical Conference to serve the Greater Bay Area, and later concentrated all of his time as pastor of Bethlehem. Pastor Cline was active, outspoken, and served for almost twenty-five years. Under his leadership, Bethlehem became a well-recognized church as a result of Pastor Cline's outreach and community involvement. Long after Pastor Cline left, the members would recall his dedication and great love for the people of Bethlehem.[104] By 1952, Bethlehem had outgrown the 16th and Magnolia Street location and they began to negotiate for the church building occupied by Zion Lutheran Church at 959 12th Street as Zion was relocating to the more affluent area of Oakland in the Piedmont hills. Bethlehem relocated to the

104. Bethlehem Lutheran History Book, unpublished.

12th Street location on October 4, 1953. The history records for Bethlehem reveal a large gap for twenty years from the early 50s until the Reverend Will Lawrence Herzfeld was installed as a full time pastor on September 3, 1974. The Reverend Herzfeld was a social justice activist who reshaped Bethlehem church into a nationally known community activist church. In 1975, the Reverend Herzfeld visited Haiti and, as a result his efforts, Bethlehem Lutheran Church sponsored sixteen Haitian refugees. By then Bethlehem was known internationally as a global mission church.

The Reverend Herzfeld was the first African American to serve on the executive staff for the Lutheran Council in the United States. Dr. Herzfeld found time to combine his duties as a pastor and adjunct professor of urban ministry at the Graduate Theological Union, Berkeley, from 1979 to 1989. Bethlehem had been a member of the Missouri Synod until 1975. Under Dr. Herzfeld's leadership, Bethlehem was one of the first African-American churches to break away from the Missouri Synod and join the Association of Evangelical Lutheran Churches because of the disputes over social and doctrinal issues. The Reverend Herzfeld also served as vice president of the Alamo Black Clergy from 1970 to 1989. The Alamo clergy were an ecumenical group that was struggling to bring new meaning to theology from a black perspective. Dr. Herzfeld also served on the board of directors of the National Conference of Black Churchmen for almost three decades while serving as a social political activist. Dr. Herzfeld found time to obtain a Doctorate of Divinity from the Center of Urban Black Studies at Berkeley in 1984 and another doctorate from Christ Seminary in St. Louis in 1984. In addition to numerous boards, he was chairperson of a subcommittee of the Mayor's Blue Ribbon commission on Crime in Oakland in 1986 to 1987, a member of the Committee on Lutheran Unity in 1981, and served on numerous other boards, including being a member of the California Attorney General's Commission on Racial, Ethnic, Religious and Minority Violence in 1987.[105] In addition to the Reverend Herzfeld's social activism and pastoral duties, he had an interest in sports. He was named chaplain for the Golden Gate Warriors professional basket team from 1987 to 1988. The positions that Dr. Herzfeld held promoted the presence of Bethlehem Lutheran Church as one of the premier churches in the Bay Area. Dr. Herzfeld made history when he became the first African American Bishop to head a Lutheran denomination in the United States, putting Bethlehem Lutheran Church in the spotlight as a first. Dr. Herzfeld was called from labor to reward on May 9, 2010 unexpectedly when he was stricken with malaria after attending the ordination of

105. www.socialarchive.iath.virginia.edu, Herzfeld, Will Lawrence, 1937 (accessed September 16, 2015).

the first female Lutheran pastor in the Central African Republic.[106] A series of pastors served Bethlehem Lutheran including the Reverend Julius Carrol, who was successful in leading Bethlehem to retire its mortgage and became debt free.[107] Like many other churches, membership has declined significantly, leaving Bethlehem struggling to continue its witness to the community.

St Paul African Methodist Episcopal Church, 1933

St. Paul A. M. E. Church was officially organized in 1933. Early history indicates that a Berkeley Mission was organized in 1926 during the administration of Bishop H. Blanton Parks, and Reverend A. Milton Ward who served as Presiding Elder. Eleven members from First African Methodist Episcopal Church, Oakland, came together and formed the Berkeley Mission with Reverend Davis serving as first pastor for three months. When Reverend Davis left, the Mission was left on the rocks, struggling for survival for seven years; however, they managed to hold on to a core group until 1933 when Reverend Elliott came and reorganized the Mission in the home of the Reverend Speese with members from Parks Chapel.

In 1934, the Reverend Arthur Moore was appointed pastor and brought an organizational leadership style including raising $250 for a church building. Reverend Moore was succeeded by the Reverend H. C. Claybrooks in 1936. Reverend Claybrooks was a great spiritual leader and Sunday School worker; however, he did not remain long. In 1939, the Reverend A. M. Ward was appointed pastor and the church name was changed from Berkeley Mission to St. Paul African Methodist Episcopal Church.[108] St. Paul benefited from the Great Migration when thousands of black men and women came to the Bay Area where work was plentiful in the shipyards. In just one short year between 1942 and 1943, membership grew from seventy-two to 185 with women representing the majority. The church was able to burn its mortgage after successfully renovating the building. [109]

In 1942, Reverend M. L. Hawkins was appointed pastor and within six months the remaining mortgage debt of $1,279, was paid off, the church building was completely renovated, a new pipe organ and baby grand

---

106. "William L. Herzfeld files," The New York Public Library Schomburg Center for Research in Black Culture, Manuscripts, Archives, and Rare Books Division, 1964–1990.

107. Bethlehem Lutheran Church 80th Anniversary Book, unpublished.

108. "F. D. Speese History of St. Paul A.M.E. Church," Oakland Public Main Library History Room Archive collection under folder Churches

109. Lemke-Santangelo, *Abiding Courage*, 160.

piano was purchased, and a four-room parsonage apartment was built.[110] A number of ministers have served as Pastor for St. Paul due to the itineracy process that rotates pastors in and out of the pulpit. St. Paul AME continues its strong tradition of social action under the leadership of the Reverend Anthony Hughes, who was appointed circa 2013. St. Paul stands as a beacon of light in the Berkeley area and the greater community.

Progressive Missionary Baptist Church, 1935

The Progressive Missionary Baptist Church was organized on January 5, 1935 by a group of thirty-five devout Christians in the midst of the Great Depression when economic conditions were especially hard. During its infancy years, the church struggled for survival, but somehow managed to earn the reputation of the "Friendly Church on the Avenue" in the South Berkeley area that stretches from Adeline and 63rd Streets down to Ashby Avenue. In the early 1940s, the old Lorin-Lincoln Hall, which was used for many events including a dance hall, was purchased by the members of Progressive for their place of worship. Progressive was one of the many churches that provided resources and connections for the black migrants during the WWII era and the Great Migration. Progressive was pastored by three ministers prior to Reverend Edward Stovall, who pastored the church beginning in the early 40s. By 1955 membership had grown to over twelve hundred. With a growing membership and finances, Progressive purchased five lots adjacent to the existing edifice, remodeled the original building, and put up an outdoor sign. With the added growth, in 1959, the church expanded its sanctuary including a library, nursery, classroom, baptistery, choir rooms, and an usher's room.[111]

Progressive was a great supporter of the NAACP and made significant contributions to college scholarships and religious camps for delinquent boys.[112] Reverend Stovall was a forward-thinking pastor who connected the church to the community.

The Reverend Stovall was commended by the California State Assembly for outstanding community service, including the Mayor's Citizens'

110. Oakland Public Main Library History Room, Archive collection under folder "Churches."

111. Progressive Missionary Baptist Church *Twenty Years of Progress 1935-1955*, Church file, Northern California Center for Afro-American History and Life.

112. Lemke-Santangelo, *Abiding Courage*, 160. Quoted from Progressive Baptist Church, *Twenty Years of Progress 1935-1955*. Church file Northern California Center for Afro-American History and Life.

Advisory Committee and the Capital Improvement and Urban Renewal Committees. The Reverend Stovall served as secretary of the St. John Baptist Association, President of the California Baptist State Sunday School and Baptist Training Union (BTU), President of the Interdenominational Ministerial Alliance, President of the Alameda County Branch of the NAACP, and President of the Berkeley Area Council of Churches.[113]

On March 23, 1961, Dr. Stovall along with the Reverends Roy Nichols, Berkley, and Booker T. Anderson met with Dr. Martin Luther King Jr. who was visiting in Oakland.[114] The Reverend Stovall was later called from labor to reward circa 1968. On September 1977, Progressive overwhelmingly elected the Reverend Earl Stuckey. The Reverend Stuckey was known for his in-depth preparation and study that went into every message, lesson, and seminar that he presented and preached on a national level. Reverend Stuckey organized Progressive around the five New Testament purposes of the church: fellowship, discipleship, ministry, evangelism, and worship. To add to the spiritual growth and organization of the church, Reverend Stuckey created Purpose Teams and Team Leaders, ordained men who shared his vision. First Lady Kay Frances Stuckey has worked alongside her husband for over forty-five years.[115]

Star Bethel Missionary Baptist Church, Oakland

The conflict of World War II was on the horizon and the Great Depression had taken a toll on the economy, but it did not stop a group of ten faithful people from coming together in the home of Sister Shirley Evans to organize the Star Bethel Missionary Baptist Church in June 1938. The black population had begun to grow, and the faithful few located a storefront in the heart of West Oakland.

The first two pastors were Reverend N. Reason, who resigned to become the pastor of the First Union Baptist Church in San Francisco, and the Reverend F. W. Watkins, who was also serving as part time pastor of North Richmond Baptist Church. The Reverend Watkins was elected to serve as the full-time pastor of North Richmond in 1938, leaving Star Bethel without a pastor for a brief time. On October 1, 1938, the Reverend George H. Henderson was called to pastor the little church that had struggled to stay alive during the hard times of the Depression with seventeen members. Under the Reverend Henderson's leadership, Star Bethel grew to exceed over three thousand members in the 1940s. The church had a great decision to

113. *Oakland Tribune*, circa 1961.

114. *Oakland Tribune*, March 23, 1961.

115. http://progressive4life.org/welcome/our_story.

make, agreeing to purchase property at 5812 San Pablo Avenue at the cost of $95,000. In the next decade Star Bethel continued to grow.[116] In 1961, the Reverend Henderson celebrated twenty-two faithful years as Pastor. By now Star Bethel had a local and national reputation for inspirational service and a choir that was known to bring the people to their feet. Under the leadership of the Reverend Henderson, Star Bethel managed to burn its mortgage on the occasion of the 23rd Church Anniversary. The Reverend Henderson was called from labor to reward circa December 1961.

On August 1, 1962, the Reverend Edward J. Boyd was called to pastor Star Bethel. Due to poor health, Pastor Boyd retired in 1973.

In 1974, the Reverend Doctor C. Cedric Claiborne accepted the call to be the fifth pastor of Star Bethel. Under his leadership the church continued the tradition of building and prospering for God's glory. Dr. Claiborne had come from successfully pastoring the Mount Zion Baptist Church in East St. Louis, Illinois and brought those same gifts of leadership and skills for kingdom building to Star Bethel. The Church purchased its first parsonage in the exclusive Oakland Hills on Coach Drive as well as three minibuses to transport and spread the gospel in the communities of Oakland and beyond. Star Bethel continued the vision of building God's kingdom as membership increased. A new edifice with four stories was built on the San Pablo property that expanded the sanctuary and had facilities for multiple uses, including a chapel for weddings and private prayer. On September 7, 1980, the church held a dedication service. Dr. Claiborne resigned September 30, 1985 and immediately founded the Canaan Christian Covenant Baptist Church, holding services at the Palmer D. Whitted Funeral Chapel in Oakland.[117] For eleven months, Star Bethel struggled without a leader until the Reverend J. L. Hudson accepted the call as the sixth pastor, coming from Pathway Baptist Church, Chicago. The Reverend Hudson was a fearless, faithful leader. He nurtured the congregation spiritually and continued the building project that began under Dr. Claiborne. On March 13, 1988, Star Bethel celebrated fifty years of faithful service in the community. The Reverend Hudson retired in January 2008.[118]

In May 2008, Dr. Earl Ward, a son in the ministry at Star Bethel, was elected as the seventh pastor. In 2009, the church celebrated its final mortgage burning, leaving the church debt free. Additional renovations included a lift for physically challenged persons. Under Dr. Ward's leadership, Star Bethel continues to be a church for the community in the community.

116. Star Bethel Missionary Baptist Church Golden Anniversary, March 13, 1988, p. 5.

117. Ibid., 6.

118. Ibid., 7.

Mingleton Temple Church of God in Christ, Oakland

In September 1939, Elder Mingleton opened a church mission at 939 Myrtle Street, Oakland, without a single member. Shortly thereafter, M. J. Lewis, Mabel King, and W. F. White joined Elder Mingleton. Slowly, other members joined including Elder William Hannibal Means and Williette Means. Elder Mingleton gave Mrs. Means permission to organize a citywide revival to draw members. The Revival was successful and Mingleton Temple became known as the Power House. German Reed Ross, a gifted musician born on a cotton farm in Hubbard, Texas, joined Mingleton Temple in 1945, becoming internationally recognized as a gifted musician, earning numerous accredited degrees, and becoming the first African-American corporate auditor for the IRS in Northern California. On October 5, 1947, during the peak of the Second Great Migration, membership had grown to the point that a new church had to be built at 529 Market Street, Oakland. Elder Mingleton was a highly gifted preacher who could draw a crowd. Unfortunately, he became seriously ill and passed on the responsibilities to Elder Leland Germany and later Elder Lafar Johnson. Elder Mingleton was called from labor to reward (date unknown). Bishop E. B. Stewart pastored the church from 1953 to 1954. The flourishing days of West Oakland came to an end during the redevelopment phase following WWII. Homes, businesses, and churches were uprooted and blacks were scattered to make way for the main post office and the new high-speed Bay Area Rapid Transit.

The Oakland Redevelopment Agency destroyed the West Oakland businesses and homes of blacks including the strip along Seventh Street, which was the heart of the black community. Mingleton Temple along with other black churches were forced to relocate.[119]

Circa 1953, the church relocated to 15th Street in West Oakland. In 1954, Superintendent V. F. Devers became the pastor, serving faithfully until he was called from labor to reward in 1981. The baton was passed to Superintendent John M. Evans to be the next pastor. Under his leadership, the church was remodeled and ministries expanded to include outreach programs. Women served a leadership role in the COGIC church and were often referred to as "Mother." Some of the great women at Mingleton Temple included Mother I. J. Mingleton, wife of founding pastor, Mother E. M. Devers, and Mother Perrodine, who united with Mingleton in 1944.[120]

119. Self, *American Babylon*, 157.

120. Mingleton Temple Church History, Oakland Public Library History Room, church files.

Part III—Great Migration 1940–1970

It is of no use for us to sit with our hands folded, hanging our heads like bulrushes, lamenting our wretched condition; but let us make a mighty effort and arise; and if no one will promote or respect us, let us promote and respect ourselves. Marie W. Stewart

The Second Great Migration—1940–1970

"From the early years of the twentieth century to well past its middle age nearly every black family in the American South, which meant nearly every Black family in America, had a decision to make . . . Historians would come to call it the Great Migration. It would become perhaps the biggest underreported story of the twentieth century. It was vast. It was leaderless."[1] Many of the migrants settled in the Bay Area for the opportunity to improve their economic conditions by working in the shipyards. Large numbers of migrants settled in the metropolitan cities of the Bay Area. Black churches exploded with the population growth. It seemed as if churches sprung up overnight; some started in storefronts and others as prayer bands in homes. It was not uncommon for Bay Area black churches to connect with southern black churches to encourage family members to come to California reassuring them that the church would help take care of them. The promise of care however, was not readily available. The majority of the black churches were not prepared to handle the needs of the migrants who needed housing. It was one thing to find employment, but the issue of finding housing in already crowded black neighborhoods loomed large. Social inequity was

1. Wilkerson, *The Warmth of Other Suns*, 8, 9.

a way of life for the black migrants seeking a better life. In 1940, the black population of San Francisco and three main East Bay Cities, Richmond, Berkeley, and Oakland, *combined* was only about seventeen thousand. Ten years later the black population of these four cities stood at roughly one hundred and seventeen thousand. The black community in Oakland, the largest in northern California before the war, experienced similar growth. With an African-American population of about eighty-five hundred in 1940, Oakland saw about thirty-seven thousand more settle there by 1945.

Richmond and Vallejo both saw their black populations jump and, in Oakland, the numbers grew from 8,462 in 1940 to 37,327 in 1945. By 1950, Oakland saw a significant increase brought on by the birth of baby boomers; by 1950, the census count showed an increase of 12.4 percent with a count of 47,562 blacks in Oakland. Berkeley Blacks increased by 11.7 percent adding up to 13,289. The 1950 census count for San Francisco City and County revealed the black population had an increase of 5.6 percent with a count of 43,502 Blacks. Richmond's black census count revealed 13.4 percent increase with a population count of 13,374.[2] One old timer recalled, "We'd go down to the 16th Street station after school to watch the people get off the trains, it was like a parade. You just couldn't believe that many black people would come in, and some didn't even have any luggage; they would come with boxes with three or four children with no place to stay."[3] They came by train, gradually moving forward out of the Jim Crow cars as the train moved west. They came by car, camping along roadsides when no hotels would take colored people. Most of them made the journey in 1942 and 1943, when the labor shortage required all hands on deck, regardless of what color those hands were.[4]

In the early 1940s with the influx of Blacks migrating to the Bay Area, they were forced to live in segregated neighborhoods. As West Oakland developed into the East Bay's principal black community in the mid-1940s, whites left in large numbers. New housing in East Oakland nearby suburbs, provided them with residential mobility.[5] In San Francisco, Instead of serving as a catalyst to improve housing opportunities, World War II stimulated white hostility toward housing integration in San Francisco and intensified black residential concentration within the African American community. This process ultimately led to the development of San Francisco's first black

2. Bay Area 1950 Census Count, Association of Bay Area Governments by cities.

3. Crouchett et al., *Visions toward Tomorrow,* 45. Cited in the Oakland Office of Community Development, Oakland 1979, p. 18.

4. Flamming, *African Americans in the West,* 166.

5. Self, *American Babylon Race,* 42.

ghetto in the postwar period.[6] Housing was not the only problem facing blacks. Competition for defense industry jobs, and other scarce resources created many of the same problems that had plagued urban areas during the First Migration. In late 1942–1943, blacks were required to show proof they had lived in Contra Costa County for at least one year, a requirement that was not applied to whites. It was no surprise that equal treatment was absent. Shipyard managers allowed blacks to head all-black crews but never to supervise whites. One Bay Area shipyard personnel director declared, "We wouldn't ask white people to work under a Negro and we shouldn't expect them to."[7] The sanctions that enforce the rules of segregation and discrimination are applied by whites to the Negroes, never by the Negroes to the whites. The laws are written upon the pretext of equality but are applied only against the Negroes.[8] Blacks were disadvantaged by separatism within the Boilermakers Union. Not only were they denied voting privileges in the business of policies governing benefits, they were denied the opportunity to attend business meetings.

World War II transformed few places in the East Bay as dramatically as West Oakland. Tens of thousands of African American migrants from the southern states, recruited to the East Bay by Kaiser, the Moore Dry Dock Company and the federal government, settled in the flatlands of West Oakland. Housing discrimination in nearby cities of Albany, El Cerrito, Alameda and San Leandro, and parts of Oakland Hills crowded black migrants into established Negro districts.[9]

Berkeley was particularly affected by the African American migration, the city's black population grew from three thousand to more than twelve thousand between 1940 and 1945. After the turn of the century, Black professionals and prosperous blue-collar workers began to settle in Berkeley.[10] With the rising tensions between blacks and whites, it became necessary for the NAACP to address the issues. Walter A. White, Executive Secretary, NAACP, spoke at Technical High School in Oakland and also Wheeler Hall, Berkeley, on "Minority Groups and the California Civil Rights Law" on Friday November 15. Mr. White frequently referred to the indifference of the Democratic senators in their treatment of the Anti-Lynch Bill. He told the

6. De Graaf et al., *Seeking El Dorado.* Broussard, *In Search of the Promised "Land,"* 197.

7. Taylor, *In Search of the Racial Frontier,* 258. The personnel director is quoted in Broussard, *Black San Francisco,* 157. See McEntire *The Negro Population in California,* Supplement 2.

8. Myrdal, *An American Dilemma,* 2:577.

9. Ibid., 53, 54.

10. Wollenberg, *Berkeley, A City in History,* chap. 7.

crowd "No Negro American will be accepted as volunteer in the Army nor in the Navy, except as mess men in the latter." Only by strong force were Negroes permitted as mechanics in aviation in some places. Yet Negroes are never discriminated against when it comes to paying taxes in support of the defense program. "This is the kind of background out of which has grown such institutions as lynching. Ninety nine point two percent of lynchers have gone free."[11]

By 1943 the City of Richmond's black population had reached fifty-seven hundred. This is a city that counted only 270 black residents three years earlier. The Great Migration was a mixed blessing with great opportunities; at the same time, it was a difficult adjustment for both the black migrants who faced intense hostility. Once again, it was the community of the Negro Church that gave the Blacks some sense of solace.

A Family Bound for the Promised Land

The children of William and Minervy Demery Taylor represents the story of many other black families who migrated from the Deep South during the Great Migration and became part of the pioneer families who helped to start churches. William and Minervy lived in poverty with their fifteen children in the Caddo Parish area of Louisiana, however they owned and farmed their own land. Minervy and William raised their children to be devout Christians who transported those values with them as they came to California, one by one.

Henry Taylor, the oldest son, quit school in the sixth grade to help support the family. In his early twenties and worked at Barksdale Air Force base in Bossier City. Henry married Viola Mayfield Harris, and together they built a shotgun house at 128 Scott Street, Bossier City, Louisiana. Like thousands of others, Henry heard about job opportunities in California and became one of the many migrants to head west in 1943, leaving his family behind to find employment and a place to live. It didn't take long for Henry to find employment as a laborer at Moore Dry Dock Shipyard, Oakland where work was plentiful, not knowing that exposure to asbestos would contribute to his death years later. Henry soon found housing in Harbor Homes, a temporary housing project located near Moore shipyard. He sent for his wife, Viola, and four young children Martha, Carolyn, Jackie, and Harris, who traveled by way of train, leaving the majority of their belongings behind with the exception of a few clothes, and a shoebox of chicken to eat on the long journey where new beginnings were in store. Martha recalled

11. Lena Wysinger, *Oakland Tribune*, November 24, 1940.

that "those were happy times, lots of friends, people lived close together, and you could talk to your neighbors through the paper thin walls in the Harbor Homes projects (temporary war housing) located near Moore Dry Dock Shipyard. If we were poor, I sure didn't know it, we had three sets of clothing each; church clothes, play clothes, and school clothes. We always had a turkey on the table for Thanksgiving, and toys for Christmas, we were rich with love, family and friends. Living in the projects had its benefits, as it fostered a close kinship of community."[12] Working in the shipyards was not happy days for most of the black workers. Henry was accustomed to discrimination in Louisiana; however, he was not prepared for the hostility that he and other Black workers would receive at the shipyard.

White workers viewed black migrants as an invading mob and routinely circulated stories of Black incompetence and stupidity. The Boilermakers Union, which controlled the largest number of shipyard crafts, excluded Black workers from its locals, effectively blocking their access to skilled crafts.[13]

Henry and Viola united with Mt. Calvary Baptist Church located in the Boilermaker's Hall on Seventh Street in West Oakland. Church served as a spiritual reservoir but also a place where Black people socialized and grew as a community. Henry became active as a deacon, and Viola worked with the missionary women's society. During the post-war years, starting in the early 50s, parts of west Oakland, and especially Seventh Street, was uprooted to make way for the Bay Area Rapid Transit District Station and post office. Businesses and every Black church on Seventh Street were destroyed because of redevelopment. The Reverend G. W. Killens relocated the church to a vacant movie theater that was sold to the congregation on 23rd Avenue and the family continued to worship at the new location until the pastor left and started a new church on San Pablo Avenue in West Oakland called St. Mathews Missionary Baptist Church.

Housing shortage became a major concern because racial covenants were still enforced. Henry and Viola managed to save enough money to purchase a small three-bedroom home in Brookfield village in Far East Oakland off 98th Avenue, which was still predominately a white neighborhood that had no black businesses or institutions; for the Taylor family, it felt like isolation. With a home and backyard, Henry did gardening, built a chicken coop, and planted apricot and peach trees By the mid-50s, shipyards throughout the Bay Area were shutting down. The family hit financial rock bottom. Without a decent education, things were looking bleak until

12. Martha C. Taylor, author, retelling a portion of her childhood.
13. Lemke-Santangelo, *Abiding Courage*, 113.

Henry purchased a red truck and started his own business of home demolition and gardening with a good business hiring others. Twelve years after the shipyard closed and had no workers, Henry was still paying union dues, through the pressure of the Boilers Union. In the mid-1950s the Reverend Titus Washington, started a house church and named it Tabernacle Baptist Church. Henry and Viola joined the church along with their children. Henry was already an ordained deacon and became a member of the Trustees Board. After serving faithfully for many years, Henry made a decision to help one of his adopted sons who had been called into the ministry to start his own church. The Reverend Jesse Davis became pastor and founder of Shiloh Baptist Church and Henry was among the first deacons.

Henry was known in the church community as "preacher." No doubt it was his whooping style and musicality in his generalized fervent prayers that caused him to be called "preacher." Children in the church knew his prayers verbatim and would recite the standard prayer in unison each Sunday during devotion as Henry prayed:

> Oh Lord, Oh Jesus, once again, and again, your poor weak and humble servant, come to you this morning with knee bent and head bowed. Lord I am not here this morning for form or fashion, neither be an outside show to an unfriendly world. I want to thank you this morning for waking me up, clothed in my right mind. Lord, I thank you that my bed wasn't my cooling board and my sheet was not my winding chamber. Lord, remember my mother in a far distant land, as she grow in age, help her to grow in your grace. Lord, remember my wife and children . . . Lord, don't forget about the boys on the battlefield. Keep them from all hurt harm or danger. Lord when I get through rising and falling, coming and going, when I have done the best I can, please find a resting place for me in your kingdom, where I can praise you forever. Amen.

The kind of generalized prayer Henry said each Sunday is a common stock of phrases and images by persons throughout the Negro lower-class religious world. Prayers of this type are often synonymous with old-fashioned or southern—such prayers were common in colored Baptist or Methodist churches of *all* status levels.[14]

Rafe Taylor Sr., second-oldest son, migrated from Bossier City, Louisiana to Oakland, with his wife Elnora and children. Shortly after arriving, he joined the Antioch Baptist church during its early stages of organization in 1944 under the leadership of Pastor Thomas. Rafe Sr. served as one of

14. Drake and Cayton, *Black Metropolis*, 620.

the first seven Board of Directors for the church when it officially became incorporated on October 18, 1945. Rafe Sr., a deacon, was often called "preacher" because of his energetic whopping style of praying. It was clear to everyone Rafe "felt the spirit" as displayed with dramatic emotionalism when leading Sunday morning devotion and Wednesday night prayer meeting and family reunion gatherings. Beatrice Taylor-Jett, Rafe Jr., and Laura Taylor-Johnson, the fourth oldest of eight children, recalled "sitting on the mourners bench, I was only eight years of age when I confessed and gave my life to Christ."[15] The mourners bench was that conspicuous spot down in the front of the church where the sinner is supposed to sit and wait for the spirit to strike.[16] Rafe Jr. echoed, "We stayed in church all day on Sundays, starting with Sunday School, eleven o-clock service, singing in the choir, three o-clock service, evening Baptist Young Peoples Union, commonly referred to as BYPU, and BTU then Sunday night service." One of his childhood friends at Antioch was Huey P. Newton who later founded the Black Panther Party. Rafe Jr. recalls their large house on Filbert Street, which was in walking distance to the church. In his adult years, Rafe Jr. served concurrently with his Father on the Deacon Board and later became chair of the Trustee Board.[17] Elmore, Eddie, and Phillip Taylor migrated from Louisiana during the 1940s and joined their brother Rafe at Antioch Baptist Church. Elmore, Eddie, and Phillip soon became deacons. Elmore met Clara in California and had three children: Larry, Billy, and Shirley. Larry served on the Deacon Board with his father, Elmore, and Uncles Eddie and Rafe. Billy Ray, the second-oldest, served briefly on the ministerial staff at Antioch. Billy Ray and Shirley did not remain within the Baptist denomination. Billy Ray became an ordained African Methodist Episcopal pastor in the Bay Area serving at various churches. Shirley joined the Taylor Memorial Methodist Church. By the late 1950s Elmore and Clara had saved enough money to purchase a home and were part of the wave of black migrants moving from West to East Oakland in the late 1950s. Urban renewal, commonly referred to as "Negro removal," was uprooting the Black community in West Oakland. It had become necessary to ease the racial covenants that held blacks in one locale. Billy Ray recalls the culture shock of going to school and living next door to white people on 52nd Avenue. He recalls that a climate of social change was beginning to take place: the freedom movement for equality emerged demanding equal access to housing and jobs; hairstyles

---

15. Laura Taylor-Johnson, interview, Aug. 11, 2014.

16. Drake and Cayton, *Black Metropolis*, 618.

17. Rafe Taylor Jr., interview, Oakland, August 11, 2014.

had gone from neat trims to large afros.[18] Eddie Taylor came to California and enlisted in the army. He was wounded while fighting in World War II and received the Purple Heart for military merit. Eddie served on the Deacon Board at Antioch Baptist Church and remained a faithful servant until he became ill.

Flenore and Nathaniel the younger brothers, came to California in the early 50s and also joined the Antioch Baptist Church. Flenore and his wife, Ernestine, relocated to East Oakland and united with Starlight Missionary Baptist Church where Flenore was a founding member and became an ordained deacon. Nathaniel, the youngest child, recalled his father, William, had passed away in the early 1950s. On one of the visits Henry made to Louisiana, his mother, Minervy, expressed to him that she feared for her youngest son's safety in the racist environment of Louisiana and to please take Nathaniel with him to California. Nathaniel recalls that "it was bitter sweet to leave momma and my sister, Sweeney behind, but I also knew I would have a better life in California." Minervy remained in Louisiana in familiar surroundings with her daughter, Sweeney, for approximately two years before relocating to Stockton, California and lived for a brief time with Tennessee, her other daughter.

Within a year after arriving in California, Nathaniel was drafted in the United States Army and eventually went abroad for two years before being discharged. Jonathan was approximately one year older than Nathaniel. He relocated from Louisiana to California along with his wife, Mary, and his daughter, Sharon. The Taylor brothers contributed to the growth of churches in Oakland, particularly the Antioch Baptist Church.

The depth of the Taylor family's contribution to church growth in Oakland is long and all of it cannot be told. What is important is that this family typifies the migrant families of the 40s who sojourned from Louisiana to California literally with no earthly goods but with a strong will to be somebody. For them, going to church was akin to being law abiding: it was the right thing to do. The family values of attending church, buying a home, and getting a good education were passed down through generations, from migrants to their children and succeeding generations. All fifteen children of Minervy and William remained strong Christians including the daughters. Five of the seven brothers became deacons in the same church. Three of the brothers became founding members of churches in Oakland.

18. The Reverend Billy Ray Taylor, interview, Oakland, August 11, 2014.

Antioch Baptist Church, Oakland

In March 1944, the Reverend J. L. Thomas called fifteen persons together at the Harlem Cleaners on 7th Street in West Oakland and organized the Antioch Missionary Baptist Church. The Reverend Thomas purchased the building at 1177 7th Street at a cost of $4500 and stated that "this is our church home." It was moved by Beatrice Walter and seconded by Mary L. Thomas that the church would bear the name Antioch Missionary Baptist Church. Gertrude Mabery gave the first dollar to the church. Articles of Incorporation were filed October 18, 1945 that stated the name of the church shall be Antioch Baptist Church of West Oakland. "The purpose shall be to promote and maintain religious services and teachings consistent with the usages and doctrines of the Baptist Church; and to promote and encourage charitable contributions to the poor and needy."[19] Two years later, the church repaid the Reverend Thomas and purchased the building, remodeling it with a baptizing pool at the cost of $2,000 Consistent with the growth of West Oakland, the church had to look for a larger facility. In April 1947, a lot was purchased at 14th and Filbert Streets at a cost of $10,500 Two years later the church marched from 1177 7th Street for the groundbreaking service and began building in July 1949. In January 1950, the members moved into the new church facility and laid the cornerstone in April 1950. In 1959, the church expanded with a new addition at a cost $45,000 and held a rededication service February 7, 1960. A great era ended when the Reverend Thomas was called from labor to reward, January 19, 1962. For a brief time, the church was managed by the deacons.[20] Deacon Rafe Taylor Sr., Chairman of the Deacon Board, took the lead. Several months later, the Reverend E. L. Cunningham was elected pastor from September 20, 1962 through December 1964. Under the Reverend Cunningham's leadership over 100 persons joined the church. In June 1964, the Reverend Robert T. George, came from Texas to conduct a weeklong revival. He was a gifted, energetic, singing preacher who could bring a crowd to their feet. It was not surprising that six months later he was elected pastor on December 9, 1964. Antioch Baptist Church was firmly rooted in the Bay Area, often hosting revivals with well-known preachers from the South. Outside of the church, the Reverend George was often visible in community affairs.[21] In 1982, he delivered a rousing speech in Oakland at a Peace and Justice Rally to stop the Regan War Machine. The title of his speech was, "Lord, I Have

19. Odelia Brown, "Antioch Missionary Baptist Church History," unpublished compiled manuscript, p. 4.

20. Ibid., 4.

21. Ibid., 5.

a Problem." The Reverend George was referring to Regan as a man who loved the war more than he loves people.[22] TheReverend George was called from labor to reward December 4, 2002. The Reverend Marvin Warren and the Reverend Gray served briefly as pastors. The Reverend Todd Wheelock serves as the senior pastor and continues to expand the ministry of Antioch into the wider community.

Activities among Negroes

Lena Wysinger, 1940s

"Activities among Negroes" was a Sunday newspaper column that appeared in the *Oakland Tribune* from 1923 through 1945. Delilah Beasley was the first black woman to write for a major newspaper for the general press. The importance of the column was on positive events and racial uplift using a variety of topics and pending issues that affected blacks, including church events, academic achievement, marriages, death notifications, as well as social changes. With this goal in mind, the column served as a major vehicle for building and knitting the community together by keeping people informed about events locally and nationally. Joseph Knowland convinced Beasley to write a regular column in the *Oakland Tribune*. She wrote from 1923 until shortly before her death in 1934; then Lena Wysinger took over the column. The purpose of the column was to portray black people in a positive way. Both Beasley and Wysinger wrote mostly about current events in the Bay area such as churches, social events, women's clubs, literary societies, and national politics. The weekly column was like a connecting link to the wider black community, notifying the public on past and upcoming events especially for black churches.[23]

Tensions for Newcomers

I was free, but there was no one to welcome me to the land of freedom. I was a stranger in a stranger land.

—Harriett Tubman

---

22. *The Black Workers Forum,* located in History Room, Oakland Public Library, April 1982, p. 50.

23. Annalee Allen, "East Bay Faces of the 20th Century," *Oakland Tribune,* August 24, 1999.

In social terms, the incoming blacks were perceived by the dominant white population as a disruptive element who "did not know their place." The *Observer* reported on March 11, 1944 that outside agitators were referring to blacks as stirring up the good niggers.

A new race problem erupted in the Bay Area as Negroes were trying to be part of the mainstream. The reverse appearance of white women driving Negro passengers, and white women waitresses serving Negroes in white men's restaurants became contentious; it just did not sit well. If that is not a potential source of trouble, we do not know what is brought about by the influx of what might be called socially-liberated or uninhibited Negros who are not bound by the old and peaceful traditions that Negroes were to stay in their place. But the trouble is that the Negro newcomer does not concede that the white man has the right to be alone with his kind. Whether race prejudice or not, the white man has the right of race prejudice if he so desires. If he does not care to associate with anyone, he is not compelled to do so. Right there is where the Negro is making his big mistake. On October 26, 1941, Lena Wysinger reported in the Oakland Newspaper *Negroes in the News*, that "A. Phillip Randolph, International President of the Brotherhood of Sleeping Car Porters, and M.P.Webster, first Vice-President and member of the committee on fair employment practices, will speak at a mass meeting at the Oakland Auditorium this afternoon at 3:00 pm. Randolph's subject will be: 'The Fight for World Democracy, and its Relation to the Negro People.' Webster will speak on 'Negro Workers in National Defense.'"

On August 16, 1942, Wysinger reported in *Negroes in the News*;

> Harvey Kerns, Executive Secretary Division of Negro Welfare, Cincinnati, arrived in Oakland August 10th for a two week analysis of the Negroes in Oakland in their relation to the social and civic welfare programs in the community. Kerns will investigate and study the relation of Negroes in Oakland to social welfare agencies, the effect of the migration of Negroes on the social structure of the community and the Negro in general. An evaluation of social work programs on the Negro will be made. Kerns was invited to Oakland by the Council of Social Agencies of Oakland.[24]

The following event serves as an illustration of the tension between blacks and whites: "A black man was stabbed in a Richmond restaurant in 1943 for refusing to give up his booth to a white patron. Blacks were often

---

24. Bagwell, *Oakland the Story of a City*, 240.

warned away or attacked for entering white neighborhoods and gathering spots."[25]

The Migration somehow fueled racial tensions. Throughout 1943, Oakland newspapers wrote about blacks as criminals and considered them "roving Negroes."[26] The *Oakland Observer* sounded the alarm in May 1943 when it announced that blacks were not patronizing downtown restaurants where formerly the first wave of Negroes in the First Migration would have never dreamed of going. A huge race riot broke out on the Oakland streets in May 1944 when over five thousand black fans of Cab Calloway were turned away; the crowd smashed windows and doors. The Twelfth Street riot was characterized in the *Oakland Observer* as blacks barging in on the white man's life, even though Calloway is a black entertainer.[27]

Trouble with the southern black migrants was not only with whites. Some old-time black residents resented the southern migrants, holding them responsible for resurgent racism. In his study of black San Francisco, Charles S. Johnson "found that nearly half of old-time black residents disapproved of newcomers because they augment[ed] racial difficulties in the city."[28] One oldtimer from San Francisco commented that the newcomers were not like the proud pioneers: "Their demeanor in their way of walking down the street . . . You could pick them out from among all the others just like that (snaps his fingers) and they needed up to nine years before they seemed to get Americanized." The last term suggests they seemed like foreigners to native San Franciscans.[29] Historian Douglas Daniels found similar sentiments among old-timers he interviewed in the East Bay. An Oakland native, John Watkins, commented that he felt like a tourist whenever he went to downtown Oakland because there were so many newcomers and they were so different from anything he knew: "Old Residents and newcomers were just like two different peoples. They were a spectacle to the extent of where we used to go down on 7th Street [in Oakland], sometimes just [to] stand and watch them." Watkins recalled them as beautiful people with different ways or modes of dress and dialogue and just different ways of being. "You see them down in department stores with overalls on, trying on fur coats and stuff like that. You'd never see any of these things before." Watkins said on one occasion he and a friend went to what we would call

25. Johnson, *Second Gold Rush*, 168.

26. *Oakland Tribune*, November 7, 1942, and September 13, 1943; *Oakland Observer*, May 15, 1943.

27. *Oakland Observer*, March 11, 1944.

28. Johnson, *The Second Gold Rush*, 168–70.

29. Interview, Aurelious Alberga, July 27, 1976, recorded in Daniels, *Pioneer Urbanites*, 171.

a soul-food restaurant. Watkins asked for a second helping of potatoes and Watkins was charged a dime more. His friend explained that Watkins had asked for "potatoes," whereas he had requested "tatoes."[30] Some of the early pioneers were embarrassed about the way the second migrants acted, feeling like they needed to be inculturated in civic pride and social responsibility.

The black newcomers also received a chilly reception from longtime black residents who felt they were not sophisticated and would destroy the gains and privileges they already enjoyed. One prewar black resident complained that "you couldn't understand them and I wasn't use to that."[31] To help the newcomers to become socialized, Frances Albrier local political activist and founder of the "Little Citizens Study and Welfare Club," held meetings in local churches to educate newcomers on their dress, language, behavior, and social mores they should know.[32] World War II had a profound impact on every aspect of life in Richmond, drastically altering black and white assumptions about the future. The coming of the Kaiser Shipyard was the most visible symbol of the war in Richmond. Shipyard work offered African Americans an economic shift upward, placing them in the midst and at times in the vanguard of Richmond's (and the nation's) economic, industrial, and social transformation.[33] The World War II black migration to San Francisco was a major shift of black migrants from the South to the West. By 1945, San Francisco's total population had increased to 827,400, an increase of 30.4 percent in five years. But, while the city's white population grew at a rate of 28.1 percent during this period, the black population had increased by 665.8 percent. Approximately thirty-two thousand Afro-Americans resided in San Francisco by 1945.[34] Whether oldtimers or newcomers, both sets of migrants were inextricably bonded as Negroes being forced to unite in the common struggle fighting for civil rights. The Great Migration had a decisive impact upon the churches bringing the oldtimers and newcomers face to face to assimilate the southern style of worship and the meager resources available for expanding their ministries.

For the most part, they united in the same churches. With the outbreak of the Second World War, the Negro press emerged as one of the most powerful forces among Negroes in America. Newspapers became the "racial watchdogs" and, with a unanimity that surprised Negroes as much as it did

30. Daniels, *Pioneer Urbanites*, 172.

31. Moore, *To Place Our Deeds*, 81.

32. Johnson, *African-American Christianity*, 170.

33. Ibid., 40.

34. *Special Census of San Francisco, California*, August 1, 1945; Broussard, *Black San Francisco*, 135.

the rest of the country, their editors began a campaign for the complete integration of Negroes into all-war-related activities.[35] Just as migration population dramatically increased, church attendance increased. Black migrants
brought their style, culture, and religion with them. Storefront churches
popped up overnight throughout the San Francisco Bay Area. The movement of Negros to cities created somewhat of a crisis in that it uprooted the
masses of Negroes from their customary way of life, destroying the social
organization that represents both an accommodation to conditions in the
rural South and an accommodation to their segregated and inferior status in
southern society. The storefront church represented an attempt on the part
of the migrants, especially from the rural areas of the South, to reestablish
a type of church in the urban environment to which they were accustomed.
They wanted a church, first of all, in which they were known as people.[36]

Nothing Could Stop the Black Church Growth

*The Black Holy Ghost roaring into some shack of a church, in
the South seizing the congregation with an ancient energy and
power—the black church, therefore, represents and embodies the
transplanted African memory.*

—Larry Neal

During the period of the 1940s the Black Church grew by leaps and bounds.
According to War Manpower Commission officials, a black Baptist church
in Shreveport, Louisiana became a coordinating center for aspiring Bay
Area migrants. Black southern preachers abandoned their churches and
headed for California, working in shipyards and starting new churches often
with the same members. Storefronts were turned into churches overnight.
Bibles, a makeshift pulpit, and a few folding chairs transformed a former
corner store into a church—these were known as storefront churches. Most
storefront churches were fitted with folding chairs, a tambourine, a pair
of cymbals, a battered piano, a religious picture of Jesus, and a red velvet
curtain hanging behind the makeshift pulpit. The photo of Jesus hanging
on the wall was a strong way of showing how storefronts were transformed
into churches. Without the photo, it could simply be a meeting room.[37] Sociologist E. Franklin Frazier commented that the storefront was an attempt

35. St Drake and Cayton, *Black Metropolis*, 401.

36. Frazier and Lincoln, *The Black Church since Frazier*, 58.

37. Sernett, *Bound for the Promised Land*, 190.

on the part of migrants to reestablish southern roots. The religious culture from the South was extended to other parts of the country. The desire for the warm and intimate association of fellow worshippers in church services was not the only reason why the storefront church flourished, it was more welcoming than the already established urbanized Negro churches that often did not welcome the newcomers.[38]

Some of the local churches were ambivalent toward the migrant community. The exact number of storefront churches is unknown, as they were not counted with accuracy. In 1942, a social investigator, J. Harvey Kerns, counted thirty-five black churches in West Oakland alone; the large number of storefront churches was an early sign of organized black migrant life in the city. New wartime churches served as employment and housing agencies for newcomers, and their ministers provided counseling for emotional, financial, and legal problems. Some of the new preachers became important community leaders. Many of the new churches were established by migrants themselves. The Reverend Guthrie John Williams, for example, migrated to Richmond from Louisiana and founded the Mount Carmel Missionary Baptist Church in Richmond in 1944.[39] In addition to founding and pastoring the Mt. Carmel Missionary Baptist Church, he presided over the Inter-denominational Ministerial Alliance, founded the Universal Non-Partisan League, which focused on desegregating Richmond's stores and business, and was a principal player in the birth of the Parchester Village. Williams, an accomplished carpenter whose application to the carpenters' union had been rejected when he arrived in Richmond, involved himself in a variety of activities dedicated to smashing segregation.[40] With the strength of black churches, messages of encouragement were preached. The message of the Double Duty Dollar—i.e., to turn the dollar around within the community—had reached the Bay Area where progressive preachers were encouraging their flock to spend their money within the community. The preacher was expected to encourage the flock to trade with Negroes. Preachers who did not preach the gospel of the "Double Duty Dollar" were liable to criticism.[41] Ministers from various denominations and churches came together in what is called Ministerial Alliances in the East and West Bay to discuss issues relevant to the communities.

38. E. Franklin Frazier, *The Negro Church in America* p 53-54

39. Johnson, *African-American Christianity*, 134–35.

40. Moore, *To Place Our Deeds*, 113.

41. Drake and Cayton, *Black Metropolis*, 2:430.

St. John Missionary Baptist Church, Richmond

It has been said that Richmond's history would not be complete without the history of St. John Missionary Baptist Church, the city's second oldest black church. World War II had begun and many people came to this area seeking employment. There was only one small black church in Richmond and it was on the north side of town. There were many black families coming to this city and that church wasn't large enough to accommodate every church-going family. In 1941, a small group of people came together and started a Prayer Band and the faithful few were motivated to organize a church. The small group continued as a Prayer Band for another year, hoping the Lord would send them a minister with a vision to organize a church on the south side of town. In 1943, a young preacher, the Reverend James Brown, joined the Prayer Band who felt their prayers had been answered. The group gave the Reverend Brown their vote of confidence to stand with him in this decision. The Reverend Brown, along with others, went from door to door soliciting funds to buy the first building on 47th Street and Wall Avenue. Six weeks after marching to the new location, they decided to name the church St. John Missionary Baptist Church.

In 1944, the Reverend James Brown was officially elected pastor by unanimous vote and in 1945 the Reverend Brown left for St. Louis, Missouri. The Reverend Robert L. Johnson became the interim pastor until the Reverend G. E. Carter was called. Under the Reverend Carter's leadership, the church was incorporated on March 1, 1946. The Reverend Carter served until 1947. Once again, the Reverend Johnson took on the task of interim pastor and was elected Pastor in April 1948. With stability in place, St. John grew as more migrants were coming to California from the South. The members went into a planning mode and built a new sanctuary at 662 South 52nd Street, Richmond. With the growth of the membership, in 1962 the church began a building fund program to purchase more land for expansion and remodeling, which began in 1966. During the remodeling phase, St. John worshiped for a brief time at Zion Hill Baptist Church until the remodeled church was completed. During the Reverend Johnson's tenure, in 1969, he had a vision that St. John should help the needy in the community. The church accepted the challenge and built a one-hundred fifty-eight unit St. John Apartments at 121 West MacDonald Avenue in Richmond. St John continued to grow under the Reverend Johnson's leadership including the organization of the Board of Christian Education, the Home Department Sunday School for the sick and shut-in, a scholarship program, the prayer warriors, membership training, the church library, and the Bond Program to expand the sanctuary to accommodate the growing membership.

On Sunday, June 19, 1983, St. John held their "On-Site Ground Breaking Service," and, on April 1, 1984, St. John held their "Entering Program" for the brand new sanctuary. Due to the large membership growth, a second service was added, and two lots were purchased for additional parking and a van was purchased for transportation. After thirty-seven years of faithful service, the Reverend Johnson's health began to fail and he retired in May 1985. In July 1985, the church elected the Reverend Lloyd Farr as Pastor and he served until May 1990. A series of pastors served until the Reverend Calvin Jones was elected to serve as interim and, after five months, was installed as pastor on Sunday, August 8, 1993. His health began to fail a few months later and he soon had to resign on the advice of his physician. On June 8, 1994, the Reverend Jones was called from labor to reward. The prayers of the church were answered when the Reverend Kevin B. Hall was elected pastor on July 29, 1994 and installed on September 18, 1994. The Reverend Doctor Hall, a San Francisco Theological Doctor of Ministry graduate, guided the church into a new theme: "A Kingdom Building Church in the New Millennium." During Dr. Hall's first year, the church paid off the debt on the parsonage and began expansion and development of an educational facility. Additional ministries were added including a Christian Board of Education, Bible study classes for all age groups, as well as training classes for deacons and ministers. Other accomplishments include the strengthening of the Tutorial Program and the inauguration of St. John's Church Leadership Council. In the meantime Sunday School attendance doubled under Pastor Hall's administration including the Marriage Enrichment Ministry and the Men's Missionary Ministry. Pastor Hall's focus was never membership-driven, but discipleship-driven. St John is today known as a Kingdom Building Church in the New Millennium. Under Dr. Hall's leadership the church has acquired the Administration Building located in downtown Richmond, a multi-million-dollar renovation and beautification project enhancing the worship center, and built the Kevin B. Hall Education building.[42]

Davis Chapel Christian Methodist Episcopal Church

Front view of Original bldg. & Congregation

The Reverend G. W. Davis

In 1942, Presiding Bishop C. H. Phillips of the Colored Methodist Church saw that there was no C. M. E. church in Richmond. That same year, he assigned the Reverend George Washington to organize a C. M. E. Church. The Reverend George Washington Davis visited the Reverend F. W. Watkins,

---

42. St. John Missionary Baptist Church History, http://www.sjmbc.org/history (accessed September 15, 2013).

pastor of North Richmond Baptist Church, and asked him to aid him in find-ing a place to rent for worship services. The Reverend Watkins introduced the Reverend Davis to Mr. Willie Myles, who rented the Reverend Davis the Club House Building at York and Gertrude Streets in Richmond for $10 a month. The Reverend B. W. McGlothen, Pastor of McGlothen Temple, and his membership worshiped with the Reverend Davis and helped in the organizing of what became known as "Davis Chapel Colored Methodist Episcopal Church" (the word Colored was changed to Christian in 1954).[43] The CME Church is similar to the AME and AME Zion denominations in that it too embraced the *Book of Discipline* used by the larger body of Methodists.[44] On the first day of worship with McGlothen, three persons joined Davis CME, members Mary Long, Liddie P. Johnson (Long's daugh-ter), and Gloria Harris (Long's grand-daughter), thus officially forming the Davis Chapel CME Church. The membership of Davis Chapel grew rapidly during the following months. During the early months of 1944, property (on the corner of 4th Street and Chesley Avenue, Richmond) was purchased from Mrs. Lillian Carrie for $300 to build a church. By the time the church had completed building, membership had grown to eighty-nine members. In 1946 the Reverend Davis was assigned to another church and a series of pastors followed him until 1948, when the Reverend S. R. H. Banks was assigned as pastor. The membership increased to 375, and it was not too long thereafter that a building program was put into motion to remodel the existing structure. A loan was secured for the building project and the church was valued at $75,000. The Reverend S. R. H. Banks served at Davis Chapel for nine years and nine months and at the end of his tenure 441 members were counted on the rolls. In May 1958, the Reverend Banks was assigned to Beebe Memorial C.M.E., Oakland, and the Reverend L. S. White was assigned to Davis Chapel. The Reverend White quickly won the friend-ship of the membership through his electrifying personality and his unusual gift for organization. With a few months, twenty-eight more persons were added to the roll. In October 1958, the Reverend S. R. H. Banks was called from labor to reward. In his memory, a Sunday School Departments was named "The Banks Department." The Reverend L. S. White was elevated to Presiding Elder of the Oakland District and, on October 10, 1958, he as-signed the Reverend Leroy Johnson to Davis Chapel who remained for four years and nine months. During his tenure 259 more persons joined includ-ing fifty-seven young people who were baptized. While at Davis Chapel, the

43. Davis Chapel CME History, http://www.spiritofdavis.com/history.htm Ac-cessed December 1, 2013.

44. Anne H. & Anthony B. Pinn *Black Church History* (Minneapolis: Fortress press2002) p 55

Reverend Johnson received 259 members and baptized fifty-seven young people. By the time the Reverend Johnson left Davis to become a Chaplain in the United States Army, six hundred persons were on the roll; quite a jump from the original three in 1954.

The Reverend L. S. White was reassigned to Davis Chapel in August 1963 and served for one year. The Reverend Herman C. Riley was assigned in September 1965. The Reverend Riley served for six years. The church grew spiritually and completed many projects both in the church and the surrounding community. The Reverend Riley was very civic-minded and during his pastorate he was President of the Greater Richmond Inter-faith Program (G.R.I.P.), President of Richmond's Model Cities Neighborhood Board, Chairman of the Crime Reduction and Prevention for Richmond, West Contra Costa Council of Churches, and other civic organizations. After the Reverend Riley was reassigned, the Reverend John H. Dorn was assigned in September 1971 and was called from labor to reward on November 25, 1971. The following pastors served from 1972 through 1994: the Reverend John B. Spearman Sr., the Reverend Winfred T. Warren, the Reverend Elonza J. Edwards, the Reverend Chester B. Tollette, and the Reverend Willie Mays. In August 1994, the Reverend Lawrence P. Lakey , the Reverend Wayne Mays, and the Reverend William Larkin served from August 2002 through 2005 On Thursday, Thanksgiving Day, November 27, 2003, at approximately 5:00 p.m., a fast-moving blaze destroyed the church building. Word of the fire spread rapidly to astonished members who showed up on the scene and witnessed their church turning into ashes. The Davis Chapel family held a meeting at the Senior Center in in North Richmond the next day. The fire destroyed a building, but it would not destroy their church: "Why should I cry for the church structure, my faith is not in the structure?" Pastor William Larkin who was the pastor of Davis Chapel at the time said, "We will rebuild, there's no question about it."[45] St. Peter CME Church, El Cerrito, just a few miles away, shared their facility with Davis Chapel for services. The Reverend Dr. Nicholas Betts followed the Reverend Larkin in August 2005. Under Dr. Betts leadership, a groundbreaking service was held, a construction loan was secured, and the dream of going back to North Richmond began to unfold. The building was erected to 73% completion thereby requiring additional funding. Davis Chapel CME continues to be a beacon of light in the community. Reverend Cassandry Redmond Keys became the pastor on July 18, 2012, and continued to rebuild the church using the spirit of Nehemiah.

45. Davis Chapel CME History, www.spiritofdavis.com/history.htm (accessed December 1, 2013).

Of the sons and daughters from Davis Chapel ten have served as pastors of their own congregations.[46]

Macedonia Missionary Baptist Church, 1943

Macedonia Missionary Baptist Church started in the home of the Reverend C. Turner on March 21, 1943, 1:00 p.m, in Richmond, California along with other persons including the Reverend A. E. Williams, the Reverend W. H. Harris, the Reverend G. G. Griffin, and the Reverend J. Johnson. One of the ministers voiced that there was need of another church in North Richmond and felt he was being guided by the Holy Spirit and God that, someday, North Richmond was going to be a great community. Feeling that the minister was being led by the Holy Spirit, the faithful few followed his lead. The church was named Macedonia Missionary Baptist Church and the Reverend G. G. Griffin was voted to serve as pastor. The membership grew from nine to fifteen hundred and became a well-organized church over a period of time.[47]

War at Home

When large numbers of black southerners arrived during World War II, the Bay Area cities finally faced the problems that had plagued eastern cities since World War I. Adjusting to a culture that rejected the black race was not an easy task. The 1940s was a time of war both abroad and at home. Migrants soon discovered that "the rules for success" were not written for them, that their place was on the bottom of the ethnic ladder.[48] While it is true that hundreds of thousands of people migrating to the Bay Area created housing shortages through the area, it must be taken into consideration that part of the problem was that Blacks were restricted by racial covenants that kept them in confined "black areas." Unable to move beyond certain parts of the cities, ghettos were formed creating a crisis in housing. Whites and blacks clashed over discrimination in the work place. While Shipyards may have provided work for blacks, they were relegated to the bottom of the ladder with regards to opportunities for promotions. But there simply were not enough houses in designated "black areas" throughout the Bay to accommodate the soaring numbers of people, resulting in ghettos forming

46. Ibid.
47. Oakland Public Library, History Room File, Oakland Churches, Baptist.
48. Sernett *Bound for the Promised Land*, 209.

at Hunters Point, along Fillmore Street, and around 7th Street in Oakland. Black migrants discovered, despite the best efforts of white San Franciscans, that their adjustment to this urban milieu was marred by racial discrimination. The Hastings Clothing Store, for example, revised its policy because of the influx of southern white and colored, and would not allow black patrons to try on suits or hats before purchases. Only after the city's interracial leadership pressured the establishment did this policy cease. Black San Franciscans discovered that racial discrimination and restrictive covenants made it more difficult for them to obtain housing in a tight housing market than for their white counterparts. Housing discrimination was widespread in San Francisco. It was hardly a coincidence that the majority of blacks resided in three census tracts in 1940.[49]

Jones United Methodist Church, San Francisco

Jones Methodist Church was founded in February 1943 by the Reverend T. J. Bridgette of the Louisiana United Methodist Conference and a group of approximately forty Methodists that came together in dedicated fellowship to create a Methodist Church in the Fillmore District, which was then largely African-American. With the cooperation of Bishop Edgar Love, who presided over the Central Conference (a national conference of Methodist with black congregations), a storefront church was organized at 1901 Bush Street. The Reverend Bridgette and the forty members named the church in honor of Bishop Robert E. Jones, the first Black Bishop in the United States of the Methodist Episcopal Church in 1920. Missing historical information leaves a wide gap from 1920 to 1944 when Articles of Incorporation of the Jones Methodist Church were filed in the office of the California Secretary of State to the time the church experienced membership growth as a result of the black population growth during WWII, when blacks came in search of war-related employment in the shipyards and other industries. By now, membership growth exceeded three hundred. The church relocated on May 27, 1945 to 1975 Post Street, San Francisco. Blacks looking for spiritual guidance to navigate through issues such as relocation and discrimination turned to churches such as Jones Memorial, where they found a sense of community and united purpose. Jones Church established a number of social programs designed to address the needs of the congregation and the surrounding community.

49. Broussard, *Black San Francisco*, 167–72.

The Jones United Methodist Credit Union was founded in 1952 as a response to red-lining (offering credit with exorbitant interest rates) and other discriminatory practices against blacks. The Credit Union began with $1,500 in assets, and was approved by the Federal Credit Union League on the basis of the good credit rating of a few members with rising assets separate from the church's operating budget. Jones Methodist came to the rescue for housing shortage in 1960 when it built 184 units of affordable senior housing for members and non-members.

Jones Memorial and Ridgeview United Methodist Churches merged July 1, 2001 in an effort to combine its ministries and to become more affective.[50]

In 1947, the resident Bishop of the California Nevada Conference appointed the Reverend Dr. Hamilton T. Boswell as pastor of Jones in 1947. The Reverend Boswell was part of the wave of African Americans who moved from the South to San Francisco after World War II. Dr. Boswell was aggressive and led with a leadership style that could get results. After twenty-nine years of service, Dr. Boswell retired in 1976 and was given the honorable title of Pastor Emeritus. Willie Brown Jr., the first African American to serve as Mayor of San Francisco said:

> When I became Speaker of the California Assembly, I began trying to talk him out of retirement. It took a while but in 1984, he agreed to serve as Assembly Chaplain, a post he held with great distinction and to the benefit of the members of that body for the next ten years, the longest tenure for an Assembly Chaplain in California history. Brown went on to say that when the nation was focused on the struggle for civil rights in the South, he helped create the civil rights movement in San Francisco.[51]

Dr. Boswell was called from labor to reward on May 6, 2007.

In 1976, Reverend Book T. Anderson Jr. of Easter Hill United Methodist Church, Richmond, California, replaced the Reverend Dr. Boswell. He served Jones Memorial and the San Francisco community until he was called from labor to reward on November 29, 1982. In 1982, Dr. James McCray Jr. was appointed as senior minister to Jones United by the California Nevada Conference. Dr. McCray previously served as pastor at Pittsburg United Methodist Church in Pittsburg, California from 1977 to 1982. Dr. McCray as well as his predecessor, the Reverend Anderson, grew up in Jones, were trained in Jones, and continued to maintain the historical

50. Jones United Methodist Church History, http://jonesumc.com/pages/history.htm (accessed January 11, 2014).

51. Boswell-Raine, *Prayers for Willie, Pathways for Daily Living*, viii–ix.

ministry and leadership of Jones that was so well known throughout the state. After twenty-six years, Dr. McCray retired from Jones Memorial UMC on March 2, 2008. Two days later, the Reverend Phillip Lawson, a retired United Methodist Minister, was assigned by Bishop Beverly Shamana as Jones's interim senior minister. In 2009, the Reverend Staci Current was appointed as senior minister of Jones Memorial. The Reverend Current is today Jones's first female senior pastor, having served as senior minister of Shattuck Avenue United Methodist Church in Oakland, California from 2001 to 2009.[52]

Sounds of the Bay Area: Secular and the Sacred

When Southern migrants came to California during the World War II era, they transported blues traditions with them. Music served as a reminder of home; it was like medicine for the soul. African-American men and women were equally important as repositories of black culture, both urban and southern rural. Minnie Lue Nichols's self-named club also became a blues staple in North Richmond. Minnie Lue's featured home cooking, like chitterlings, greens, chicken, and sweet potato pies, while showcasing local blues musicians and national celebrities, like B. B. King, Bobby Blue Bland, Jimmy McCracklin, Ray Charles, and James Brown.[53]

Charlie Yardbird Parker, famous jazz saxophonist and composer, frequented the Bay Area during the 40s. Parker once replied to a question about his religious affiliation that he was a devout musician. Even T-Bone Walker's friends were convinced that he would become a preacher when he stopped singing because of the way he sang the blues. They said it sounded like a sermon. The blues singer Alberta Hunter testified that to her the blues were almost religious, like a chant. The blues are like spirituals, almost sacred.[54]

San Francisco, Oakland, and Richmond were the hot spots for musical performances: blues, jazz, spirituals, and gospels. Harold "Slim" Jenkins, a black Louisianan, moved to Oakland during World I opened what would become the most celebrated black nightclub on the West Coast. The club had a large show room, a first-class restaurant with a huge banquet room, a market, and a liquor store. Slim Jenkins's club earned the reputation as a black-and-tan club because it catered to a mixed clientele. Ivory Joe Hunter, Etta James, the Platters, Cab Calloway, Percy Mayfield, and Sugar Pie De Santo are just a few of the famous entertainers to appear at Slim Jenkins

52. Jones Memorial United Methodist Church History.

53. Moore, *To Place Our Deeds*, 132–33.

54. Levine, *Black Culture and Black Consciousness*, 236

Supper Cub. The Swing Club was another popular location on 7th Street in Oakland. Billy Eckstine, T-Bone Walker, Count Basie, played there as well as the Villa's, the Clef Club. Seventh Street was a haven for black folks.[55] Seventh Street was Harlem West with a solid base. One of the great attractions for Black music is the "call and response" that connects the artist with the performer as they share the experience together. "Anybody here know what I'm talking about?" "Do you feel me?" "Do you know like I know?" Before long, it seems as if the performer is serving up a sermon, similar to having church on Sunday morning.

T-Bone Walker, blues singer, said, "The first time I ever heard a boggie-woogie piano was the first time I went to church even the sermon was preached in a blues tone while the congregation yelled amen."[56]

The 1940s was also the age of the big swing bands; some played at the Oakland Auditorium. While Oakland downtown flourished, so did 7th Street in spite of unwritten racist laws that contained them to West Oakland.[57] Clubs like the Continental and Rumboggie Room in Oakland opened its doors in 1945, hosting famous celebrities such as Johnny Fuller and Jimmy McCracklin, Big Mamma Thornton, James Brown, Ray Charles, and Ike and Tina Turner to name a few who entertained to a packed audience. The Fabulous Ballads were formed in 1961, making their first appearance at the Rumboggie. Raincoat Jones, a bootlegger who was a loan shark, helped to fund a series of nightclubs in Oakland. Oakland was also known for cultural dancing. Ruth Beckford, native Oaklander, opened up the Ruth Beckford African-Haitian dance company and founded a recreational modern dance department for the Oakland Parks and Recreation Department, the first of its kind in the United States.

Esther Mabry was twenty-two years old when she came to West Oakland from Texas during the Great Migration in 1942. After working for Slim Jenkins for several years, Esther opened her own restaurant across the street, calling it Esther's Breakfast Club, and later renamed it Esther's Orbit Room.[58] Esther's was a popular club middle-class people as well as cab drivers and railroad and shipyard workers frequented for food—including getting a salad tossed fresh at the table. Al Green and Etta James were among the iconic legendary blues singers that performed at Esther's. Mabry

55. *Sights and Sounds Essays and Celebration of West Oakland* (California Dept. of Transportation: Caltrans 1997) p 318

56. Shapiro and Hentoff, eds., *Hear Me Talkin' to Ya: The Story of Jazz by the Men Who Made It,* 247.

57. Nations, *Swingin on the Golden Gate,* 7–12.

58. *Festival at the Lake Guide 1988: Communities in Action,* located in Oakland Public Library, History Room, Blacks, Business 1988.

was nicknamed the "Great Lady."[59] One of the popular entertainment locations in Oakland was the Lincoln Theatre. It was a popular Negro theater
opened in 1921 and operated by Joseph and Elizabeth Freeman. It was the
only theater where blacks could see a movie and be treated with respect.
The T. & D. Theater, located on Broadway in Oakland, only allowed blacks
to sit in the last fifteen rows.[60] Music in the Bay Area blues evolved from
soft inflected jazz during World War II when it came to be a style closely
identified as East Bay Rhythm and Blues due to the migration of blue-collar
musicians from out of state.

Across the Bay, San Francisco was known more for jazz than blues. In
1929, Henry Starr, an Oakland-born musician was the first black entertainer to get on a radio show in San Francisco. He accomplished this in an age
when American apartheid (in the form of segregation and Jim Crow laws)
prevented black entertainers from being hired.[61] The San Francisco Union,
Local 6 of the American Federation of Musicians chartered in 1897, denied
African-American musicians membership. In 1924, black musicians were
granted a charter to do business as Local 648 headquartered in Oakland.[62]
The Fillmore District became occupied by blacks during the Great Migration. Billie Holiday, Louis Armstrong. Lionel Hampton, Duke Ellington,
John Coltrane, and other headliners jammed at dozens of jazz clubs such
as Shelton's Blue Mirror, Texas Playhouse, Club Flamingo, Leola Kings Bird
Cage, and the renowned Fillmore Auditorium. While the Fillmore was big
in name, it was small in geographical area, only about ten-square blocks
that was jammed with clubs, pool halls, and theaters, and a few churches.[63]

The Fillmore became the hub of black life by 1930 and the preferred
residential area for black residents. The narrow strip along Fillmore Street
from McAllister to Sutter, bordered by Divisadero Street and Webster Street,
in particular, became the focal point of black activity.[64]

Berkeley did not share in the limelight of jazz or black entertainment;
most Berkeleyans would come to nearby Oakland to 7th Street, or went to
the Fillmore District for jazz.

The sounds of gospel music found a popular place in the Bay Area.
Based on traditional choir and quartet singing in southern churches, a
cappella gospel music enjoyed an upsurge in popularity as southern black

59. *Inside Bay Area*, June 1, 2010.

60. www.http://cinematreasures.org/theaters/5094 (accessed September 20, 2013).

61. Thompson and Deterville, *Images of America Black Artists in Oakland*, 12.

62. Praetzellis and Stewart, eds., *Sights and Sounds*, 301.

63. Adkins, *Images of African Americans of San Francisco*, 64.

64. Broussard, *Black San Francisco*, 30.

migrants formed new singing groups that toured local communities. Ship-yard workers formed gospel groups like the Singing Shipbuilders Quarter (Richmond), Rising Stars Singers (Oakland), and the Paramount Singers (San Francisco). These two groups, whose members came primarily from Texas and Louisiana, laid the groundwork for later Bay Area gospel groups like the Golden Stars, the Golden West Singers, the Swanee River Singers, the Spartonaires, the Oakland Silvertones, and many others.[65] Church mass choirs began to cut records under the leadership of pastors like G. W. Killens and Carl Anderson. Opal Nations said Bishop Louis Narcisse sounded like a saved and sanctified blues singer. Blues and gospel music both expressed the struggles of life. Charles Albert Tindley wrote, "I'll Overcome Someday," was popular during the Civil Rights era. Betty Reid and her husband Mel Reid opened the first black gospel and blues record store in West Oakland in 1945. Two years later, Mel acquired time on Berkeley's KRE radio station and broadcast a weekly thirty-minute gospel program called "Religious Gems." Mel Reid opened a second store on Sacramento Street in Berkeley, where it remains today. Mel's uncle, Paul, took over Mel's radio spot and added "Spirituals at 6 a.m." in 1957. Mel, Betty, and Paul presented Gospel Extravaganzas at the Oakland Auditorium during the 1950s. They also held quartet battles and choir competitions. During the 1950s, black Bay area churches began to broadcast live, gaining a reputation for outstanding preaching and mass choir singing. The Reverend George Killens's two-part sermon, "The Cross," and his congregation singing "Father I Stretch my Hands to Thee,"', led by Reverend Killens, Mount Calvary Baptist Church, Oakland, were among the first recordings to be made by churches in the Bay Area.[66] Mount Pleasant Baptist Church, Oakland, under the musical direction of Bessie Mack, made a name for itself singing gospel songs. Mary Bolden was well known for her singing with the J. L. Richards Specials and the Voices of Evergreen, a mass choir of Evergreen heard for fifteen minutes on Sunday nights on radio station KWBR. Oakland's Evergreen broadcast on KWBR, St. John Missionary Baptist Church, Oakland, and on KLX, Mt. Zion Spiritual Temple, KLX. Among the churches that broadcast on KBLX were El Bethel Missionary Baptist Church, San Francisco, Double Rock Baptist Church, San Francisco (featuring Pastor Victor L.Medearis), St. John Missionary Baptist Church, Oakland (featuring Pastor Dr. Carl Anderson), and the Antioch Baptist Church (featuring the Reverend R. T. George, a master preacher and musician). Sunday night was the time when all ears were tuned into the radio to hear old-fashioned preaching and singing.

65. Johnson, *African-American Christianity*, 140.

66. Ibid., 39.

Jumpin' George Oxford was one of the beloved D. J.'s of the 1950s. His focus was on race records, catering to blacks as did Bouncin' Bill Doubleday on KWBR and Don Barksdale, former-basketball-star-turned D. J. in the late 1950s, who was the owner of the Sportsman on Grove Street and the Showcase on Telegraph Avenue, both in Oakland.

Ray Dobard moved from New Orleans to Berkeley during World War II. Dobard established a music publishing business, providing a chance for locals to get their music on "wax" and to a larger audience. Many of Dobard's fine gospel sides featured King Narcissee, the Golden West Singers, and others. Jesse Jaxyson moved to West Oakland in the 1930s. A member of the First Church of Religious Science, Jesse followed a healthy diet and did not drink or smoke. Jesse became an accomplished keyboardist and played during worship service. He met Clarissa Mayfield, a choir member at his church, and together they set up a radio repair shop at 1606 7th Street, Oakland. He had a room converted into a makeshift recording studio that he ran along with Bob Geddins. "Bob Geddins, called the 'Father of Oakland Blues,' began pressing records at his West Oakland plant at 8th and Center Streets."[67] Groups like the Rising Star Gospel Singers began recording on Hemby's Pacific Records imprint. Geddins picked up Rising Starts soloist Tommy Jenkins, Lowell Fulson, and the Pilgrim Travelers and recorded them along sides commissioned by A. B. Strong, a gospel singer from San Francisco. Geddins began to press music and soon hosted a blues and rhythm record show over KWBR.[68] Overall, black music, whether secular or sacred, has been the voice of the common folks and their struggles for hope in the midst of despair. The sacred and secular sounds of the South were transported from the South to the Bay Area and expressed the struggles that continued for blacks folks.

First Union Baptist Church, San Francisco

First Union Baptist Church was organized March 18, 1944 as a small storefront church at 1643 O'Farrell Street, San Francisco, by the Reverend P. S. Osborne of Macedonia Baptist Church and the Reverend M. L. Price of Galveston Texas, both migrants. The church started with a membership of seven, with the Reverend Nathaniel R. Reason serving as the first pastor. It was soon discovered that the first name selected for the church had to be changed from First Baptist Church because another church in the city was known by that name. As a result, the word "Union" was added to First

---

67. Praetzellis and Stewart, Eds, *Sights and Sounds,* 301.

68. Nations, *Swingin on the Golden Gate,* 38–39.

Baptist resulting in the name being changed to First Union Baptist Church. With a growing membership, various projects were started to raise funds to purchase a new church. The first building fund started with $47.50 and grew from a small seed of money to where a building could be purchased at 2398 Geary Blvd. on December 23, 1946. The church secured a ten-year mortgage. However with a significant growth in membership, brought on by the Great Migration, the mortgage was paid off in seven years and a mortgage burning ceremony was held in July 1953. With the increase of membership, more space was needed. The Women's Auxiliary started a new building fund of $300 with the dream of moving to a more modern and spacious location that had space for educational classrooms and a parking lot. The Reverend Nathaniel Reason was called from labor to reward on June 12, 1968 before the dream became a reality.

Deacon Willie B. Smith held the reigns from June 12, 1968 until February 23, 1969. During this period, the church purchased a parsonage. On February 24, 1969, the Reverend Henry L. Davis Sr. was called to be the pastor. The efforts for securing a larger location had not stopped. Groundbreaking for a new church was held on Easter Sunday, April 18, 1976 and on December 19, 1976 Pastor H. L. Davis Sr. led the congregation to the brand new edifice at 1001 Webster Street, San Francisco.

Once again, with good management, prayer, and determination, the church paid off its mortgage in six years and held a mortgage burning ceremony in 1985, with construction well under way for new classrooms. The church managed to purchase additional property to expand its ministries. Pastor Davis was called from labor to reward on May 8, 1984. Once again, Deacon Smith took the leadership role in keeping the church together. The Church elected the Reverend Henry L. Davis Jr., son of the former pastor, on March 18, 1985. From July 2000 until January 20, 2002, Deacon George Booth took the lead role for the church while a pastoral search was conducted. On January 21, 2002, Pastor DeWayne A. Byrdsong was elected fourth Pastor and served through December 30, 2009. Once again, the church was without a pastor and Deacon George Booth, Board Chairman, took on the role of congregational leader. On October 10 2011, the First Union Church family elected the Reverend D. E. C Matthews as Pastor.[69]

The Church for the Fellowship of All Peoples

In the later part of 1943, the Reverend Alfred G. Fisk, PhD, a Presbyterian clergyman and professor of philosophy, brought together a few persons

69. First Union Baptist Church History.

from various races and denominations to start a church that would bridge the gap between races, cultures, and faiths. In the meantime, Dr. Fisk was trying to lure Dr. Howard Thurman to be a part of the leadership of the church.

On October 5, 1943, Howard Thurman received the first of a series of letters from Dr. Alfred G. Fisk, Professor at San Francisco State College. Fisk told Thurman the Presbyterian Board of National Missions was going to provide them rent-free space in a former Japanese Presbyterian Church at 1500 Post Street. The Fillmore District in San Francisco once largely occupied by Japanese Americans were forcibly relocated to concentration camps during WWII, leaving businesses, churches, and residential housing vacant.. A. J. Muste, a well-known pacifist and national secretary of the Fellowship of Reconciliation, had resigned his position to become the co-pastor and was looking for someone to co-pastor with him. He wrote to Dr. Thurman seeking recommendations. He emphasized, "But we don't want it to be any sense run by whites for Negroes. It should be of and by and for both groups."[70] Dr. Thurman was employed as Dean of the Chapel and professor of Religion at Howard University in D.C. and his wife Sue was involved as founder-editor of the *Aframerican Women's Journal*. A. J. Muste's letter was appealing to Thurman, though he expressed concerns about the role he would have in the leadership of the church. With fears calmed from Muste that Thurman would be the co-pastor, he resigned from Howard, saying, "[W]e would be pioneers in California a century after the gold rush of 1849."[71]

Fellowship Church's origins started in the heart of the Fillmore District. The formal inaugural service for the Church for the Fellowship of All Peoples took place on October 8, 1944 at the First Unitarian Church in San Francisco, the only white church in the city that would lend its endorsement and its sanctuary for the event. There were no precedents established or traditions, so they started from scratch. In the early years, with the financial support of the Presbyterian Church, the group of less than fifty members worked to understand that unique mission of the new church. They relinquished financial support from the Presbyterian Church in favor of an independence that would allow an interfaith vision to flower. The worship service had liturgical dancing as an expression of worship, an English handball choir, and art exhibits of the creative expressions of the members. Thurman's core message in his sermon included the development of the inner resources needed for the creation of a friendly world of friendly men. The sermon included the elements of instruction, guidance, inspiration,

---

70. Thurman *With Head and Heart*, 139.

71. Ibid., 140, 143.

conviction, dedication, and the challenge that love could grow.[72] The second location for the church belonged to the Methodist Filipinos. The third location was the Art Colony on Washington St., before finally settling on Larkin Street, where it was purchased from St. John's Evangelical and Reformed church that had been organized by Richard and Reinhold Niebuhr's father who had come from Germany.[73] The church's congregation was predominantly white and was not attractive to black people. Despite Thurman's optimism and dedication, Fellowship Church had only a marginal impact on San Francisco's race relations. Racism was very much a part of the climate. The major hospitals were closed to black physicians except for work as janitors and orderlies. Dr. Thurman was not exempt from racism. He went to the Stanford University Hospital to visit one of his sick white church members. He was stopped by the desk nurse who was obviously confused and questioned him as to why he was visiting a white patient as the mixing of races was not well received. The private nurse assigned to the patient welcomed Dr. Thurman and reaffirmed that the patient was expecting him. On one occasion, a white congregant wanted to host a reception in her affluent Nob Hill home and was prevented by the tenants who didn't want non-Caucasians in their building. There were very few mortuaries servicing the needs of the black community. When an elderly member of the church died and the service was to be held at the oldest mortuaries, the management was upset when they found out Thurman was the minster. They were candid about their feelings saying that if "Negro members of your church attend her service and see you officiating they may decide that when they die, they too could be buried from our parlors and that they would never do."[74] The Church for the Fellowship of All Peoples did not achieve the success that both Thurman and Dr. Fisk had in mind. It became apparent that both black and white races felt more comfortable sticking with their own race.[75] Dr. Thurman left in 1954 for a tenured position as Dean of Theology at Boston University, but returned to serve as Minister Emeritus until his death in 1981. The Revered Dr. Dorsey Blake served two years as the minister prior to his installation in October 1994. Mrs. Sue Bailey (Howard) Thurman presented Dr. Howard Thurman's robe to Dr. Blake, which had not been worn since Dr. Thurman's death—it was a symbol of her trust in his leading the congregation.[76]

72. Ibid., 160.

73. Ibid., 149.

74. Thurman, *Head and Heart*, 157.

75. Howard Thurman, *Footprints of a Dream*, 43–44.

76. http://www.rhn.org/historyfellowship.html, (accessed May 20, 2014).

Providence Baptist Church

Providence Baptist Church had a humble beginning when the Reverend
Freeman B. Banks, from Omaha, Nebraska, met with Mr. J. S. Pough in a
San Francisco café and discussed the idea that a Baptist church was needed
south of Market Street in San Francisco. The idea came into reality with the
Reverend Banks becoming the pastor. The first worship service was held
in the Washington Street Hotel on 4th Street in San Francisco. The small
congregation moved to the Old Majestic Theater at 365 3rd Street and eventually purchased the property for $25,000. The organization of the church
started with the Reverend Banks forming a Sunday School and appointing
Eli Evans as superintendent, Estena Robinson as Church Clerk, and Ancil
Johnson as Director of the Baptist Training Union. The Deacon Board was
organized and Deacon J. S. Pough was appointed Treasurer and Chairman.
Louis H. Narcisse, who later became nationally known as Bishop Narcisse
and founder of Mt. Zion Spiritual Temple in Oakland, was appointed musician. From 1943–1950 the church continued to be methodically organized
with a Women's Missionary Union, the Laymen and Brotherhood, Saturday
Night Bible Class, Sunshine Band, Junior and Senior Red Circles, and Young
Women auxiliaries. In 1949, the congregation made the final payment on
the church property located at 365 3rd Street. A Youth Department was
organized under the direction of Alice Johnson. Evidently, a major disagree-
ment brewed in the church, to the point that a lawsuit was filed to dismiss
the Reverend Banks. After two years of litigation, the Reverend Banks was
dismissed and the Reverend Clinton W. Rogers was elected Pastor. In 1958,
the congregation purchased the land with an old house at 1601 McKinnon
Avenue and began to have plans drawn for the new church. The new church
was built and, in 1959, the congregation marched from 365 3rd Street to
1601 McKinnon Avenue. In 1961, the Reverend Rogers was replaced by the
Reverend J. A. Hester, who served as minister-in-charge until October 7,
1961. On July 28, 1962, the Reverend Calvin Jones Sr. was elected pastor
and installed four months later on November 25, 1962. Under the Reverend
Jones Sr.'s leadership, five years later, on October 8, 1967, the mortgage was
burned. New ministries continued to be added to the church.

On April 21, 1974, groundbreaking ceremonies were held for the
Education and Recreation Center and the building was dedicated in May
1975. In 1987, the Reverend Calvin Jones Jr. was elected Assistant Pastor.
On December 31, 1990, Jones Sr. retired with the honorable title of Pastor
Emeritus. The Reverend Calvin Jones Jr. was elected Senior Pastor on March
22, 1991 Jones Jr. had an impressive background, having earned a Master
of Divinity from Harvard in 1983, and having played defensive back for

the Denver Broncos from 1973 to 1976. Following his father's retirement in 1990, organizational changes were set into motion as Jones Jr. merged the choirs into the Voices of Providence. He also merged the Youth and Young Adult Choir and renamed that singing unit Voices of Imani. The Providence Foundation was organized and many programs have operated through it. A homeless shelter was founded that is well known. Nearing completion is the senior citizens complex to be opened at a date to be determined.[77] The Reverend Jones works tirelessly as he ministers to families and youth. He formed the Providence Foundation of San Francisco, a collaborative foundation with the church to provide a multitude of services. In 2004, he established a youth outreach program at the San Francisco Juvenile Hall where he ministers to assist with life-altering skills.[78]

New Providence Baptist Church, San Francisco

New Providence Baptist Church was organized by the Reverend Clarence E. Scott circa April 1945 in the Presbyterian Church at 19th and Connecticut Streets in San Francisco. From there the church moved to #1 Kohala Road, San Francisco. The church made several moves: one from Divisadero and Geary Streets, using the Hall of the Most Worshipful Sons of Light; several years later the church relocated to Bush and Laguna Streets and then to 1408 Farrell Street into a remodeled church. The Black enclave in the Fillmore District was hard hit when the San Francisco Redevelopment leveled the neighborhood by uprooting homes, businesses, and churches, dissolving a close-knit community New Providence was targeted to be uprooted, even though the church was beautifully remodeled. The church relocated once again to 309 Lyon Street, where it remained for several years. The Reverend Scott and the members continued to keep the faith as Pastor Scott had a vision of someday erecting a beautiful edifice. With the support of the faithful members and the help of God, Pastor Scott's vision became a reality in 1974 when the members marched to the new location at 218 Granada Street. Membership grew and the church expanded and remodeled to include stained-glass windows, new furniture, classrooms, and a church library. In October 1995, the church's million-dollar mortgage was burned. Pastor Scott was called from labor to reward on October 1998 having served for fifty-three years. Pastor Scott always had the church's best interest at heart. Nineteen days prior to his death, he recommended the Reverend Michael

---

77. Jones United Methodist Church History.
78. History of the Providence Baptist Church.

Gilmore to succeed him. On March 29, 1999, the Reverend Gilmore was installed as pastor of New Providence. New Providence continues to grow.[79]

Bethlehem Missionary Baptist Church, Richmond

Bethlehem Missionary Baptist Church was organized on April 8, 1945 in Richmond in the home of the Reverend and Mrs. Nathaniel Phanor. Two months later a groundbreaking ceremony was held on June 9, 1945. The church was built and a dedication ceremony was held December 9, 1945 and the cornerstone was laid July 19, 1948. The Reverend Nathaniel served from 1945 to 1955. On April 15, 1957, Dr. Abraham Henry Newman was elected pastor. Under his leadership the church grew strong in ministries and in the community. A Board of Christian Education and the Active Youth Development project were implemented. During the years 1975 through 1985, the church hosted citywide revivals and became active in evangelism and prison ministry. On December 20, 1981, the church celebrated its mortgage-burning ceremony.

The next ten years, Bethlehem continued to grow and attract members. The ministerial staff and Deacon Board increased and the women's ministry was enhanced with two new circles. Pastor Newman was an active pastor beyond the community. He served as the 9th President of the California State Baptist Convention, served two terms as Moderator of Progressive Baptist Missionary Educational District Association, and was Chairman of the Board of Directors, National Baptist Convention, USA, Inc. Pastor Newman was called from labor to reward December 10, 2003. After Reverend Newman's death the church set out to reorganize the Boards of Deacons and Trustees. Church bylaws were drafted and adopted on August 30, 2004, and a pulpit search committee began the search for a new pastor. The Reverend Dr. Alvin C. Bernstine was elected pastor in 2006. Bethlehem is today a magnet church that draws a large membership and influence in the community.[80] Dr. Bernstine is an esteemed pastor, prophet, and professor. Bethlehem serves as the West Contra Costa site for the Leadership Institute at Allen Temple.

79. New Providence Baptist Church History, http://www.newprovidencesf.org/aboutHISTORY.html (accessed April 2, 2015).

80. Bethlehem Missionary Baptist Church History, www.bethlehemmissionary-baptistgchurch.org/.

Evergreen Baptist Church, San Francisco

In 1945, the Reverend Ruth Johnson stated that God led him to go to San Francisco to build a church between two mountains. The church started with only a Sunday School, which was held in Reverend Johnson's home at 2501 Ingalls in the south Basin of San Francisco with twenty-six persons. In 1946, Pastor Johnson located a storefront building at 6270 3rd Street, San Francisco, and that became the beginning of the Evergreen Missionary Baptist Church with the seating facing a mountain. Pastor Johnson was not shy about challenging his parishioners to focus on having a Christ-like attitude and he organized and was the overseer of all church auxiliaries. Many pastors, ministers, and teachers have come through Evergreen under the leadership of Pastor Johnson.

The Reverend Johnson suffered health challenges and stepped down in June 1991. That same year the Reverend Christopher Jones was elected. The Reverend Johnson felt well enough to attend and gave him the pastoral charge. The Reverend Jones resigned in March, 1995. That same year, the Reverend James Greenwood was called as the Pastor. Under the Reverend Greenwood's leadership the church experienced a reorganization with additional ministries; the Ruth Circle was re-organized and Vacation Bible School and the Youth revival were added to the ministries.

The church purchased property adjacent to the church. The Reverend Greenwood resigned in 2002 and relocated to San Antonio, Texas to care for his ailing mother.

Minister Dexter Landers served as interim pastor until 2003 when the Reverend Damien Epps was elected pastor. Evergreen continued to grow spiritually. After five years of dedicated service, the Reverend Epps resigned in July 2008. In August 2008, the Reverend Jackey J. Wilson Sr. was asked to serve as the interim pastor. In October, two months later, the Reverend Wilson Sr. was voted as pastor of the congregation. On October 19, 2015, Evergreen will celebrate its seventh Church Anniversary year.[81]

Mount Zion Spiritual Temple, 1945

It's nice to be nice, and let others know you are nice.

—BISHOP KING LOUIS H. NARCISSE

---

81. Evergreen Baptist Church History, http://www.evergreenbaptistchurchsf.org/ebc-history.

The Mt. Zion Spiritual Temple was founded by King Louis H. Narcisse in 1945 in a storefront at the corner of 14th and Peralta Streets, Oakland, with fifty folding chairs. King Louis H. Narcisse was born in Gretna, Louisiana across the Mississippi River from New Orleans on April 27, 1921. When his father died, Narcisse moved to New Orleans where he was steeped in Roman Catholicism and the cult of voodoo. After moving to California, Narcisse worked at the naval shipyard on Mare Island. Narcisse was a gifted musician who could sing, play the piano, and preach. He was crowned by bishops from the Church of God in Christ at an Oakland ceremony in 1956. Mt. Zion Spiritual temple was organized with a strange mixture of Catholic ritual, Protestant practice and Holy Roller jubilee. The power and glory of the movement was centered on its founder and spiritual leader: Narcisse's church court was composed of princesses dressed in regal white robes, bishops in full regalia, princes, Superiors, Reverend Mothers, a Queen, and Mothers and missionaries decked out in black tuxedos. All paid dues to retain their titles and few challenged this during the early, more lucrative years of the King's reign.[82]

Over the years, Narcisse befriended people of power and worldwide reputation. These included Mahalia Jackson who guested at his mansion, Little Richard Penniman, plus a string of former California politicians from the governor on down. King Narcisse recorded for various recording studios including Jaxyson, who ran a radio repair shop on 7th Street, as well as the Ollie Hunt label in San Francisco, and the King ended up on wax at John Dolphin's Hollywood Records studio on West Pico Boulevard in Hollywood in 1953. Narcisse became part of a gospel group with an old Louisiana friend, James Wiltz, and formed a gospel quartet called the Rising Stars. The first three recruits for the group were all from Louisiana. They were able to record on Bob Geddins's Oakland-based Big Town label. The Rising Stars became one of the Bay Area's most beloved and successful quartet groups.[83] In 1955, King Narcisse recorded at Mount Zion Spiritual Temple with his own Mount Zion Spiritual choir. King also waxed for Ajax, a local one-man studio in Oakland-off-Broadway. His most memorable and well-known song was "Give Me Wings Lord," otherwise known as "Two Wings." In the mid 50s, King Narcisse put words and music to his motto "It nice to be nice" for the minuscule concert on the record label Shirley, about which little is known.[84] King Louis H. Narcisse, also known as the Grace Bishop, lived in a twenty-four-room pink palace in Oakland's Piedmont district. Making no

---

82. Nations, *It's So Nice to Be Nice*, 10.
83. Ibid., 11.
84. Ibid., 13.

apologies for his extravagant lifestyle at the expense of poor people, Narcisse said, "I have built a solid foundation here at Mt Zion . . . I have labored hard, made sacrifices and suffered," saying this outward manifestation of worldly gain is necessary. "The diamond rings, the flashy cars attract attention . . . they were given to me by God." He also believed that a show of substance is beneficial to the flock. "I want golden robes and slippers here, but that is to prove to the people that they can have things here on earth."[85]

Narcisse has other religious beliefs to put before his followers, including: 1) we should worship the Spirit of God every day, not on just a special day; 2) the burning of incense in the home will drive out evil spirits, 3) there is a blessing in oils and holy waters; and 4) if you are pure and right, good will always conquer. When the Rolls-Royce was presented to him in 1962 as a delayed 40th birthday present from his followers, he stopped traffic for blocks.[86]

In January 1961, King Narcisse led a fifteen-car motorcade to the inauguration of President John F. Kennedy. Before leaving Oakland he appeared before a crowd of four hundred outside City Hall, many of whom pressed bills and silver into his bejeweled hands. Throwing the cash onto his red carpet the King proclaimed: "I was asked during a recent television interview how I manage to get money, well, it's like this, people just give it to you."[87]

Blessed bread is passed out by Narcisse to eager followers on Monday morning rituals at one of Mt. Zion properties. He says of ceremony: "It is symbolic of life, food and creation. It is more than just bread—it becomes a spiritual blessing. There are people who will not take a trip or have surgery without my blessing." He confided, "There are those who live, breathe and die by my words." People flock to Mt. Zion for the main event with services conducted by temple functionaries before the King arrives. Shortly after his grand entrance, he heightens the mood by leading the congregation in song with his rather pleasant tenor voice. Narcisse expresses the belief that he has descended from the prophets of biblical times, having been given a "time element" on earth. "I believe there could not have been His Grace, King Louis H. Narcisse, until this day," he says. "Just as there could not have been other religious leaders until their day. I am a gifted person. I have the gift of prophecy. I have the gift of healing." There are those among the followers, however, who claim even more. He is credited with returning sight to the sightless, curing the incurable, and, one day in 1952, restoring to life an Oakland man. Unfortunately, these miracles

85. Robinson, "The Kingdom of King Narcisse," 114.
86. Ibid.
87. Ibid., 115.

have gone unrecorded by either the responsible press or medical science. I do not ask you to believe it.[88]

> While it is assumed that Narciss [sic] is a man of God, he does not feel obligated to reaffirm his patronage when he steps into the pulpit to preach . . . rather, Narciss [sic] comes to the development of sermon units with a different set of generating principles. In effect Narciss [sic] has significantly altered the customary three-tiered configuration that places the African-American preacher in the mediating position between God and the congregation . . . for in addition to the Lord's Prayer, he uses the Hail Mary, both chanted antiphonally, during the course of his sermon. The explanation offered by a follower was that the Hail Mary allowed Narciss [sic] to honor men and women, the Lord and His Mother. The Narciss [sic] configuration recognizes that the Spirit of God can descend on himself and his congregation concurrently but that he has a special obligation to instruct his congregation to the interpretation of God's visitation.[89]
>
> According to the *Oakland Tribune*, November 27, 1970, King L. H. Narcisse, founder of Mt. Zion Spiritual Temples, will receive the Afro-American Association's Leader of the Year Award at an Achievement 70 gathering at 7:30 p.m. tomorrow at the Sequoia Lodge 60 Joaquin Miller Court.[90]

King Narcisse was called from labor to reward in Detroit from a heart attack on February 3, 1989. "After his death, the King's body was flown from Detroit to Oakland, where a three-and-a-half-hour service was held, conducted by the Reverend A. L. Cobbs at the Mt. Zion Spiritual Temple. Following the funeral, the King's bronze casket was placed inside an antique hearse, and four black horses driven by John Jenkel dressed in black tails and top hat lead [sic] the procession towards downtown Oakland. The entourage drove seventeen miles to Rolling Hills Memorial Park where the King was placed in the ground."[91] *The San Francisco Gate* reported on September 28, 2004 that the Mt. Zion church building was destroyed by fire.

88. Robinson, "The Kingdom of King Narcisse," 112, 114, 115, 118.

89. Davis, *I Got the Word in Me and I Can Sing It*, 69, 70, 72, 3, 87.

90. *Oakland Tribune*, November 27, 1970..

91. Nations, *It's So Nice to Be Nice*, 13.

Mt Calvary Baptist Church, Oakland

Mt. Calvary Baptist Church was organized on March 4, 1945 at 1315 7th Street by a determined group of people who were migrants from the South. The Reverend H. W. Watson was elected pastor. The invitation was extended to fifty-two men and women. Henry and Viola Taylor, migrants from Louisiana, were among the first members.

Itolev Hudson was among the first migrants from Louisiana to join Mt. Calvary. At a later time, she was active in the church, president of the missionary council, a member of the missions department, served on the Missions Board, and sang in the choir. As a good and faithful servant, she served willingly whenever and wherever there was a need.[92] The church records reveal that deacons were allowed to continue as a deacon after being voted on each January. Henry Taylor was reinstalled on January 28, 1947. The members sang several familiar songs; "I Heard the Voice of Jesus Saying," "This Little Light of Mine," and, finally, "I Shall Not Be Moved." The scripture reading was Psalms 78:1–3. Six months after the Reverend Watson was elected pastor of Mt. Calvary, he resigned after being called to pastor New Hope Baptist Church. Shortly after, the Reverend George Washington Killens was elected pastor of Mt. Calvary. Mt. Calvary quickly grew, becoming one of the largest churches in Oakland. The Reverend Killens had a powerful voice and was among the first singing, firebrand preachers to have his entire congregation record. His early RPM recording in 1947, *Father I Stretch My Hands to Thee*, was recorded in concert at Oakland's Civil Auditorium. It set the stage for many other successful Bay Area churches to record live in a church atmosphere. Carrie-Mae Anderson, resident pianist for Mt. Calvary, had brought Odessa Perkins to California. Ms. Perkins became one of the most well-respected gospel contraltos in the San Francisco Bay Area. While a member of Mt. Calvary, Perkins joined The Spiritual Gospel Singers, an all-male aggregation. Marie Marbles and Joe Tugwell sang with Perkins in the Mt. Calvary Baptist choir.[93] After having rented the Hall since 1945, in 1952, Reverend Killens convinced the congregation to purchase the Boiler Makers Hall. One year later, the church was forced to sell because urban renewal was destroying 7th Street and other West Oakland areas making way for a new freeway, post office, and for mass transportation. Mt. Calvary relocated at 1445 23rd Avenue, a former movie theater. In 1956, the Reverend Killens left Mt. Calvary and became pastor of St. Matthews Missionary

---

92. www.fouchesfuneralhome.com/obituaries/Itolev-Hudson.

93. Nations, *The Odessa Perkins Story*, 2. http://www.opalnations.com/files/Perkins_Odessa.pdf (accessed March 2, 2016).

Baptist Church at 3129 San Pablo Avenue, Oakland. A large group left with the Reverend Killens including Odessa Perkins and many members of the congregation.[94]

The Reverend Killens served at St Matthews from 1956 until his retirement in 1972. He was called from labor to reward circa 1975 at the age of sixty-eight. Funeral services were held at the Mt. Calvary Baptist Church on 23rd Ave. The Reverend S. J. Scott, Pastor of St. Paul Baptist Church, officiated. The Reverend Benjamin Carroll Sr., born in Holly, Louisiana, was elected pastor of Mt. Calvary in August 1981. In June 1983, he attended the National Baptist Convention in Memphis, Tennessee. On June 26, 1983, while preaching at the First Baptist Church, Memphis, he collapsed in the pulpit and was called from labor to reward on June 27, 1983 at the Baptist Memorial Hospital in Memphis. The church suddenly found itself without a pastor. Since that time, a series of pastors have presided as Pastor.[95]

Echoes of Port Chicago: A Tragedy in the Bay Area

The Black man cannot protect a country, if the country doesn't protect him.

—Henry McNeal Turner

A number of the men that were killed in the tragedy at Port Chicago were members of local Bay Area churches. The background for the tragedy was tragic in itself. Blacks working at the shipyards were frequently given the least desirable graveyard shift and the most dangerous and unpleasant assignments. In spite of their having attained the same high level of skill as whites at welding or other crafts, they were segregated into auxiliary unions; in the Brotherhood of Boilermakers, for instance, auxiliary members had to pay dues, but could not vote in union elections.[96] Port Chicago is located in Concord in Contra Costa County, just ten miles east of Richmond and thirty miles north of San Francisco. On the night of July 17, 1944, over 4,600 tons of explosive bombs were being loaded on two merchant ships. Around 10:18 p.m., a series of explosions from the bombs went off, sent shock waves that could be felt as far away as Nevada. Three hundred and twenty sailors were killed instantly, including 202 enlisted African-American sailors who

94. Ibid., 9.

95. Obituary of the Reverend Benjamin F. Carroll—Funeral held at Mt. Calvary Missionary Baptist Church July 2, 1983.

96. Bagwell, *Oakland*, 234.

had little training in handling explosives and munitions. In some instances, the black soldiers were required to move ten tons per hatch per hour. After the explosion, white officers were given thirty days leave and blacks were not given leave, exposing the bare ugly truth about racism in the United States during World War II. Fifty black men were charged with mutiny, punishable by death for refusing to load ammunition in an unsafe work environment. Shortly after the explosion, seeking to deflect charges that the Port Chicago base was segregated, the Navy brought in two divisions of White sailors to load munitions, but they weren't assigned to work with black soldiers. A munity trial was held and, after only two hours of deliberation, two hundred and eight black men were court-martialed and were found guilty of conspiracy and sentenced to eight to fifteen years in prison with a dishonorable discharge.

Thurgood Marshall, who was working as legal counsel for the NAACP, sat in on the last few days of the proceedings and later argued, "This is not fifty men on trial for munity. This is the Navy on trial for its whole vicious policy towards Negroes."[97] While the Port Chicago 50 were later hailed as heroes, the Navy never officially exonerated them of mutiny. President Bill Clinton issued a pardon to sailor Freddie Meeks in 1999, but the others died without having their names cleared. Some, such as Joseph Small, had actively refused to seek a pardon. "That means, you're guilty, but we forgive you," he said before his death in 1996.[98]

Post War Traumatic Stress in Black Neighborhood

Black people have been traumatized and psychologically wounded. This is something we cannot discuss enough at this historical moment.

—BELL HOOKS

After six years and one day, World War II ended on September 2, 1945. World War II was both a blessing and a curse for black people. In the post-war decades, racial tensions were at an all-time high; it was the beginning of the ending of the black insulated communities. Through the mid-1940s, signs announcing, "We Refuse Service to Negroes," sat in the windows of many hotels, bars, and restaurants, particularly in the areas of downtown

97. *Bay Area News Group,* July 17, 2014.
98. *Bay Area News Group,* July 17, 2014.

close to West Oakland and in cities like Albany and San Leandro.[99] The un-employment lines were long and, instead of a large postwar out-migration, San Francisco's black population continued to grow between 1945 and 1950. The federal census reported 43,460 blacks in San Francisco, a staggering 904 percent increase from the 1940 population.[100] Once the war ended, not only did the majority of the newcomers stay in their newfound homes, but many more would follow and San Francisco's African-American population would continue to grow, increasing by 11,000 between 1945 and 1950.[101]

After the war, black women experienced the highest unemployment rates—more than 40 percent in the Bay Area. With the closing of defense industries, the debilitating effects of postwar unemployment and economic dislocation were most glaring in small boomtowns like Richmond. Many migrant women viewed postwar unemployment as a product of white eco-nomic policy, designed to encourage migrants to leave the Bay Area. By 1946, Richmond had the highest proportion of unemployment claimants anywhere in the Bay Area. Post-WWII, some natives felt that migrants would leave. The withdrawal of social services in war housing areas in De-cember 1945 further disadvantaged poor working-class families.[102]

A journalist wrote that "carloads of families toting their mattresses, pots and pans, tables and chairs were seen leaving housing projects. Howev-er, most migrants remained as their standard of living spiraled downwards. Many who held on to their jobs became the working poor as overtime, and working hours were cut below 40 hours."[103] In the meantime, housing discrimination remained a serious problem. Meanwhile the San Francisco Redevelopment Agency was uprooting black residents in the Fillmore, and the same was occurring in West Oakland. To make matters worse, racial covenants were still in place that restricted blacks from living in certain ar-eas and landlords were charging exorbitant rates.

By the end of the war, Oakland operated three permanent and eleven temporary projects, of which four "had mixed racial occupancy, seven were all-white, and three were all-black. All three of the black projects and a fourth nearly all-black one were located in West Oakland. All of the white projects were located in or near East Oakland."[104]

---

99. Self, *American Babylon Race*, 58.

100. Broussard, *Black San Francisco*, 204.

101. Miller, *The Postwar Struggle for Civil Rights*, 13.

102. *San Francisco Chronicle* June 8, 9, 17, 24, 1953.

103. Richard Reinhardt, "Richmond: The Boom That Didn't Bust," *San Francisco Chronicle*, August 16, 1953.

104. Rhomburg, *No There There Race*, 99.

The *San Francisco Chronicle* reported that "nearly 12,000 people a week were lining up at the unemployment office to collect twenty dollars in weekly unemployment benefits. In the spring of 1947, overall unemployment had dropped to 8,000, but black unemployment as a percentage of the total had risen by forty percent, to 2,250 or twenty-eight percent of the total. Seventy-five percent of unemployed black men and 40 percent of unemployed black women had been shipyard workers."[105]

What added to the burden of employment was that the majority of migrant workers in the shipyards were not trained beyond the menial work they performed as shipyard workers. Even if they were prepared, discrimination remained prevalent. In 1944, Kaiser employed around forty-seven thousand workers, by the spring of 1946, the workforce was less than nine thousand.[106] Most blacks were not prepared for the aftershock of unemployment.

In August 1949, West Oakland resident Lola Bell Sims wrote to Harry Truman: "Just now here in Oakland the colored people are much confused and very unhappy thinking that they are going to lose their all and all by the U.S. government taking their property by force whether or not they want to give it up."[107] To West Oakland residents like Ms. Sims, property ownership meant a home where they could have shelter in their old age. And now it appeared that a partnership of the city of Oakland and the federal government, made possible by the Housing Act of 1949, planned to condemn their property, acquire it through eminent domain, and redevelop vast stretches of the city's principal lack neighborhood. The attention gave homeowners like Ms. Sims reason to worry because she and a generation of Jim Crowed African Americans owned or rented homes in the oldest, most deteriorated sections of the nation's cities, now the targets of renewal programs.[108]

The ending of the war was not the end of black church growth in the Bay Area, however. Blacks remained and continued to flow into the area. From storefronts and tents to house churches, Black church growth in the Bay Area continued in spite of problems and hurdles.

105. *San Francisco Chronicle* 18, 1946.

106. *FEPC, Final report,* p 78;

107. Lola Bell Sims to Harry Truman, August 30, 1949, File 605, Box 30, Files of the Housing and Home Finance Agency National Archives, Record Group 207.

108. Self, *American Babylon Race,* 137–38.

Faith Presbyterian Church, Oakland

The Presbyterian State and National Boards were aware of the fact that there were Negro members of the Presbyterian faith in San Francisco and the East Bay area who did not have a Presbyterian church in a less affluent area to serve the people. The Reverend John Dillingham, a Presbyterian minister, had been assigned to Oakland to explore the possibilities of developing a Presbyterian Church in West Oakland to serve the Negro Presbyterian population who were without a church. As a result, a group was brought together and the official service for Faith Presbyterian Church was organized at the First Presbyterian Church in Oakland on April 28, 1946. The Reverend W. M. Clauson, Moderator of the San Francisco Presbytery, presided. Following the sermon by the Reverend Dr. Ralph Marshall Davis, Pastor of First Presbyterian, the moderator received the new members and presided over the elections and ordination of the elders, which now constituted the official beginning of Faith Presbyterian as an organized church. The Reverend Dillingham was the first pastor, Leola Burke, a member of Faith Presbyterian, was the first black woman elder in Northern California, and Themus Spencer was the First Clerk of Session. Other elders included Arthur Isom, J. C. Price, and Earl M. Jett. The first deacons were Eloise Isom, Ella Jett, Sarah Harris, A. W. Gordon, Susie Means, Grace Grand, Helen Perkins, and Robertha Wells. The first location for the church was at 13th and Market Streets in the West Oakland area before moving to 55th and Gaskill Streets in North Oakland. On August 31, 1949, the Session approved forty individuals as charter members. Through the years, a number of pastors served Faith. Among them was the Reverend Frank Pinkard who moved the church to 430 49th Street in 1974. In 1981, the Reverend Ophelia Manney became the first African American woman to be ordained in the San Francisco Presbytery and served as interim pastor in 1981.

In 1983 a new era was ushered in when the Reverend Frank Jackson became pastor. The Reverend Jackson gave the church new directions in mission, community involvement, spiritual healing, and in spreading God's word. Faith Presbyterian has worked hard to build positive relations with all ethnic groups, making significant contributions in African American / Korean community relationships. In 1991, Oakland experienced a devasting firestorm that burned homes to the ground and took lives. Faith opened its doors to become a refuge for many who had become homeless. Faith has made major contributions to the community. In 1997, Faith Presbyterian along with Allen Temple Baptist Church and Lafayette-Orinda Presbyterian Church provided financial resources to rebuild two churches in Boligee, Alabama that had been destroyed by arson. The Reverend Frank Jackson was called from labor to reward September 11, 2009. The church continues with interim ministers as the congregation carefully selects the next installed pastor.[109]

Friendship Missionary Baptist Church, San Francisco

Friendship Missionary Baptist Church was organized on August 18, 1946, under the leadership of the Reverend Eli Leroy Evans Jr. in a storefront at 1545-A Post Street, San Francisco, California, with his wife, Mrs. Millie G. Evans, and four children. From this number, the church began to grow as new members joined weekly. The organizational structure for the church began to take place as Mrs. Millie G. Evans organized the first choir with Sisters Bowie, Jean Austin, and Savannah Crawford. Mrs. Edythe Moore was the first pianist. Willie Robinson served as the first Usher's President. A piano and other church furniture were purchased by the Reverend Evans.

Isaiah Martin and Albert Reese were ordained as deacons by Pastor Evans. The Reverend W. R. McDonald joined in the late 1946 to assist with the spiritual growth of the membership.

In the early spring of 1947. Mrs. Evans became seriously ill and was called from labor to reward in May 1949. During the postwar years, the church continued to grow and relocated to 1525-A Post Street. After the three-year lease expired on December 24, 1949, the church was offered property at 1257 Octavia Street and later was given financial assistance to build. On May 6, 1951, the members raised $45,000, making it possible for the groundbreaking services on May 6, 1951 for a new church. On November 4, 1951, with Articles of Incorporation attained and the official name of the church changed to First Friendship Institutional Baptist Church, the congregation, led by Pastor Evans, officers, and choir, marched from their storefront building to a newly erected church joyfully singing, "We're Marching to Zion." Pastor W. A. Holly and the Foothill Baptist Church was the guest church. The Conroe Bay Area Extension College was placed in the church facility. Shortly thereafter the name of the church included the word "Institutional." Dr. Evans strongly believed in preparing persons for leadership. He served as the first dean of the branch of the college called "Industrial College" that focused on training ministers and missionaries. Local ministers were given certificates and used their training to help them start other churches. Among the rising stars who graduated from the college included the late Reverends J. L. Richards, W. A. Holly, D. J. Ridley, J. A. Strickling, and the Reverend Malone and Henry McBride, all who

109. Faith Presbyterian Church History Anniversary.

founded some of the leading churches in the Bay Area. In 1959, the City
of San Francisco served notice that Friendship had to relocate because of
redevelopment. The church relocated to 501 Steiner Street on December
4, 1960, with a mortgage of around $192,000. On August 26, 1979, a mort-
gage burning ceremony was held using the theme "God's Watchman" from
Jeremiah 1:9. Dr. Amos C. Brown Sr., Pastor of Third Baptist Church of
San Francisco, was the guest minister. Under Pastor Evans's leadership, the
church sponsored Friendship Village, a low-rent housing development that
opened in October 1970. Pastor Evans served as Chairman of the Board of
Directors and Flora B. McRay managed the complex from July 7, 1971 until
her retirement in 1989. Pastor Evans's health began to fail, and he selected
the Reverend Weltham L. Hudson to serve as his assistant. The Reverend
Evans was called from labor to reward May 1, 1985. Following the Reverend
Evans's death, a series of ministers served as interim pastors. In March 1991,
the Reverend C. C. Coleman was elected Pastor and installed on September
15, 1991. Friendship had earned a name as a church that prepared others
for serious study. The Reverend Coleman organized the "Christ for Lunch
Bunch" Bible study with people from other churches attending. The Reverend Coleman served until October 1, 1995. The Reverend Charlie Crier
succeeded the Reverend Coleman and served as interim for several years.
On March 7, 1997, he was elected pastor and served until June 30, 2001.
On December 21, 2001, Floyd W. Trammell Jr., MDiv, was called to be Pastor and was installed on April 21, 2002. Through his theme, "Vision and
Mission," the Reverend Trammell challenged and led the Friendship Family
to address the spiritual, economic, social, and cultural needs of the community. Under Pastor Trammell's leadership, Friendship has grown; new
deacons and praise dancers have been added, women have been included as
preachers, Christian education has expanded, and improvements have been
made to the facilities of the church.[110]

Galilee Missionary Baptist Church, San Francisco

The Reverend S. W. Jackson was the founder and organizer of Galilee Missionary Baptist Church of San Francisco in October 1946. World War II had
come to an end and, surprisingly, numerous Negroes remained in the Bay
Area, creating a need for additional church growth. The church was originally named Shiloh Missionary Baptist Church Number Two. However, er-
rors made by mail carriers with the former Shiloh congregation forged the

110. Friendship Missionary Baptist Church History, http://www.ffibc.com/834120
(accessed March 2, 2016).

need for a name change. The church changed its name to Galilee Missionary Baptist Church. In the early 1960s, the church was physically moved on large trucks several city blocks from Galvez Street to 1901 Oakdale Avenue. The move was an ambitious undertaking as the women and men of the church donated their time and talents to the building's reconstruction. A series of pastors served Galilee after the Reverend Jackson was called from labor to reward. The Reverend Dwayne E. Fisher, serves as the Senior Pastor and continues the leadership of Galilee reaching into the community with church ministries.[111] Galilee is one of many churches that were uprooted during the redevelopment era following the war.

Evergreen Missionary Baptist Church, Oakland

In July, 1947, The Alameda Church Council sent a letter to the Alameda Community Church declaring the pulpit vacant. At that time there was no black church in Alameda, and the Reverend J. L. Richards wanted Alameda Community Church to become a black Baptist Church pastored by a black minister. The Reverend J. L. Richards, along with a small group of Christian believers, met in the Reverend Richard's home on July 27, 1947 for the purpose of organizing a Black Baptist Church in Alameda. The name Evergreen was submitted and approved and the new church became known as the Evergreen Missionary Baptist Church. On August 10, 1947, the Reverend Richard was installed as Pastor of Evergreen Missionary Baptist Church and the Reverend W. M. Clark of the Mt. Zion Baptist Church, Oakland, led the installation service. By now, the church had relocated from Alameda to Oakland. Without a permanent place to worship, the members moved to several places in the West Oakland area before finding a permanent location at 408 West MacArthur Blvd, Oakland on February 24, 1957. The new location was the former church home of the Church of Latter Day Saints and was purchased for the sum of $97,500. Buildings formerly occupied by white congregations became available during the white flight to suburban areas. Evergreen quickly became one of the leading churches in Oakland. As the church grew, additional property was purchased adjacent to the church for a parking lot. On July 23, 1972, Evergreen held its mortgage burning service. The Reverend Dr. S. M. Lockridge, Pastor of Calvary Baptist church, San Diego, was the guest speaker.

On October 27, 1984, the Reverend James L. Richard was called from labor to reward after thirty-seven years of faithful, dedicated leadership and service. The Reverend William Scott served as interim pastor from

111. Galilee Missionary Baptist Church History.

November 1984 to April 1985. At the suggestion of Sister Mary C. Bolden, the church held a special prayer meeting to have a new pastor. On January 1, 1985, a pulpit selection committee was established, which recommended the name of the Reverend Frank Pinkard Jr., a son of Evergreen, as the new Pastor. The Reverend Pickard had served as Pastor at Faith Presbyterian prior to his election on April 9, 1985. An impressive installation service was held Sunday, May 19, 1985 with the Reverend Joseph Randolph Richardson, Pastor of El Bethel Baptist Church, San Francisco, giving Pastor Pinkard the Pastor's Charge. The Reverend J. L. Johnson, Pastor of Elizabeth Baptist Church in Richmond, delivered the installation message. The Reverend Pinkard's first sermon as pastor was "Moving into the Future with God." Pastor Pinkard's first Appreciation Service was held October 16–19, 1986.

Improvements were made to the church including an elevator and the J. L. Richard Terrace; a Senior Citizen and Handicap Housing Complex consisting of eighty units for the aged and handicapped was dedicated on November 6, 1988; the Mother Irene Cooper Terrace, another Senior Citizen and Handicap Housing Complex consisting of forty units for the aged and handicapped was also established.

On Sunday, July 27. 1997, Evergreen held its 50th Golden Jubilee Anniversary Service. Dr. E. Edward Jones, former President of the National Baptist Convention of America, was the guest speaker. On that day, the groundbreaking ceremony for the new sanctuary was held. Three years later, Sunday, July 23, 2000, the congregation marched into a new state-of-the-art sanctuary, which was added to the existing church. On June 24, 2007, under the leadership of Bishops Robert "Bob" Jackson and Ernestine Cleveland Reems, the title "Bishop" was bestowed upon the Reverend Frank Pinkard. In May 2009, Bishop Pinkard celebrated his twenty-fourth year as Pastor of Evergreen.[112]

Bethel Missionary Baptist Church, Oakland

The Reverend Herbert Guice was born August 7, 1913 in Rentisville, Oklahoma. In 1921, he became affiliated with the First Baptist Church of Rentisville and remained there until his family moved to Kansas City, Missouri in 1923. In 1942, the Reverend Guice relocated to Oakland and on October 24, 1943 he received his license to preach. He was ordained at the St. John Baptist Church, pastored by the Reverend James Brown. He later moved his membership to Bible Fellowship Baptist Church where he served as

112. Evergreen Baptist Church Anniversary Celebration Book—A Brief History Oakland Public Library History Room File Churches.

Assistant Pastor. The Reverends O. P. Smith and Herbert Guice were highly respected in the Eastbay as men of integrity and fighters for justice along with their uncompromising way of preaching the gospel.

Dr. O. P. Smith had a strong influence on Dr. Guice and encouraged him to become a senior pastor; their relationship was a tight bond until the Reverend O. P. Smith was called from labor to reward circa 1971. Dr. Herbert Guice took Dr. Smith's advice to heart and the journey of Dr. Herbert Guice as Pastor of Bethel Missionary Baptist Church was birthed. Bethel Missionary Church started from an organized body known as the Estuary Community Church. The Organizer and first Pastor of the Estuary Community Church was the Reverend J. L. Richard, who served from 1945 to 1947. The first worship services were held in the Estuary Housing Projects Tenant Activity Building, 339 Singleton Avenue, Alameda, California, under the supervision of the Alameda Council of Churches. The second Pastor was the Reverend R. D. Garrison, who served from 1947 to 1950. In March 1950, the church was without a pastor and a pulpit committee was set up to work with the Alameda Council of Churches to secure a pastor to fill the vacancy. The committee was made up of Brothers James Brown and P. D. Odom and Sisters Mary Cain, Lillie Martin, and Georgia Wishups. On June 12, 1950, a special business meeting was held and elected the Reverend Herbert Guice as Pastor. As a Baptist minister, the Reverend Guice felt strongly that he could not work effectively in a Community Church. He was assured by the Alameda Council of Churches that if he would accept the position as Pastor, they would assist in every way possible to establish a Baptist Church in Alameda. In February 1953, the Reverend O. P. Smith, the Reverend Guice's mentor and pastor of Bible Fellowship Baptist Church, sent five persons with letters to assist with the organizational service. Among the early organizers were Mrs. Eulee Guice, Maggie Willis, Beatrice Singletary, and Misters C. W. Willis, Lewis Clark, and ministers serving on the organization Board including the Reverend O. P. Smith, A. O Bell (Pastor North Oakland Baptist Church), G. H. Henderson, C. E. Henderson, and W. L. Cook. In February 1953, the approval of the Alameda Housing Authority and the Alameda Council of Churches was given for a Baptist church to be organized. On Wednesday evening, March 4, 1953, Harold Camping, Chairman of the Project Work Committee of the Alameda Council of Churches, gave a special address. During the event, the adoption of the Church Covenant and Eighteen Articles of Faith were held. On the night of the organization, 186 members united by Christian experience. It was motioned by Jack Johnson and seconded by Hattie Bryant that the Reverend Herbert Guice would be the Pastor of the newly organized church. The name "Bethel Missionary Baptist Church" was submitted by Pastor Guice who used Genesis 28:

19—"He called that place Bethel"—as the foundation for the church name. Shortly thereafter, a building fund was established to purchase a permanent location for worship. The temporary projects were being torn down after the war, and the majority of the blacks were relocating to Oakland.

In November 1958, the church was able to purchase a forty-thousand square-foot lot on 69th Avenue and Rudsdale Street, Oakland, at the cost of $43,000. A little more than a year later, under the leadership of Dr. Guice, Bethel took a loan from Trans-Bay Federal Savings and Loan Association for $156,000 On Sunday afternoon, August 30, 1959, groundbreaking ceremonies for the new location were held at the new location. It was a proud moment for the Reverend Guice as he shoveled the first dirt for the new construction before a capacity crowd including dignitaries from the Mayor's Office, along with the Reverends J. L. Richards and his mentor the Reverend O. P. Smith and others who were present for the grand celebration. During the period of construction, the Reverend C. J. Anderson, Pastor of St. John Missionary Baptist Church, extended his hospitality to allow the Bethel Church family to meet in their property at 720 Filbert Street for approximately six months.[113]

On Sunday, August 7, 1960, at 7:30 a.m. the Bethel Church family gathered at 339 Singleton Ave. in Alameda, the site of their first church location, for one hour of prayer and thanksgiving. The congregants proceeded from Alameda by individual cars to the second location, 720 Filbert St. in Oakland for a second prayer gathering. After the second prayer gathering, the members formed a motorcade and drove to 6901 Rudsdale Ave. in Oakland, the site of the new Bethel Church. The key to the church was presented to Pastor Guice by Senior Deacons' Chair, Barnett Bolton, as the congregation gathered at the front entrance. The Bible from the previous building was placed upon the pulpit by Deacon Napoleon Sims.

The cornerstone for Bethel was laid on June 3, 1962. With the exception of $18, the finances of the church was depleted; the greatest work lay ahead: paying off the mortgage.

On August 2, 1970, the mortgage-burning services revealed that the mortgage of $150,000 was amortized over a period of twenty years; however, it was paid off within ten years. Pastor Guice delighted in saying that "the mortgage was paid off without one chicken being fried, and no rabbit had to lose its foot because regular tithes and offerings paid the mortgage off." The joyous mortgage-burning service celebration included the appearance of Dr. Marcus Foster, the first black Superintendent of Oakland Public School, Barney Hilburn, an Oakland Board of Education member.

113. *Oakland Post Newspaper* August 6, 1970.

Other dignitaries along with a standing-room crowd witnessed this historical celebration. The Reverend O. P. Smith delivered the evening sermon.[114]
Bethel Church is known for encouraging its youth to get a sound education.
Dr.Guice established the Bethel Church Job Placement Program in 1971,
providing full-time and part-time job placements for twenty-five hundred
young people and adults. Dr. Herbert Guice was inspired to build an elementary school after learning about the alarming school dropout rate that
starts in elementary school. In 1983, Reverend Guice formed a committee
from members in the church who held professional jobs for the purpose of
building a Christian Academy for pre-school through sixth grade. The Dr.
Herbert Guice Christian Academy became a reality when it was completed
in 1997. Over the years, over five million dollars have been raised for college scholarships. Some of the recipients became doctors, lawyers, school
principals, business owners, and pastors.

Mrs. Mable Williams served for over forty years as Dr. Guice's secretary. She was an outstanding role model and served in many capacities. She
was affectionately known as "Able Mable" because she was never too busy or
tired to give of herself.

Dr. Herbert Guice was called from labor to reward at the age of ninety-
four on February 13, 2008. In honor of his spiritual guidance, social justice
involvement, and civic participation, a resolution was passed to rename a
portion of Rudsdale Street between the intersections of 69th Avenue and
73rd Avenue as Herbert Guice Way. Prior to his death, the Reverend Guice
recommended two sons of Bethel, the Reverends Vincent Martin and Frank
Darby, for consideration to succeed him. The Reverend Frank Darby was
elected and serves today as pastor of this historic church.[115]

St. John Missionary Baptist Church, Oakland

St. John Missionary Baptist Church was organized on July 6, 1947, in an old
revival tent on Magnolia Street in West Oakland with a small group of eight
persons. Dr. O. P. Smith, Bible Fellowship Baptist Church, was the revivalist
who encouraged the Reverend Carl Anderson to start a church from the
revival. At the onset, the Reverend Anderson encountered resistance; a City
of Oakland ordinance stated at that time that a tent revival could not go

114. Ibid.

115. History of the Bethel Missionary Baptist Church 36th Anniversary, *Oakland
Post*, August 6, 1970, City of Oakland Agenda Report March 11, 2008, U.S. Congres-
sional Records, Vol. 153, no. 2, pp. E35–E36, January 5, 2007. The History of the Bethel
Missionary The Baptist Church 36th Anniversary.

beyond thirty days. The young Anderson would not be denied and City officials renewed his permit for thirty additional days. Shortly thereafter another attack came when some black prominent pastors told him, "Partner, you can't make it, take these few members you have and join one of the boys churches." The Reverend Anderson replied, the "boys didn't send me." Sixty days later, the twenty-five-member congregation was given access to the Seventh Day Adventist Church at 34th and Market Streets in Oakland by Pastor R. W. Nelson. Six months later, February 27, 1948, St. John relocated to the Watson Building at 952 8th Street where services were held for two years. As early as 1949, Dr. Anderson increased the church's outreach evangelism through radio broadcast. St. John's Radio ministry soon became the number one radio religious broadcast in Northern California. Originally "The Gospel Call Hour" was broadcast on radio station KLX, KWBR, and, finally, KDIA. Dr. Anderson continued to expand the ministry of St. John by adding a Sunday-morning live broadcast called "The Period of Mediation." Radio listeners were very familiar with Dr. Anderson's famous quotes: "What God can't do, just can't be done," and "Hold on old soldier." Later Dr. Anderson increased the presence of St. John with a live Sunday television morning broadcast as the first Bay Area African-American church on television. It was noted that approximately 40 percent of the growth of St. John's congregation during the 1950s through the 1970s was the direct result of these radio and television broadcasts. St. John was known locally and nationally for its unique music ministry. The choir grew to over two hundred voices in the early 1970s, receiving numerous awards and honors.

Gerald Davis described Dr. Anderson as "well-thought of and well-regarded in the Bay Area as a *good* preacher." In many ways, he is the prototypical contemporary urban African-American preacher blending the sophistication and savvy of the successful urban politician and businessman with the earthiness and mother wit of the Black Southern rural church tradition.[116]

In 1950, the church purchased its first building located at 720 Filbert Street for a purchase price of $29,000 with a down payment of $1,000. The Filbert Street location was home for St. John for nine years. However, Dr. Anderson had his eyes on a stunning edifice located at 36th and Adeline Streets, which was the St. Andrews Catholic Church. Dr. Anderson began to pray, "Lord if you give me this building to worship in, I'll give you a better service.". His wife, Rosabelle, commented, "Rev, the Lord is not going to give you the building those people are worshiping in."[117] In 1958, St. Andrews

116. Davis, *I Got the Word in Me and I Can Sing It*, 1.

117. Great S. John Missionary Baptist Church History—Oakland Public Library

sat vacant because of urban renewal. With the Filbert Street church in the process of being remodeled to accommodate the growing membership, Dr. Anderson heard the voice of the Holy Spirit while in the pulpit one Sunday morning that said, "Hurry and move the congregation." One morning as Dr. Anderson was on his way to church, he drove past St. Andrews as was his custom. He noticed something that had not been there before, a "For Sale" sign in front of the building. In his jubilant excitement, Dr. Anderson stopped his vehicle, jumped out, retrieved the realtor's sign, and threw it into the trunk of his car and proceeded directly to the real estate office. Plans were set into motion and, eventually, with approval, the church was purchased. Dr. Anderson soon learned that the building had been vacated by the Catholic Diocese because the State of California had plans to construct the 580 freeway that would involve relocating the church. It was also during this same period that the City of Oakland notified Dr. Anderson that a new project entitled Urban Renewal would impact all of West Oakland and in particular the location where St. John was located on Filbert Street. Dr. Anderson was now faced with what seemed an insurmountable problem. Black West Oakland was slowly being destroyed. Memories of West Oakland were profoundly shaped by the rupture of redevelopment. West Oakland was a beautiful place until the city, with a decree to clean out West Oakland, came through. Physical destruction for new transportation routes shaped people's mental and emotional maps of West Oakland.[118]

Dr. Anderson and his congregation was faced with the daunting task of having St. Andrews Church physically moved from 36th and Adeline Streets to the 19th and Market Street location, which had previously been purchased by Dr. Anderson. Dr. Anderson moved quickly by having his two apartment buildings demolished at his own expense and donated the land to the church; making room for the new edifice to be relocated.

While the idea seemed feasible to Dr. Anderson, not everyone was as optimistic; as the logistics were akin to crossing the "Red Sea." Negotiations began with the Ahen House Moving Company, then permits were granted by the City, and the move was set into motion by strategically cutting the former Catholic Church into three sections for the move down San Pablo Avenue to Market Street. Street closures were coordinated out of concern for traffic, streetlights, and telephone wires. The dramatic relocation of the building was the biggest television news story of that day. Once the church was relocated, it became apparent that a dining facility and Christian Education wing was needed. The men provided the labor and the cost of

History Room, File Draw Churches.
    118. Self, *American Babylon Race*, 157–58.

completely refurbishing and furnishing the church building.[119] In 1959, on Easter Sunday morning, with his faithful congregation behind him, Dr. Anderson led St. John from the Filbert Street location to a beautiful completely refurbished building at a cost of $318,000, of which $7,400 was spent on stained-glass windows.

St. John was not exempt from tragedy. In 1993, a six-alarm fire gutted the church. The fire could be seen from miles around. Appeals were made to the congregation and other sister churches for help in rebuilding the church. Dr. Herbert Guice and his congregation, Bethel Missionary Baptist Church, donated $20,000 to assist in the rebuilding project. Two years later, December 24, 1995, Dr. Anderson led the members back into their rebuilt and improved sanctuary.[120]

The history of St. John cannot be told without mention of the renowned music ministry of Dr. Carl Anderson and the St. John choirs. In the early 1950s, the Echoes of Zion Choir was founded, growing to nearly two hundred voices in the early 1970s and that, over the years, received numerous awards and honors.

Dr. Anderson was called from labor to reward September 1, 2000 at the age of eighty-two. He was memorialized by government and church leaders. The Reverend Dr. J. Alfred Smith Jr. gave a moving eulogy while many others expressed their sorrow and love for the fallen icon.

After four years without a pastor, including two years of a pastoral search, the congregation appointed the Reverend Dr. Gregory Payton to succeed Dr. Anderson. The Reverend Gregory Payton was no stranger to St. John, having been a longtime member and a popular youth minister, and was installed on January 19, 2005 by Dr. Melvin Von Wade.

Continuing in the legacy of Dr. Anderson, the Reverend Doctor Payton established his own leadership style. Without delay, he called for forty days of prayer to begin the healing process. St. John, now known as Greater St. John Missionary Baptist Church, continues to be a voice for the community.[121]

Liberty Hill Missionary Baptist Church, Berkeley

On February 8, 1948, Liberty Hill Missionary Baptist Church was organized by the late Reverend I. H. Lewis in his home at 1628 Alcatraz Avenue, Berkeley. In attendance was his wife, Tiny Lewis, Joe Ann, Brother Neal, and

119. St. John Missionary Church History, 2.
120. Ibid., 3.
121. Greater St. John Missionary Baptist Church History Files.

A. Lewis. Later they borrowed the Good Shepherd Hall at 1823 9th Street, Berkeley for the first meeting place where ten new members joined the church.

Other ministers who were instrumental in helping the Reverend Lewis organize included the Reverend Clark (Pastor of Mt. Zion Baptist Church, Oakland), the Reverend J. L. Thomas (Pastor of Antioch Baptist Church, Oakland), the Reverend H. Watson (Pastor, New Hope Baptist Church, Oakland), and the Reverend E. E. Stovall (Pastor, Progressive Baptist Church, Berkeley).

In May 1948, Liberty Hill Missionary Baptist Church purchased its first property at 834 Delaware Street, Berkeley. The church grew quickly and steadily and, by 1951, a larger building was needed. The church secured a location at 997 University Avenue, Berkeley, the former Grace Bible Church. In 1964, the Reverend Lewis tenured his resignation and, that same year, the Reverend W. C. Ellis was elected pastor. In 1967, Liberty Hill liquidated its indebtedness from a building fund account that was established for the purposes of remodeling and developing a new building. In 1971, the old building was demolished, making way for a brand new edifice. In the meantime, Liberty Hill held services at a building located at 8th and Hearst Streets, Berkeley.

In December of 1971, the new church was completed and the congregation dedicated the building; it was a joyous time for the church as they returned to the new edifice. A Junior Deacon Board was instituted as a means for preparing the youth for service. In April 1975, Liberty Hill joined the National Baptist Convention of America, Inc.[122]

In September 1979, Pastor W. C. Ellis resigned as pastor after being called to pastor the Mt. Pleasant Baptist Church in Fresno. One year later, September 1980, the Reverend James Williams was elected Pastor. Thirty-eight years after the founding of the church, an annual homecoming service was instituted to celebrate the blessings of the church. In June 1986, Liberty Hill once again liquidated its indebtedness and held a mortgage burning service.[123]

In February 1987, Dr. Marvis V. Peoples was called to assist during a period of serious illness of Pastor Williams, who was called from labor to reward that same month. On March 15, 1987, the Reverend Dr. Marvis Peoples was elected Interim Pastor. Dr. Peoples, a lifetime educator and retired Oakland School principal, immediately began to reconstruct the Christian

122. Liberty Hill Missionary Baptist Church History files, provided by Liberty Hill Missionary Baptist Church.

123. Ibid., 2.

Education Department. Dr. Peoples had served as Dean of the Christian Board of Education at Mt. Zion Missionary Baptist church. Dr. Peoples established a Christian Social Concern Committee to address issues that impact the community, such as getting the City to install a traffic signal light at the corner of 9th Street and University Ave. where the church is located.

On July 12, 1987, Dr. Marvis Peoples was elected Senior Pastor. The first salaried church secretary and minister of music were approved and added to the pastoral staff. On November 1, 1987, the official installation service of the Reverend Dr. Peoples was held at the Allen Temple Baptist Church, where he was ordained and considered a "son" of Allen Temple," where he previously served on the Board of Christian Education.

As the church became more organized administratively, annual reports were printed in booklet form in January 1988, and the Deacon-in-Training program was instituted. On April 8, 1988, the Narcotics Anonymous committee began weekly meetings. A series of new ministries were added to the church to serve the greater community including a prison ministry and convalescent ministry Liberty Hill Missionary Baptist Church continues to thrive under the powerful and spiritual leadership of the Reverend Dr. Marvis Peoples.[124]

Mount Carmel Missionary Baptist Church

The first meeting for the Mount Carmel Baptist Church was held on February 25, 1948 by the founders, the Reverends James Owens, T. Adams, and Mr. Cleveland, along with other unnamed supporters who met in the Harbor Homes temporary shipyard projects on Moorship Avenue. The inaugural song, "Jesus Keep Me Near the Cross," was sung and the Scripture reading from Matthew 16:17–18 was read by Mr. E. Cleveland. The Reverend James Owens then explained his vision for the church. The Reverend Owens was led to read the miracle at Mount Carmel in 1 Kings 18:17–46, which became the inspiration to name the church Mount Carmel Baptist Church. Pastor Owens then appointed officers for the church and the first offering was $4.50. Without a building to meet in, the church rotated locations. The second meeting was held in the home of Gladys Brooks, 879 Wood Street, in West Oakland. At a later unknown date, Mt. Carmel moved to 17th and Peralta Streets and worshipped with the Mary Springfield Baptist Church (with the Reverend J. N. Jacobs, Pastor). On July 3, 1948, Mt. Carmel relocated to 810 Chester Street in Oakland and remained at that location for fifteen years. As the years progressed, the membership continued to grow

124. Ibid., 4.

and ministries were added to the church. In 1960, Mt. Carmel moved to East Oakland and purchased two lots on 81st Avenue. On Sunday, February, 10, 1963, a groundbreaking ceremony was held. In the meantime, an invitation to hold worship services was extended to Mt. Carmel by the Reverend Ed Nation, Pastor of Alpha Tabernacle Baptist Church, at the corner of 79th Avenue and East 14th Street. On March 15, 1964, Mt. Carmel marched into their new location and, on February 22, 1981, Mt. Carmel held a symbolic mortgage-burning ceremony, making Pastor Owen's vision of a mortgage burning become a reality. The Reverend Owens was called from labor to reward, circa March 1981. The Reverend Bennie Giles was elected on January 30, 1981 and served until January 1984. During his tenure he organized the Youth and Young Adult Department. The Reverend Lloyd Farr was elected as Pastor July 29, 1984 and served until June 9th, 1985. The reasons for his short tenure were not revealed in the church history. East Oakland had undergone a major demographic shift. Drugs had infiltrated the surrounding community where the church was located, but it did not stop the growth of the church under Dr. Redeaux who was elected Pastor on October 28, 1985 and advanced the church's involvement into the wider community. Dr. Redeaux was called from labor to reward on February 9, 2006. The Reverend Andre T. Green was elected Pastor on, May 16, 2006.[125]

Double Rock Baptist Church, San Francisco

The Reverend Victor L. Medearis organized the Double Rock Baptist Church in 1949, San Francisco, at the Double Rock Housing Authority Recreation Center, 1375 Donner Avenue. The area became temporary housing during the early stages of WWII and the Hunters Point Navel Shipyard was nearby. The Reverend Medearis named the church after two gigantic boulder-type rocks sighted in the bay nearby. The Reverend Victor and Mrs. Gladys Medearis both worked as a team teaching Sunday School, witnessing beyond the walls of the church to children throughout the Hunter's Point housing area, inviting the residents to church services, and so on. More children than adults joined the church. Pearlie Hawkins helped to train the older children and taught them to become teachers of God's word. Pastor Medearis organized a Junior Choir and Mrs. Medearis organized the children's choir and the usher board. As Double Rock grew, the Reverend Hershel P. Randall became the Associate Pastor. The newly formed Deacon Board was chaired by Deacon Norris Gipson followed by Leon Jones, Claude Arnold and others. Prior to pastoring Double Rock, as early as 1943, Victor

125. Mt Carmel Missionary Baptist Church history files.

Medearis managed the Paramount Singers, a popular Bay Area male quartet singing group known to attract as many as six thousand people to the Oakland Auditorium. He was a gifted singer who was also a multi-talented harmonica, keyboard, and guitar player. In 1953, property was secured on Shafter Ave. and a groundbreaking ceremony was held September 27, 1953 and symbolically Mrs. Medearis turned the first shovel of dirt. One year later, in December 1954, the church family proudly marched into the new edifice located at 1595 Shafter Avenue, San Francisco. San Francisco was making drastic changes in the Fillmore through redevelopment in the early days of the Civil Rights Era following WWII. In the 1960s, Double Rock hosted musicals on Sunday afternoons with great gospel artists such as Mahalia Jackson, Cleophus Robinson, the O'Neal Twins, Sam Cooke, the Soul Stirrers, the Clara Ward Singers, the Caravan Singers, the Blind Boys of Alabama, and other noted artists. From 1950 to 2002, Double Rock developed a strong radio ministry on KSAN, KDIA, and KFAX local radio stations that broadcast Black churches and Black music. The neighborhood where Double Rock Church is located has seen its fair share of crime with drug infestation. The Alice Griffith Public Housing Development built in the early 1960s has not been maintained by the city very well.

The *San Francisco Examiner* interviewed the Reverend Victor Medearisin 1965. The article was titled "The Ghetto Can Get You But It Didn't Get Him." The Reverend Medearis said, "The most important key to success-especially for a Negro is vocabulary. Without a vocabulary, you can't communicate in our society and without communication how can you accomplish anything . . . Don't believe everything you hear . . . It's impossible to communicate with higher authorities unless you let them have some kind of hold. What's vital is that you don't let them own you."[126]

Prior to retirement, Pastor Medearis served as Founder and Pastor for over sixty years. God's work continues under the leadership of Reverend Reynard H. Hillis.[127]

---

126. *San Francisco Examiner*, September 5, 1965.

127. Double Rock Baptist Church, history files, submitted by Minister Ernestine Smith.

Beauticians, Barbers Oakland, circa 1940s discussing unionization

Oakland Auditorium

Bossier City Baptist Church, Louisiana, 2nd row 6th person, Viola Taylor 3rd row 1st person Rafe Taylor & 5th person Henry Taylor

Minervy Taylor. Mother of migrants from Louisiana to California

Henry and Viola Taylor Migrants from Louisiana

Preacher unknown in 1940s

Siblings Della and Elmore Taylor Oakland Ca.

Elnora and Rafe Taylor, Migrants from Louisiana

Carolyn Sue, Harris and Jackie Taylor, Harbor Homes late 1940s

Harbor Homes School 1949

Henry Taylor MoreDryDock Shipyard worker in 1940s

Betty Taylor Bell and husband James Bell, Migrants from Louisiana

Part IV—Civil Rights Era and beyond— 1950s–1972

The Civil Rights Movement that rearranged the social order of this country did not emanate from the halls of the Harvards and the Princetons and Cornels. It came from simple unlettered people who learned that they had the right to stand tall and nobody can ride a back that isn't bent.

—Dorothy Cotton

The Civil Rights Era and Beyond

The change in the Negro's mentality about harsh treatment began to boil over during the 1950s. Negroes began to object to discrimination, separate-but-not-equal schools, eating at separate lunch counters, riding in the back of the bus, Jim Crow laws, housing, jobs, and other areas of mistreatment. Negroes began to verbalize their feelings in forums that would give them equality. In other words, no longer were they going to sit idly by and be treated as subhuman or chattel; those days were coming to an end.[1]

The Civil Rights Movement was a struggle for full equality on all levels for African Americans, starting from slavery, continuing through the Emancipation, Reconstruction, Jim and Jane Crow, and segregation, and culminating in the 1950s. The pace for equal rights picked up dramatically in the 1950s. On a national level, most are familiar with the Birmingham and Selma March. Civil rights activities in the West suggest that long before World II, nineteenth century black parents fought school segregation

1. Drake and Cayton, *Black Metropolis,* 763.

in California. Westerners confronted job discrimination, housing bias, and de facto school segregation. As a result of pervasive discrimination, "black westerners engaged in direct-action protests; demonstrations, sit-ins, boycotts, and other civil disobedience activities to eliminate discrimination."[2] WWII may have ended, but a real fight and struggle for civil rights was just getting underway across the nation.

In San Francisco blacks were denied employment at all levels. The first black fireman was not hired without a ruckus until 1955. For decades, blacks complained that they were denied employment opportunities solely because of their race in San Francisco. The Fair Employment Practice Committee corroborated the charges. Blacks were excluded from driving cabs for white companies in San Francisco because employers feared that the public would resent the close physical contact.[3] One of the watershed cases during the 1950s regarding housing discrimination was the case of Mattie and James Charley Jr. Banks v. City and County of San Francisco Housing Authority. Of the seven projects the Authority managed, only one, Westside Courts, was open to African Americans. The couple applied and were denied without reason to move to the North Beach housing project located near Fisherman Wharf having met all qualifications. An up-and-coming young black lawyer took the case before the San Francisco Superior Court to Judge Melvyn I. Cronin, who ruled that the "neighborhood pattern" was illegal and void and in violation of the Fourteen Amendment.[4] The success of this case was a stepping-stone for Terry Francois, a young black attorney, who served as the San Francisco chapter president of the NAACP who had earned a reputation as a civil-rights activist and politician with a law office in the predominately black Western Addition area of San Francisco. He was later elected to the San Francisco Board of Supervisors.

William Byron Rumford Sr., a Bay Area resident and owner of Rumford pharmacy in Berkeley, was elected to the California State Assembly in 1948. In 1959, Rumford was instrumental in the passage of the California Fair Employment Practices Act that eliminated practices of discrimination in employment and otherwise against persons of color. This bill proved to have weaknesses as discrimination continued on the housing front. Rumford then initiated the California Fair Housing Act, known as the Rumford Act (AB 1240). The Bill proved to be one of the most significant laws protecting the rights of blacks and other people of color to purchase housing

2. Taylor, *In Search of the Racial Frontier*, 280.

3. Ibid., 218.

4. Mattie Banks v. San Francisco Housing Authority, "Statement of the Court: affidavit of Mattie Banks, No. 15685" *San Francisco News*, October 1, 1952.

without being subjected to discrimination. By the early 1950s, black leaders were demanding that white politicians get involved on racial issues if they wanted the support of black voters. An aspiring white candidate like Phillip Burton grasped the message and endorsed a wide spectrum of civil rights issues. The Reverend F. D. Haynes of Third Baptist Church, had a congregation of over 4,000 members. He used his influence as both a minister and community leader to push his candidacy for the San Francisco Board of Supervisors. Though he was unsuccessful, he was impressive for a black candidate in the early 1950s. He became an ally in cosponsoring an FEPC bill, though it died on the desk of Governor Knight.[5] The Bill proved to be one of the most significant laws protecting the rights of blacks and other people of color to purchase housing without being subjected to discrimination.[6]

On the other side of the bay, black Richmondites were waging war against unfair housing. The Reverend Guthrie John Williams, pastor of Mt. Carmel Missionary Baptist Church and an accomplished carpenter, had been rejected for admittance to the Carpenters Union. Williams was founder of the Universal Non-Partisan League and President of the Interdenominational Ministerial Alliance and was influential in the black community. Amos Hinkley, a white incumbent, was running for re-election for the Richmond City Council seat wanted the endorsement of Williams and the black vote. In exchange for his endorsement, Hinkley arranged for Williams to meet his close friend, Fred Parr, a white businessman and housing developer. This was a critical meeting for Williams as it allowed him to discuss the housing problem blacks were experiencing. As a result, Parr agreed to develop a housing area, which later became known as Parchester Village.[7] Parchester Village, a development built in northwest Richmond, represented a compromise on the issue of residential desegregation.

Following WWII, the common cry for black Americans was fair housing, better education, voting, freedom from police brutality, the right to live wherever they could afford, and equal employment opportunities. Equally important by the end of the 1950s and early 1960s was the War on Poverty program by President Lyndon B. Johnson, which was a response to national poverty in America. A series of programs to relieve the burden of poverty included The Social Security Act, Community Action Programs, and the Head Start program to help young children from low-income families with economic and health issues. The Black Panther Party started a free breakfast program in 1968 in West Oakland to provide healthy meals for children in

5. Jacobs, *A Rage for Justice: The Passion and Politics of Phillip Burton*, 64-65.

6. Broussard, *Black San Francisco*, 237.

7. Moore, *To Place Our Deeds*, 114.

a safe loving environment. The "Survival Program" included medical check-ups through doctors who supported the program.

Most importantly, the Civil Rights Movement, which was a response to discrimination against blacks during the early 50s, began as a political movement, but it raised questions for the Black Church. How would the Black Church respond to social issues raised as a result of the Black Power Movement and the Civil Rights Movement? How would the Black Church effect change? What would be the message from the pulpit with regards to a theology of liberation? A form of militancy had surfaced with the cry for "Black Power." How then would the Black Church respond to the new demands placed on it? Indeed these were trying times.

The Death of the Negro Church—the Birth of the Black Church

The Civil Rights Movement of the 60s, while politically motivated, raised fundamental issues for the Black Church and for American Christianity as well as new challenges for the Negro Church. Black people were redefining themselves from Negro to Black.

Following the March on Washington in August 1963, black people were losing hope that full integration and equality would take place. Malcolm X had said living in America was not a dream but a nightmare. Stokely Carmichael, Student Nonviolent Coordinating Committee, along with other black civil rights activists began to come into prominence, rising to power to show racial political solidarity and that the non-violence approach used by Dr. King Jr. was ineffective. Black power represented a new challenge for the Negro Church with regards to separating the gospel from a Euro-centric religion that had been oppressive to Negroes in order to develop a black Christian theology that would bear witness from a black perspective, namely, that of justice, liberation, power, and social responsibility.

Black clergy were forced to reexamine their response to black power when the Christian faith was being tested in improvised black communities.[8] Eventually the term black replaced the term Negro to describe black people. All over America, the Negro Church accepted being reborn with the name Black Church, which is a radicalized conscious departure from the critical norms that made the Negro Church what it was. It was a call to Christian responsibility and human dignity and therefore logically inconsistent with the limitations of Negro-ness. Yet the Negro Church that died

8. Cone, *For My People*, 22.

continues to live on in the Black Church born of its loins, flesh of its flesh, for there are no disjunctions in religion.[9]

To understand the power of the Black Church it must first be understood that there is no disjunction between the Black Church and the Black Community. The Black Church, then, is in some sense a "universal church" that has become more than the spiritual face of the community. It stands for social change from a gospel of liberation that is also political. The Black Church is the gathered community for social change that stands for freedom from all kinds of captivity that enslave black people.

Urban Black Diaspora—
They Bullied and Bulldozed Communities

In the summer of 1949, anti-public housing waged a fierce, emotional, and often misleading campaign directed at black homeowners in West Oakland. Real estate groups working through the local CHP branch rented sound trucks to tour the neighborhood blaring, "Your homes are about to be torn down; you will have no place to live; public housing will not admit you; go down to the city council meeting and fight this menace."[10] The African-American community along 7th Street, once considered Harlem West known for its jazz clubs, churches, grocery stores, pharmacy, and restaurants, was bulldozed during the 1950s to make way for urban renewal and the Interstate Highway programs. The effect it had on poor black areas such as West Oakland was devasting as blacks West Oaklanders were being bullied out of their homes to make room for the connecting highways, mass transportation, the Bay Area Rapid Transit District (BART), and a large post office creating boundaries and barriers for the community.

Landon Williams, born in West Oakland in 1944, had a paper route down 7th Street. "I can remember how vibrant 7th Street was on both sides. I can remember a little cleaners, you know, meat markets, grocery stores, liquor stores, furniture stores . . . and they wiped it out and the ground lay fallow for like ten years." Tom Nash, an African-American reporter and newspaper publisher, said, "Johnny bulldozer ran through all of those homes that it took those people a lifetime to acquire."[11]

The postwar era was a dark time for Bay Area black communities; neighborhoods became blighted and unemployment and housing created

9. Lincoln, *The Black Church since Frazier*, 106.
10. Johnson, *The Second Gold Rush*, 219.
11. Self, *American Babylon*, 137, 159 .

a new postwar poverty era. Racial covenants kept blacks confined in little deteriorating boxed neighborhoods, while whites were able to move wherever they desired. The government may have called it urban renewal, but blacks called it Negro removal. For many blacks it was obvious that black neighborhoods were targeted for urban renewal and the real reason was racism. Tarea Hall Pittman of the NAACP and the Reverend Solomon Hill, Pastor of the First AME Church in Oakland, responded by announcing an independent study of displaced persons. The Reverend Solomon Hill, became embroiled in a heated debate for the rights of blacks to have decent housing: "Don't continue to push these people into a vicious circle and then blame them for being there." The Reverend Hill's anger was rooted in the ten-year battle to retain and improve postwar housing in the East Bay for the poorest black workers.[12]

The Reverend W. Lee La Beaux, Pastor of the Canal Project's Providence Baptist Church in Richmond, remarked, "Ultimately, our people will be driven away . . . Sometimes I am sure that's what the people running this town really want." It had come to light that the Canal and Terrace War Apartments were targeted for demolition. Black religious leaders and black tenants staged a protests demanding priority in public housing.[13]

Thousands of families were displaced from war housing in Richmond, Berkeley, and Oakland. Through the assistance of a professional relocation specialist to find housing, many of the families were shifted to Oakland, thus removing "problem" families from Berkeley and Albany.[14]

Across the Bay in San Francisco, approximately 60 percent of the residents in the Fillmore were blacks when the Urban Renewal and Redevelopment declared it a blighted area. The San Francisco Redevelopment Agency bulldozed the Fillmore's thriving black neighborhood. Most postwar blacks found themselves locked out. The core black communities in the Bay Area were left to decay, leaving the Urban Renewal project an opportunity to uproot thousands of blacks from their homes; though war-time housing was viewed as temporary for some, blacks had looked at the housing as their permanent homes until they could do better. The Reverend Arnold Townsend, who has lived in the Western Addition for more than forty years, said, "It was not true that black folks chose to sell their homes, we were denied the opportunity to secure home improvement loans, we had no choice but to sell or crumble." Communities were wiped out. The residents were

12. Ibid., 145-46.

13. Richard Reinhardt, "The Boom That Didn't Bust," *San Francisco Chronicle*, August 20, 1953.

14. Ibid., 229, 230.

bullied with eminent domain.[15] The impact of black neighborhoods being destroyed and uprooted influenced the need for black churches to relocate and follow the patterns where the black population was relocating. It was during this era that radical pastors in the Black Church were beginning to preach a gospel of liberation in response to discrimination. Blacks throughout the Bay Area and beyond were uprooted for urban renewal. Communities were destroyed, churches were uprooted, and families displaced. An equally significant aspect of urban renewal was the geographical expansion of black churches in other areas.

Neighborhoods in Transition

Urban renewal included the white flight, leaving inner cities with further decay as thousands of whites fled inner cities and purchased or rented homes, whatever their money could afford. At the same time, many blacks were getting on their feet and able to move from decaying black neighborhoods. Racial covenants were slowly being lifted with the outmigration of whites who were headed for suburbia. Urban sprawl began to populate areas in the East Bay to remote suburban areas in Contra Costa and Solano counties. With the displacement of blacks and with racial covenants slowly being lifting, homes and businesses were vacated by whites who were leaving East Oakland by the droves. During the early 1950s, the Woods, Edwards, Taylors, Hobbs, and Burgess families were among the first families to purchase homes in Brookfield Village near the Oakland Airport. Barbara Johnson was among seven black teenagers to attend Castlemont High School in far East Oakland graduating in 1953. With the construction of the MacArthur Freeway (I-580) a noticeable pattern emerged that divided the city into flatlands and foothills stretching a racial barrier where whites lived above Bancroft Avenue while blacks lived below E. 14th Street. Clergy began to protest about the apathetic manner that blacks were treated, saying they would protest "until the walls of council of indifference come tumbling down." The few whites that tried to hang on to their houses, were hounded by real estate agents to sell so they could resale the houses at twice the price.[16]

The changing demographics in Far East Oakland created new spaces for black churches in storefronts because of white neighborhood stores closing. East 14th Street, starting around the 73rd Avenue area, became a prime location for black storefront churches as the neighborhoods were

15. Leslie Fulbright, *San Francisco Chronicle*, July 21, 2008.

16. *California Voice*, November 3, 1967; June 28, 1968; Hunter *Housing Discrimination in Oakland*, 44–56, 70.

experiencing transition. With the shift in demographics, Allen Temple Baptist Church would no longer be the lone black church in Far East Oakland. Jon P. Bloch, a professor of sociology at Southern Connecticut State University in New Haven, said storefront "churches often appeared in communities or neighborhoods in decline; as businesses moved or folded, storefronts become available for rent, possibly for a relatively inexpensive amount. While many say neighborhoods are 'over-churched,' these small churches have proven to be tentacles of support for new black communities."[17]

Cosmopolitan Baptist Church, Oakland

In the early 1950s, black churches were now spreading into Far East Oakland with the migration of blacks relocating from West Oakland. The Reverend George Wildy organized the Cosmopolitan Baptist Church on April 8, 1950 after serving as pastor of Allen Temple Baptist Church from 1929 to 1950. The first services were held at the First Christian Science Church located at 98th and East 14th Streets. After a year, the Reverend Wildy and his members relocated to the Elmhurst Baptist Church at 90th and Holly Streets, holding worship services on Sunday afternoon. Later, the church was able to purchase a lot in the 900 block of 85th Avenue, trusting that the funds for building would eventually come. The Elmhurst Baptist Church sold their property to the Reverend Wildy. The church was eventually moved in two sections to the 85th Avenue location.

The Reverend Wildy, a skilled carpenter, renovated the church and membership increased significantly. He resigned on February 2, 1956. Shortly after Wildy's departure in 1956, the church conducted a pastoral search and elected the Reverend George Houston in August 1956 and continued to prosper as they began a comprehensive building program and a G. J. Houston Scholarship fund for young people attending college. After the death of the Reverend Houston, the Reverend Larry Ashley, a son of Bethel Missionary Baptist Church, was elected Pastor in 1999. Cosmopolitan is known throughout the Bay Area for its compassionate ministry for the least and lost. The Reverend Ashley has ordained qualified ministers both male and female to the gospel ministry.[18]

17. *Bridgeport Newspaper*, September 1, 2012.
18. Cosmopolitan Baptist Church History.

Easter Hill United Methodist Church, Richmond, 1951

After the war, a small group of Richmond residents began to meet in the apartment of Jones and Mattie Mann to explore the possibilities of forming a Methodist church on the southside of Richmond as blacks were being uprooted on the northside. Among those gathered were John and Marie Griffin, Charles and Nola Bridges, Everett and Rosa Mae Pendleton, James and Romance Mann, Samuel and Augustine Williams, and the Reverend F. H. Busher, Pastor of St. Luke's, who were exploring the possibility of a black Methodist church. On November 7, 1950, the group came together for a fundraising banquet that was held at St. Luke's Church to finance the new church. The banquet raised $1,600, which was used to purchase property at 30th Street and Hoffman Blvd. The name Easter Hill was selected because there was a hill between 28th Street and Hoffman Blvd. that served as the site for Easter Sunrise Worship and because Easter Hill housing development was located nearby. On February 15, 1951, the Reverend Wilbur R. Johnson, of Boston Massachusetts, became the first pastor of the newly organized church, which was fondly referred to as "The Little Brown Church."

The Reverend Busher, who had been with the church in its infancy stage, wanted a non-denominational church that would attract both Baptists and Methodists. The Reverend Busher had earned the nickname "Pusher Busher" because of his forward style of leadership. The idea didn't set very well with the Reverend Johnson who persuaded the Reverend Busher, and the other concerned persons, to recognize the church's Methodist roots and call the new congregation a Methodist church, so that it was clear to persons joining that it was a United Methodist Church. Unfortunately, as in so many cases in black neighborhoods, the California Highway Transportation Department, through eminent domain, purchased the property for highway expansion. The church relocated to 39th Street and Cutting Blvd. and, on December 25, 1957, held the first worship service in the newly built church. This would be their home until 1956, when the State of California purchased the site for highway expansion. Pastor Johnson continued his outstanding leadership until his appointment to the Southern California Conference in June of 1959. In June 1959, the Reverend Booker Anderson was appointed pastor and served until 1969. Under his leadership, Easter Hill became known as a Social Justice Church. Dr. Martin Luther King Jr. and other activists spoke at Easter Hill. Civil rights rallies and community meetings were also held at Easter Hill. The church facilities were improved and a parsonage was built at 55th and Bayview Streets. In June 1969, Pastor Anderson was appointed to the Joint Strategy and Action Committee of the Methodist Church and was also elected to the Richmond City Council. In

July 1976, the Reverend Anderson replaced the Reverend Dr. Boswell at Jones United Methodist Church, San Francisco. The Reverend Anderson served at Jones United until he was called from labor to reward on November 29, 1982.

In 1969, the Reverend Dr. A. Edward Bell was appointed pastor and served until 1971. During the interim period the Reverend Amos Cambridge, the Reverend Max Brown, and the Reverend David Houston served as interim pastors.

In 1973, the Reverend C. King was appointed pastor and served until September 1977. The Church experienced a significant growth in the Children and Youth Ministries. Pastor King left Easter Hill to become the Director of Campus Ministries for the Wesley Foundation in Nashville, Tennessee. The Reverend Amos Cambridge Jr. returned and served as interim pastor until a permanent pastor was appointed. In 1977, the Reverend Ronald E. Swisher was appointed as pastor and served until 1990. Under his leadership the church's young adult membership increased. The Mann-Swisher Hall was built and the Parsonage Mortgage was liquidated. In June 1990, Pastor Swisher was appointed District Superintendent, Delta District of California-Nevada Conference.

The Reverend Dorothy Williams was the first African-American female pastor ordained by the California-Nevada Conference and became Easter Hill's first female pastor in June of 1990. During her two-year stay, the Reverend Williams developed a strong spiritual ministry. In June 1992, she retired from parish ministry.

The Reverend Phillip Lawson was appointed to Easter Hill in June 1992. He is one of the century's great civil rights leaders and social gospel preachers. Among his many accomplishments, in 1965, he recruited a group of seminarians to participate with him in the Selma to Montgomery March for voting rights. It would take a second book to talk about his accomplishments for human rights. In 1997, Easter Hill purchased the property between 36th and 37th Streets on Cutting Boulevard, formerly the James McMillan Pharmacy and Professional Building. "Mr. McMillan was Richmond's first black pharmacist and later won a seat on the city council."[19] The Reverend Billye Austin, the Reverend Dr. Antonia Jones-Bryant, and the Reverend Carol Estes, three female pastors of Easter Hill, all received their degrees from accredited seminaries. In 1998 the Reverend Billye Austin was appointed as Easter Hill's first Associate Pastor, having been a member since 1988.

19. Moore, *To Place our Deeds,* 120.

The Reverend Phillip Lawson retired July 1, 2003, and the Reverend Billye Austin was appointed Senior Pastor and continued in the tradition of Easter Hill's legacy of spiritually based social justice ministries. The Easter Hill East Bay Community Development Corporation is organized and receives nonprofit Federal 501 (c) 3 status. The Reverend Dr. Donald Guest continues to serve as the pastor of Easter Hill since 2012, bringing a strong social justice background. Easter Hill has a strong academic support for middle and high school students, from basic to advanced Spanish to sign language. Easter Hill prides itself as a church that welcomes all people.[20]

First Baptist Church of Parchester Village, Richmond, 1951

Parchester Village, a development built in northwest Richmond in 1949, was the first subdivision in the city where Blacks could purchase homes. Parchester Village represented much more than a place to live. It offered African Americans tangible proof of their strength as a community and of their expanding political relevance in the larger population.[21] The First Baptist Church of Parchester Village was organized in February 8, 1951 in the home of the Reverend Luther and Mother Lothell Thomas near Thomas Drive and McGlothen Way in Richmond with fifteen members. (McGlothen Way was named after the founders of the McGlothen temple.) After worshiping in the Thomas home for two years, the membership grew and a larger facility was needed. The church located land at 3900 McGlothen Way and groundbreaking ceremonies were held in the summer of 1953. It was a joyous day when the members marched from the Thomas home to the new church building.

The Reverend Thomas served until November 1961. In 1962, the Reverend Vivian Harris was elected Pastor and remained until he was called from labor to reward in June 1964. Under his leadership, a mortgage-burning ceremony was held. In November 1964 the Reverend M. J. Jackson was elected Pastor and served until September 1971. The Reverend Robert J. Riley was appointed as interim minister. In August 1972, the Reverend Joseph Harold Jr., member at Bethlehem Missionary Baptist Church, Richmond, was called as Pastor and served until he was called from labor to reward in August 2005. The community and the church are closely knitted. Parchester Village residents initiated a number of community programs that reinforced their sense of collective strength and individual accomplishment. In 1950, the Parchester Veterans' Wives Club bought a house

20. Easter Hill Methodist History.

21. Moore, *To Place Our Deeds*, 113, 116.

in the tract and converted it into a recreation center where residents held meetings, celebrated birthdays, and commemorated special anniversaries. Mary Simmons, an early Parchester resident and member of the Wives Club recalled that Parchester Baptist Church was the place where a lot of those seeds of self-worth got planted for many black children. The church's activities insured that the flowers of Parchester weren't left to grow wild.[22] On January 29, 2006, the Reverend Dr. Johnnie B. Jones, member of Bethlehem Missionary Baptist Church, was called as pastor. From First Baptist three daughter churches emerged: Zion Hill Baptist of Rodeo, Paradise Missionary Baptist Church of Oakland, and Grace Baptist of Berkeley. First Baptist of Parchester Village continues its service to the community, spiritually, socially, and in terms of its orientation toward social justice.[23]

Pleasant Grove Baptist Church, Oakland, 1951

On March 6, 1951, a faithful group of Christians met in the home of Aly and Laura McJimpson in Oakland for the purpose of forming a church. Among the charter members were J. E. Bell, Eola Bell, Pete Farlow, Cillar Farlow, Rosie Hicks, Annie Spencer-Lewis, Willie Johnson, Cornelius Perkins, Ollie Nicholson, and Bernice Taylor. The first church was located at 952 8th Street. The council was under the direction of the Reverend R. B. Blackmore, Pastor of the Kingdom Land Baptist Church, Richmond, California. Upon the suggestion of Cillar Farlow, the church was named Pleasant Grove Missionary Baptist Church. The church received its charter on December 20, 1951 and was incorporated by Attorney Thomas L. Berkeley of Berkeley, California on February 15, 1952. The Reverend James H. Henderson Jr. of Tallulah, Louisiana was called as the first pastor until May 1956. The membership grew from 26 to 125. In 1953, an old house was purchased and remodeled for a church. The Reverend Henderson resigned in good faith, and returned to Tallulah to serve as a pastor in his hometown. In June 1956, the Reverend Willie L. Bernstine was called to be the pastor. Under Pastor Bernstine's leadership, membership increased and extensive exterior remodeling was done. The church affiliated with the Progressive District Association, Tri City Ushers Alliance, as well as the National Baptist Convention. In July 1963, the Reverend Bernstine resigned to accept another charge. On March 30, 2001, he was called from labor to reward. The Reverend Arilee

22. Wenkert, Magney, and Templeton, *An Historical Digest of Negro-White Relations in Richmond, California*, 53.

23. http://www.parchester1stbaptistchurch.org/church-history/index.html (accessed September 20, 2013).

Hightower accepted the call to pastor on January 3, 1964, as the third pastor of Pleasant Grove. The Reverend Hightower was a dynamic preacher and city leader. He immediately set out to have the old structure demolished, and a permit was obtained to build a new church. Like so many properties in West Oakland, the church was confronted with problems from the Redevelopment Agency, which was literally taking properties away from the black community. On the positive side, Pastor Hightower did not lose sight of keeping the church together and found a temporary location at 7th and Henry Streets to worship. Pastor Hightower was determined not to let the Redevelopment Agency undermine their goal of building a new church in West Oakland. He took the matter directly to City Hall. Church members marched and protested to the Oakland City Council and held open prayer service in the Rotunda City Hall. After much prayer and faith, the walls of bureaucracy and politics fell and the building for a new edifice started. On June 30, 1966, the congregation marched from their temporary location at 7th and Henry Streets to the new building at 1124 Adeline Street.

Popularity of the church remained high; the Membership grew from 215 to over 800. An accountable budget system was established, all encumbrances were met without delinquent indebtedness, and a mortgage-burning ceremony was held a few years after the church was rebuilt. Pastor Hightower retired April 1991 with a large gala farewell for his years of service. His retirement included elected officials and many members from other churches who praised him as a man with a program, vision, and a plan. The Reverend Hightower was called from labor to reward, October 7, 1997. The Reverend Henry Perkins, a son of Pleasant Grove served for a brief period and was called to be senior pastor of First Baptist Church, Pittsburg, California, in 1991.

In September 1994, another son of Pleasant Grove, the Revered Thomas A. Harris III was called to be the fourth Pastor.[24] In October 2015, the City of Oakland received a nuisance complaint from "gentrifiers" who cited the church's "joyful noise" was annoying. The complaint was resolved in favor of the church.

Church by the Side of the Road, Berkeley, 1956

The Church by the Side of the Road was founded by the late Reverend Dr. Alexander Stephens Jackson II and organized on April 17, 1956 as an Interdenominational Community Church for all People. His motto was "Never allow a visitor to leave as a stranger." The first services were held in the South

24. Pleasant Grove Baptist Church, Souvenir Program Book, May 28, 2001.

Berkeley YMCA at California and Russell Streets. The church was organized to fulfill the Reverend Jackson's dream of having a "Church By The Side of The Road" dedicated to being a friend to all people of all races and faiths. Charter members included Irene Ferguson, Maurice Gibson, Bernice and George Hill, Earl Grinstad, Olga Hartman, Addie Jackson, Alexander S. Jackson III, Lucille Lane, George Oliver, Leslie Pope Rand, Willia Mae, Savedra and Vemeida Thompson, Bernice and Fred Williams, and Barbara, Roberta and Shirley Williams.

On May 13, 1956, the first church service was held in a former Episcopalian Mission on the corner of Grove and Russell Streets, Berkeley, where services were held for the next two-and-a-half years. In 1959, the Reverend Jackson along with a few dedicated members including the Reverend John Knox Hailey and the Reverend Costello Moore who were part of the ministerial staff purchased the Knox Presbyterian Church at 2108 Russell Street, Berkeley. In 1973, the mortgage was burned. The responsibilities for fiscal management came under the newly organized Trustee Board, with Dr. James A. Watson as Chair and Dr. Charles Calloway as Vice-chair. Sabbath School, Vacation Bible School, Young Adult Christian Fellowship, Adult and Youth Choirs, and a tithing plan were implemented. The Men's and Women's Leagues were organized to be responsible for the fellowship programs of the church.

The Women's League was organized into Circles of Women (Naomi, Lydia, and Dorcas) to promote Bible study and fellowship among communities of members and friends. Senior women of the church served as a pastoral aide committee to Pastor Jackson. The committee consisted of Edna Wade, Eva Goosby, Mary Williams, Pearl Ward, Alice Campbell, and Bernice Yates who served faithfully as Pastoral Aides to the Reverend Jackson. The well-known musician and vocalist Phillip Lee Reeder became the first Minister of Music. The gifted and talented Jacqueline Butler Hairston organized and directed the first Women's Choir.

Renovations and memorials have been made to the church building including a prayer chapel dedicated to the memory of Felix Goosby, a memorial window that was installed behind the choir loft in memory of a dedicated teacher of children Leslie Pope Thomas, the Fellowship Hall that was named in honor of the Reverend Dr. Martin Luther King Jr., and a scholarship fund that was established by Abbe and Marsha Foster in honor of Dr. Marcus Foster, who was assassinated while serving as the Superintendent of Schools, Oakland. The Reverend Jackson retired in 1974 and was honored with the title of Pastor Emeritus. The Reverend Jackson recommended the Reverend Charles H. Belcher as his successor. The church was elated and unanimously voted to call the Revered Belcher as the second

Pastor. The Reverend Jackson was called from labor to reward in February 1976. During the Reverend Charles H. Belcher's tenure, an "Opportunity Witness Fund" was established to fund the expansion of service programs and to finance building repairs, as remodeling was needed. A memorial window was installed in the Fireside Room in memory of the Reverend A. S. Jackson. An adjacent property was purchased and served as the Education Building. The Reverend Belcher served until June 1976. In 1977 the Reverend Dr. A. Edward Bell was called as the third Pastor of the church. A new ministry was launched to feed the needy by providing nutritious meals. Under Reverend Bell's leadership, the church was able to burn the mortgage on the Educational Building. A generous bequest was left to the church by the Lonnie Price Poindexter Jr. family to establish an endowment fund for the church. Reverend Bell served the church until 1989. In 1990, the Reverend Dr. George C. L. Cummings, a renowned scholar and author, was called to serve as the fourth Pastor. Under his leadership, the church membership and ministries grew. In 1993, the church was reorganized and developed an affiliation with the American Baptist Churches, USA, Inc. A Minister-in-Training Program was established in conjunction with the American Baptist Seminary of the West in Berkeley, California where Dr. Cummings served as Dean/Professor. The Church was restructured to include a Church Council and a Board of Deacons was established to assist the Pastor in the spiritual oversight of the church. Deacon Jonathan Staggers served as the first Chair of the Board and Deacons and Juanita Papillion served as vice-chair. A Board of Educational Ministries was also established. The music ministry was enhanced with the talented Janice Maxie Reid and world-renowned Terrence Kelly. The Reverend Dr. George C. L. Cummings tenure with the church concluded in 1996. Membership declined when Dr. Cummings left as many of the members left with him, including the Minister of Music, Terrance Kelly. The Associate Minister, the Reverend Kathy Patton, served briefly as Interim Pastor. In March 1997, retired Bishop Roy Nichols of the United Methodist Church was called to serve as Interim Pastor along with his wife, Dr. Ruth Richardson Nichols, who worked as a team to reunite the splintered church. Dr. Johari Jabir was hired as Minister of Music during this period. Much healing took place with the careful spiritual guidance of Bishop Nichols. Bishop and Mrs. Dr. Nichols fulfilled their task and returned to their lives of retirement after November 30, 1998.

On December 1, 1998, the Reverend Dr. Arthur S. Scott, a son of Allen Temple, became the fifth Senior Pastor and served until June 2002. During his tenure, a Teenage Pregnancy Prevention/Parenting Program was established by the late Reverend Dr. Julia Bums-Robinson.

Following Dr. Scott, the Reverend Chery Ward and the Reverend Dr. James Stewart (Pastor Emeritus, McGee Avenue, Berkeley) both served respectively as Interim Pastors between 2002 and 2004.

On May 30, 2004 the Reverend Doctor R. Thomas Coleman was installed as the sixth Pastor. During his tenure at the church, Dr. Coleman established "The Biblical Rules of Order" as the guiding light in the spiritual functioning of the church's vision and mission as the living body of Christ. "Trustee and Deacons Day" were added as annual celebrations. The Youth Ministry and Children's Church were restored. The Youth Programs thrived under the leadership of the appointed Youth Minister, the Reverend John Adams. Dr. Coleman honored the aging Reverend James Stewart by nominating him to have the Doctor of Divinity Degree bestowed upon him by the American Baptist Seminary of the West. In the same fashion, Dr. Coleman received approval from the congregation to confer the status of Emeritus upon Deacons and Trustees who had served honorably for many years in their capacity.

In October 2010, The Church by the Side of the Road sponsored a trip to the Holy Land. Eighteen people took the trip, which was preceded by an in-depth Bible Study Class. The Reverend Barbara Galloway Lee was the spiritual guide for the trip to Israel. Dr. Stewart remained as an honored assistant to the Pastor until he was called from labor to reward August 6, 2011. Much growth and progress was made under the leadership of the Reverend Dr. Coleman who served the church faithfully until March 2011. Associate pastors were very active in maintaining the continuity of worship service and fulfilling congregational needs until a pastor could be installed. Reverend Dr. Coleman was called from labor to reward October 14, 2012.

In December 2011, the Reverend Dr. Ambrose F. Carroll Sr. accepted the call as Interim Senior Pastor and was later elected Pastor in May 2012. He brought enthusiasm and spirit-filled biblical messages during the worship services. Dr. Carroll immediately began studying the history of the church and connecting with the community. Innovative ministries have been implemented and others continued.[25]

Church of the Good Shepherd, Oakland, 1956

On October 21, 1956, a group of seventeen members disunited their membership from Beth Eden Baptist church over the selection of the Reverend Dones to be pastor of Beth Eden. The first meeting took place in the home of Mr. and Mrs. Eugene P. Lasartemay. The group quickly grew to forty-two

25. Church by the Side of the Road Church History.

persons and functioned under the name "Progressive Religious Workers," which held their first Sunday worship service on February 24, 1957 at the Oakland Jewish Community Center. On March 10, 1957, the forty-two members were officially organized as "Church of the Good Shepherd" in the Lasartemay home by the Reverend W. C. Sample, Pastor of Pilgrim Rest Baptist Church, San Mateo, and renowned theologian the Reverend Dr. Henry H. Mitchell.

June 1, 1958, the Reverend James H. Stewart, a respected Bay Area pastor, accepted the call to become the first Pastor. His tenure ended August 1967. For almost three years, the church was without a full-time pastor. The Reverend W. C. Sample served as Interim Minister from November 5, 1967 until August 24, 1969. The Reverend Paul Thompson became the second Pastor on March 1970 and served until May 25, 1972. From October to the present time a number of ministers have served as pastor. On March 30, 2015, the Reverend Dwayne Eason was installed in a joyful celebration to a capacity-filled audience.[26]

Seventh Avenue Baptist Church, Oakland, 1958

Seventh Avenue Baptist Church was first organized by the Reverend V. M. Bailey along with a group of followers in the home of S. B. Mence at 975 107th Avenue in Oakland. On Monday, June 16, 1958 at 7:45 p.m., the group met in the auditorium of the Saint Rest Baptist Church of Oakland, California with the Reverend J. W. Jacobs, Pastor.

Letters to organize the church came from three members of the Saint Rest Baptist Church, namely, Jean Anderson, Earnest Franklin, and V. Franklin. The Reverend O. P. Smith, Pastor of Bible Fellowship, acted as moderator and called for a motion that the sixty-eight persons be organized in a church. The name of the newly organized church was established as the Ebenezer Missionary Baptist Church Incorporated. Reverend Vivian M. Bailey was elected pastor of the church with an overflow of attendees for his installation. Reverend Bailey was a dynamic leader who helped to organize the South West Region of the Progressive National Baptist Convention and served as its vice president. Bailey was tragically murdered in the church in 1963 by a deacon of the church who admitted to the assault. From November 1963 to April 1964, the church was without a pastor as the members were in deep mourning needing time for healing.

In May 1964, the church called the Reverend Joseph Sutton II to serve as Pastor. The church was revitalized with the powerful teaching

26. Church of the Good Shepherd Brief History.

and preaching of the Reverend Sutton. The church organized the Board of Christian Education, Board of Evangelism, Service Committee, the Nurses Guild, and a Hostess Committee. The Reverend Sutton served until October 28, 1968. During his tenure the church was renamed Seventh Avenue Baptist Church to reflect the location of the church at 1740 7th Avenue, Oakland. The cornerstone was laid on November 6, 1966. The Reverend A. E. Williams of Los Angeles officiated. Prior to the Reverend Sutton's retirement, Deacon C. T. Johnson confessed his call into the ministry and preached his first sermon with the blessings of the Reverend Sutton. Deacon Johnson was ordained as a minister and installed as the Pastor on July 7, 1969. Under the Reverend Johnson's leadership, the ministries and membership continued to grow. On Sunday, October 1, 1972, a new baptismal pool was dedicated by the Reverend Echles as four candidates were baptized. A scholarship fund was organized to honor the late Reverend Bailey.

In 1978, the church purchased a vacant lot across from the church to be used for parking. The following year, the church purchased a bus to serve the elderly and youth. Seventh Avenue Baptist Church was known as a refuge for feeding the hungry and helping to provide clothing for needy families throughout the community. After forty years as pastor, the Reverend C. T. Johnson retired in 2013 and was bestowed the honor of Pastor Emeritus. The Reverend Jeffery Kirton was elected pastor.[27]

Bethany Baptist Church, Oakland, 1960

Bethany Baptist Church was founded by the Reverend Huey W. Watson after he resigned from New Hope Baptist Church, Oakland, with a sizeable following of over two hundred members in 1959. The first organized meeting for Bethany was held at the Baker's Mortuary in the Gladys Memorial chapel on February, 9, 1960. The group selected Bethany for the church name and officially elected the Reverend Watson as Pastor as long as he desired. With a sizeable following, officers were elected and the task of reorganizing a new church began. The following Sunday, February 14th, the first Sunday School and worship services were held. The Reverend Watson's sermon title was, "They Had a Mind to Work." Forty-two more persons joined the fellowship on that day. The Reverend Watson encouraged the congregation by saying, "I'm not wrapped up in a building, I'm concerned about people, and I will stick a spade in another piece of ground." The congregation continued to grow and relocated to St. George's Hall at 24th and Grove Street, Oakland, and began the task of looking for a lot to build a brand new church.

27. Seventh Avenue Missionary Baptist Church History book.

Fortunately, in August 1960, Mother Ella Hunt told the Reverend Watson about a vacant Key System Bus lot at 55th and Adeline Streets, Oakland. It was just what the church needed. After fundraisers, negotiations began to purchase the lot. In May 1961, the Articles of Incorporation were filed in the City of Oakland, Alameda County, and forwarded to Sacramento, along with a list of charter members and members of the Board of Trustees. Groundbreaking services were held Sunday October 15, 1961. The Reverend A. J. Iverson, Pastor of Paradise Baptist Church in Los Angeles, was the guest speaker. With work continuing, the lot became a place to gather on Saturdays for fundraising. Home cooked meals such as barbecue, chicken dinners, head cheese, ice cream, collard greens, cornbread, and cakes proved to be profitable means for a fundraiser. Members and non-members alike sacrificed and gave generously to add to the fund raising efforts. An architect was selected and worked closely with the pastor and members to draw up building plans including wheelchair accessibility for the physically challenged. Through the help of black realtor S. B. Odell a loan was secured and granted in March 1964, and the next month the Romley Construction Company began work on April 7, 1964. On Sunday, October 18, 1964, a motorcade consisting of the Reverend Watson, contractors, officers, and members gathered for the ribbon cutting. The Reverend J. T. McCullum, Pastor of New Hope, was guest speaker for the occasion. The Cornerstone for the church was laid on Sunday, August 26, 1973 with the Reverend Will Hardeman as guest speaker and the Reverend J. S. Pough the Grand Master in charge of the ceremony. The Reverend Watson recognized his health was beginning to seriously fail him. He called the deacons, trustees, and others to his home to request that a scholarship be established in his name. The Reverend Watson was called from labor to reward August 18, 1978. With the passing of the Reverend Watson, the church was without a leader for several years. In April 1980, Dr. M. J. Williams was installed. The church celebrated its mortgage-burning service on March 8, 1981. On January 14, 1998, the Reverend Williams was called from labor to reward while preaching at an annual revival in Oklahoma. The Reverend C. H. Reynolds took the helm in 1998 and, two years later, he was called from labor to reward on February 16, 2000. For a brief period, from November 30, 2000 until May 2003, the Reverend Robert E. Daniels served. Dr. Tyrone Pitts, General Secretary of PNBC (Progressive National Baptist Convention), came from Washington D.C., to help the church in procedures and guidelines for a smooth transition. The Reverend Dr. L. P. Lewis, son of Allen Temple Baptist Church, served as the interim pastor for six years. September 12, 2010, marked a new phase in the life of the Bethany Baptist Church as the Reverend Johnny M. Leggett was installed as Pastor. Under his leadership, much restoration and healing has taken place; Bethany has also deepened its outreach ministries to the community.[28]

Paradise Missionary Baptist Church, 1960

By the early 1960s, the Bay Area was experiencing a transitional phase as blacks were moving from the flatlands of West Oakland into the northern and Far East Oakland areas. The Black Power movement was in full swing, black liberation theology was being preached from pulpits, and the climate in Oakland and surrounding areas was being permeated with talk about an upcoming Black Panther party and the white flight from cities to surrounding suburban areas was well under way. Pictures of black children within a three-year period from 1958 to 1961 in school yearbooks from elementary to high school in areas showed an increase of black students in areas where they had been forbidden due to housing discrimination. Paradise was the second black church in the Brookfield area since WWII. As early as 1951, there were four Black families that had elementary school age children enrolled at Brookfield Elementary School, a primarily white school. Reverend Titus Washington, of Alameda, founded the first black church in the early 1950s in the Brookfield area in the home of the Boykins on Makin Road prior to Reverend Johnson founding Paradise. He went from door to door soliciting black members who were still traveling back to West Oakland to attend church as well as new unchurched members. Within three years, he had moved his small congregation to 10115 Edes Avenue and named the church "Tabernacle Baptist Church." Whether or not the East Oakland Church of God in Christ pastored by Bishop Elder Mark Clifton Sr. was the second church is not clear.

Paradise Baptist Church started with humble beginnings in February 1960 when he planted a church in the Columbian Gardens Community in Brookfield off 98th Avenue on Empire Rd. The Reverend William C. Johnson had served as an assistant pastor at the First Baptist Parchester Church of Richmond. The Reverend Johnson was not shy when he went from door to door in the community along with four volunteers to tell the residents about the new church plant. By the end of May 1960, sixteen persons agreed that a place of worship was needed in the area. A meeting was called and the dream of Pastor Johnson became a reality as the Paradise Baptist Church mission was organized. The Reverend Johnson used his Veterans Administration Certificate to purchase a home at 215 Sextus Road, which

28. Bethany Baptist Church History, www.bethanybaptist.org/bbc_history (accessed October 16, 2013).

was converted into a small church for worship services. Later, a house was purchased at 9670 Empire Road, across the street from Sextus Road, and in November 1963 the small neighborhood congregation moved into its new location. By 1968, a number of residents in the community had joined and a larger facility was needed. The members purchased additional property, however, by 1970, even that building had become too small for the growing congregation. Thus the building of a new sanctuary started. With a loan for the property, along with members who poured financially into the new building project, the church was completed and, on August 20, 1972, the members joyfully marched into the new sanctuary. Pastor Johnson was elated and told the membership how God was going to use Paradise to make a difference not only in Columbian Gardens, but also Paradise would be the "salvation of Oakland." Over the next ten years, with significant growth, Paradise was able to secure a full-time pastor, administrative assistant, part-time personnel, maintenance personnel, and numerous volunteers. In 1988 Pastor Johnson expanded the evangelism ministry and hired the Reverend Leon McDaniels Sr. as the full-time Evangelism Coordinator. The spark and enthusiasm found in the Reverend McDaniels spread throughout the entire church body. In addition to church growth, Pastor Johnson established the Wistar Redemption and Recovery Program, which started as an eighteen-month residential substance-abuse facility for men and then was extended to women, illustrating that Paradise would indeed be the light in its community and the "salvation of Oakland." In addition to constructing a new worship center and the Ministry Recreation and Business Center, the Paradise Baptist Church family has come a long way since its humble beginnings in 1960. The Reverend C. William Johnson's vision came to fruition under the leadership of Pastor Leon McDaniels Sr.[29]

On September 17, 1993, the Reverend Johnson was called from labor to reward, leaving the Paradise family with heavy hearts. The experienced Reverend Leon McDaniels Sr., who was already serving the church, was installed as the pastor a month later. Pastor McDaniels, being committed to the same principles as Pastor Johnson, resolved to make a significant difference not only in the Columbian Gardens Community but also to all of Oakland. As the church continued to grow, in 1966, it became clear that a larger facility was needed. Using the book of Nehemiah for the biblical instructions on how to accomplish the construction of a new state of the art church, the task of building began. The members believed that if God could build a Tabernacle in the wilderness with Israel, surely God could build a

29. Paradise Baptist Church History, http://www.pbc5star.org/about-pbc/paradise-history (accessed March 4, 2016).

church in the city of Oakland with Paradise. As a result, Paradise began a multi-million dollar building project and a groundbreaking ceremony was held on August 17, 1997. Despite a few obstacles and increased building costs, once again, the members abundantly blessed the church financially for a new state-of-the-art worship center. The building was completed, and the new Paradise Baptist Church Worship Center located at 9704 Empire Road in Brookfield Village, a residential district that once prohibited blacks from living there, was complete—or so it seemed. The church once again set out to build the second phase for a new Ministry Recreation and Business Center to meet the spiritual, social, educational, domestic, recreational, and business needs of our community: a four-million-dollar, thirteen-thousand-five-hundred square foot facility with a full kitchen, snack bar, arcade, gym (including women's and men's showers), book store, fellowship hall, conference room, youth room, classrooms, computer lab, and administrative offices. The new facility was designed to further expand the stewardship of the Paradise Baptist Church from its members to the surrounding community and to nurture and develop the next generation of disciples.

Two other charismatic churches were planted in East Oakland during the late 50s and early 60s; Bishop Clifton founded the East Oakland Church of God in Christ, on Edes Avenue in Oakland. Apostle Ray Mack founded the East Oakland Faith Deliverance Center Church in January 1967. The church was first located at 8901 MacArthur Boulevard before moving into the bowling alley at 73rd and E. 14th Streets, Oakland. The bowling alley was completely renovated. Apostle Mack reached out to the communities all over the Bay Area. He transported families by buses, vans, and cars seven days a week. A daily broadcast on KFAX radio started and people gave testimonies about miracles of healing from incurable diseases, and testified that they had been set free from drug and alcohol addiction. In 1982, Apostle Mack founded the Raymond Edward Mack Christian Academy, grades K–12. The corner of 73rd Avenue and E. 14th Street is heavily trafficked with drugs, crime, and poverty. In the midst of it stands the ministry of the Deliverance Church where restoration is taking place.

Harmony Missionary Baptist Church, Oakland

Harmony Missionary Baptist Church was founded and organized during turbulent times locally and nationally. The nation was morphing from legalized segregation to equal rights for minorities and affirmative action. There were deep scars and wounds from the organized discrimination tactics to uproot black communities. In addition to blacks moving to Far East Oakland, they were also beginning to occupy parts of North Oakland and Berkeley. Norvel Smith commented, "You came into West Oakland, and if you really made it, with a civil service joy or something, you moved into South Berkeley."[30] The Reverend I. H. Lewis organized Harmony Missionary Baptist Church on May 17, 1964 and held its first services at the Veteran Hall at 1970 Chestnut in Berkeley before relocating to Grove Street, Berkeley and again relocated to 1916 Woolsey Street. The numerous moves can be explained as result of the Transportation Highway constructing the Grove-Shafter freeway in the locations that Harmony was occupying and the strong possibility that the Reverend Lewis was unaware about the proposed redevelopment plans to destroy homes and properties in those areas. A fire destroyed the Woosley location, leaving the members without a worship location. The Reverend Lewis was determined to continue services and personally purchased property at 4113 Telegraph Avenue, Oakland, securing a permanent location for Harmony in 1979. Realizing that his health was rapidly declining, Pastor Lewis selected A. L. Cobbs from First Corinthian Missionary Baptist Church in Oakland to succeed him and, in November 1979, the Reverend A. L Cobbs was installed as Pastor. Within a short time, the church experienced exponential membership growth as he was not only a powerful preacher but was also someone who had a vision to see Harmony grow. The church purchased passenger vans, conducted outreach ministry through live radio, expanded its facility with a family center and additional classrooms, purchased a four-plex building on Linden Street, and added a stair lift for disabled persons. Pastor Cobbs served for thirty-one years until he was called from labor to reward on April 5, 2011.[31] The church continues its ministry under the leadership of the Reverend Albert L. Cobbs Jr., Senior Pastor.

Early Years of Huey P. Newton: A Different Look

Revolutionary suicide does not mean that I and my comrades have a death wish; it means just the opposite. We have such a strong desire to live with hope and human dignity that existence without them is impossible. One of the most long-lasting influences on my life was religion

—HUEY P. NEWTON

30. Self, *American Babylon*, 50.
31. Harmony Missionary Baptist Church, 50th Year Anniversary.

With the exception of his revolutionary side as co-founder of the Black Panther Party, very little has been written about Huey P. Newton's involvement in the church. While Mr. Huey P. Newton was not a minister, there was a part of him that upheld Christian values in that he was instrumental in starting the Free Breakfast Program for some of the poorest children in Oakland that eventually spread nationwide. Equally important were the sickle-cell programs and free ambulance services for those who could not afford it. Huey Newton grew up in West Oakland in a strong religious family. The Reverend Walter Newton, his wife Armelia, and seven children were part of the Great Migration coming from Monroe, Louisiana in the early 1940s. The Reverend Walter Newton was a Baptist preacher and had been a sharecropper. Shortly after arriving in Oakland, the Reverend Newton and family united with Antioch Baptist Church in West Oakland. The Reverend Thomas, founder of Antioch believed in the power of prayer and kept a constant reminder on the pulpit that "Prayer Changes Things." The church members, mostly migrants, were also a group of people that believed in the power of prayer. Even though prayers were directed toward God, praying together for each other's strength was a powerful, shared community practice.[32] As an associate minister, the Reverend Newton would spend time preparing his sermons. However, once in the pulpit, the Holy Spirit took over and the script was never looked at again. One of his favorite messages was the prodigal son. Huey said, "He terrified me with tales of fire and brimstone and how sinners and the unrepentant would end up in a lake of fire as he waved his arms around."[33] The Bible was constantly read to the Newton children by the Reverend Newton who influenced his children through inspiration. As a junior deacon Huey was able to occasionally sit in the deacon's seats feeling a sense of empowerment. He was also a member of the Baptist Young People's Union, the Young Deacons, the Junior Choir, and faithfully attended Sunday school and worship services weekly. On rare occasions, he experienced sensations of holiness of security and of deliverance—though he never shouted, the emotion of others was contagious. There were times when Huey thought of becoming a minister, but he gave it up after studying philosophy in college as he began asking questions about the concept of religion and the existence of God. "I began to question not only the Christian definition of God, but also the very foundation of my religion. I saw that it was based on belief alone, the soundness of which was never questioned."[34]

32 Newton, *Revolutionary Suicide*, 38–39.

33. Ibid., 37.

34. Ibid., 38.

The Other Side

When Huey's high school years came to an end, doubts and troubles surfaced while attending Oakland City College in the fall of 1959 as he struggled with an inner turmoil. After Huey grew a beard, his father disapproved and gave Huey an ultimatum to shave his beard or leave. "I just fled."[35]

Huey P. Newton and Bobby Seale co-founded the Black Panther Party for Self Defense in Oakland on October 1966. After seeing police brutality in the Watts community, the nonviolent approach of Dr. Martin Luther King Jr. rejected, and the conscious rising of the Black Power Movement was brewing, the time was ripe to start a movement. After meetings at Seale's house and the North Oakland Service Center, both worked collectively to come up with a survival plan for black oppressed people in the United States under the "Ten Point Manifesto" platform of "What We Want, What We Believe." Among the major themes in the Manifesto were: freedom, full employment, decent housing, education that reaches the true history of Black people, Black men being exempt from military, an end to police brutality, the release of Black men from prison, Black people being tried in a court of their peer group, and land, bread, housing, justice, and peace.[36] During the turbulent 60s of revolutionary change, the Black Church was being made aware of its power as a change agent for social action. It is in this context that some of the aforementioned points on the Ten Point Manifesto were similar to the struggles of the Black Church who were fighting for social justice.

St. Augustine Episcopal Church in Oakland became the home of the first Free Breakfast for School Children Program where members of the Panther party cooked and served food to the poor. Father Neil, Pastor of St. Augustine's, became the Panther's spiritual advisor. Father Neil interpreted program goals and needs of the Panthers by creating a bridge with the wider community; assisting in implementing community programs of the Panthers, including health clinics, food and clothing distribution, and prison visitations. The Panthers celebrated Father Neil with a barbeque before he left in 1974, to accept a position on the staff of the Presiding Bishop at the National Headquarters of the Episcopal Church in New York.[37] St. Augustine Episcopal Church was one of many churches in the Bay Area that was involved in the turbulence of the 60s. Huey Newton earned a BA from U. C. Santa Cruz in 1974, and earned a PhD in history from the same university

35. Ibid., 58.

36. Hilliard, *Huey: Spirit of the Panther*, 31–32.

37. www.staugepiscopal.org/about-us/history.aspx (accessed September 20, 2013); Lena Wysinger, *Oakland Tribune* July 21, 1940; autobiography of the Reverend David R. Wallace located in the Oakland Public Library History Room, church files.

in 1980. He had written several papers including, "Can Religion Survive?" His doctoral title was, "War against the Panthers: A Study of Repression in America."[38]

On August 22, 1989, Dr. Huey Percy Newton was murdered in West Oakland, not too far from where he grew up. His funeral celebration of life was held at the Allen Temple Baptist Church. The Reverend Dr. J. Alfred Smith Sr. officiated. The obituary program never referenced Newton's affiliation with the Black Panther Party. Words of remembrance on the back of the program read: "Huey P. Newton had many roles in his relatively short life. He lived just long enough to have been an unknown idealist, a popular and heroic champion of the oppressed, a brilliant and controversial polemicist and ultimately one who was as despised by some as much as he was loved by others."[39] Huey once said, "We will touch God's heart we will touch the people's heart and together we will move the mountain."[40]

National Committee of Black Churchmen

The rise of the Black Power movement had a profound effect on the Black Church. In 1966, the National Committee of Negro Churchmen, later renamed National Conference of Black Churchmen, began as an ad hoc group of ministers who had come together and wrote a "Black Power Statement" that represents the beginning of a radical theological movement toward the development of an independent black perspective on the Christian faith that was published in the New York Times, July 31, 1966. [41] Black radical clergy were gathering in different regions to discuss religion, theology, and how the Black Church would respond to the Black Power Movement. More than three hundred persons assembled for a landmark event at the Claremont Hotel in Berkeley for the Third Annual Convocation of the National Committee of Black Churchmen, hosted by the Alamo Black Clergy of the San Francisco Bay Area in November 1969. Among the attendees were the Reverend Hazaiah Williams (President-Director of the Urban Center for Black Studies), the Reverend J. Metz Rollins Jr., the Reverend Dr. Samuel B. McKinney (Pastor, Mt. Zion Baptist Church, Seattle, Washington), the Reverend Howard A. Bryant (Pastor of First Baptist Church, Daly City), the Reverend Hamilton T. Boswell (Pastor, United Methodist Church, San

38. Hilliard, *Huey: Spirit of the Panther*, 254.

39. Donn Granville, "In Remembracnce," in celebration of the life of Dr. Huey P. Newton, obituary, August 28, 1989.

40. Newton, *Revolutionary Suicide*, 333.

41. Cone, *For My People*, 12.

Francisco), the Reverend Charles H. Belcher (Pastor, Downs Memorial United Methodist Church, Oakland), the Reverend J. W. Bryant (Pastor, Gethsemane Missionary Baptist Church, Oakland), the Reverend W. L. Hertzfield (Pastor, Bethlehem Lutheran Church, Oakland), the Reverend Booker T. Anderson (Pastor, Easter Hill United Methodist Church), the Reverend J. Alfred Smith (Representative of the Ministers and Missionaries Benefit Board of the American Baptist Convention), and others. The all-male clergy addressed itself to the black perspective and the need for black churchmen to develop a new and creative style of black churchmanship. The Reverend Gayraud S. Wilmore articulated four interrelated dimensions for a new style of mission:

> 1) The renewal and enhancement of the Black Church in terms of its liturgical life, its theological interpretation, its understanding of its mission to self, to the white church, and to the nation. 2) The development of the Black Church, not only as a religious fellowship, but as a community organization . . . to address the problem of estrangement, resignation and powerlessness in the political, cultural, and economic life of the black community. 3) The projection of a new quality of life that would equip and strengthen the church as custodian and interpreter of that cultural heritage rooted in the peculiar experience of black people in the United States and the faith that has sustained them for over two centuries on these shores. 4) The contribution of the Black Church, out of its experience of suffering and the yearning for freedom, of that quality of faith hope and love that can activate, empower, renew, and unite the whole Church of Christ.[42]

As a result of radical clergymen gathering, it was the beginning of a new form of the gospel being preached from the pulpits: Black Liberation Theology.

Center of Hope Community Church, Oakland, 1968

Bishop Ernestine Cleveland Reems, daughter of Bishop Elmer Elijah (E.E.) and Matilda Cleveland is one of the outstanding pastors in the United States. Bishop Reems was raised by parents who were intensely committed Christians. In 1951, she began to travel to every major city in the country with her brother, the Reverend Elmer Cleveland Jr., to preach the gospel. Although she was not able to preach in the church of her childhood, because women were not accepted as preachers, only as missionaries and teachers, Reems

---

42. *Post Newspaper,* November 6, 1969.

never lost sight of her priorities, her focus, and her desire to minister from her own pulpit. In 1968, Reems purchased an old shoe store in Oakland in a drug-infested neighborhood. She continued her travels across the country to evangelize and raise money to open a church on the property. With the funds she collected Reems built a platform and purchased an organ, a piano, and carpeting. The initial congregation was only four members. However, by the year 2000, the Center of Hope had exceeded fifteen hundred members. In 1988, Bishop Reems founded the E. C. Reems Women International Ministries (ERWIM) with headquarters in Oakland. The goals of the ministry was to motivate, instruct, and challenge women to reach their maximum potential in Christ to meet the demands of the twenty-first century. The church outgrew its location on 98th Avenue and relocated to MacArthur Boulevard. Bishop Reems's ministry extends globally to Haiti and throughout South Africa, though her primary commitments remain within her local community. In 1990, she opened a fifty-six-unit, senior housing complex, the E. E. Cleveland Manor. Bishop Reems said in an interview that a prostitute had posted herself in front of the church, waiting for a customer. Reems informed her, "Honey, you can't do that here—this is a church." The woman replied that she was hungry and needed to buy food. Bishop Reems felt the event was a message from God. With the help of federal and city funds including private donations, Bishop Reems purchased a seventeen-unit facility to operate a transitional housing program for homeless single women with children that also offers job training and childcare. In 1998, Bishop Reems established the E. C. Reems Gardens, a one-hundred-and-fifty-unit, affordable-housing complex. By 2000, Bishop Reems managed more than eighteen million dollars for various social programs and in the process transformed the neighborhood near the Center of Hope Church. In 2000, her husband of forty-one years was called from labor to reward. Through tears and a broken heart, she continued to minister.

Bishop Reems outreach to the community did not stop with housing projects. In September 1999, the Ernestine C. Reems Academy of Technology and Arts School in Oakland was established. The school promotes a child-centered, community-learning environment dedicated to developing academic excellence in core subjects, leadership, and technological skills. Bishop Reems's impact has extended beyond her local community through Kingdom Builders Ministerial Alliance, an organization she founded to mentor leaders of urban ministries. She supports missionary projects in Haiti and throughout South Africa. Bishop Reems has encouraged others who later became national figures.

Reems befriended T. D. Jakes, and asked him to preach at her church, an honor for Jakes who had not achieved national recognition. Reems was an important friend to Jakes and encouraged him during a period of frustration with ministry.[43] She has touched the world through her dynamic preaching, teaching, writing books, and has devoted her life to God's ministry. Bishop Reems retired as Senior Pastor of Center of Hope in 2004 and passed the mantel of leadership on to her son, the Reverend Brondon Reems, and her daughter-in-law, Maria, who were installed as pastors that same year. The mighty mission of Center of Hope continues to be a magnet for the community. The Paul Reems Computer Academy and Educational Facility Training Program for youth bears the name of the deceased husband of Bishop Reems.[44]

Brookins AME Church, Oakland, 1968

On Sunday, December 29, 1968, thirty laypersons, most of whom were members of Parks Chapel African Methodist Episcopal Church, met for the first time to develop plans for the establishment of a Mission in the Eastern Sector of Oakland. The first worship service of the Lay Mission was held on Sunday, January 5, 1969 at the East Oakland Chapel of Jackson Funeral Home with the late Elder Alexander White Sr. presiding. On February 24, 1969, the Mission membership selected the name of Everett Chapel AMEC and the subsequent official board appointed Elder Alexander White Sr. as a spiritual leader. During the mid to late 1960s, there was also another African Methodist expansion group in development in the East Oakland community. A group of laypersons similar to the Everett group organized and selected the name Bryant Chapel AMEC that was admitted to the California Annual Conference at its 1969 annual session. The 1976 session of the General Conference of the AMEC and the subsequent appointment of the Rt. Reverend H. Hartford Brookins would have a profound effect on the work and progress of the East Oakland AMEC and the growth and development of African Methodism already begun there. Bishop Brookins moved to complement the efforts and work already under way. As part of the master plan to effect a body of lay persons capable of building a substantial physical structure and lending itself to the process of building a major congregation in the AMEC tradition, Bishop Brookins considered Williams Chapel AMEC in addition to Everett and Bryant Chapel as a joint tool in this project of expansion.

43. Lee, *America's New Preacher*, 30.
44. Ernestine Reems, Center of Hope Church biography, *In the Storm*, excerpts found in http://www.answers.com/topic/ernestine-cleveland-reems (accessed September 15, 2013).

In October 1977, Bishop Brookins met with the congregation of Williams Chapel and others to consider a plan to merge Williams Chapel, Bryant Chapel, and Brookins Church into one church and also to locate a suitable church structure in East Oakland. One month later, Bishop Brookins met with Presiding Elder R. A. Washington and the members of the conference Board of Trustees for the purpose of establishing a fact-finding committee for the proposed venture to serve the three congregations. Williams Chapel and Bryant Chapel both approved the merger proposal with Everett Chapel but did not agree to join the proposed merger. Subsequently a large portion of the two congregations transferred their membership over to the new expansion project. Together, two full congregations and a substantial representation of the third made the East Oakland AMEC concept a reality. At the August 1978 annual conference, Bishop Brookins, Presiding Elder R. A. Washington, the fact-finding committee, and laypersons alike gathered at 2201 73rd Avenue (the selected site for the new church location) for a groundbreaking ceremony. St. Paul AMEC in Berkeley and Bishop Brookins consummated the two groups into one body. In October 1978, the Reverend G. Mansfield Collins was assigned as Pastor the East Oakland AMEC Concept. Later that year the name given to the church was Brookins AMEC in honor of the Bishop Brookins who worked tirelessly to bring the church into fruition. The Reverend Norman D. Copeland was assigned to pastor Brookins in August 1980. Under his administration, the church was reorganized and a great deal of work was done in preparation for construction of a new church at the 73rd Avenue site. The Reverend Edgar E. Boyd was assigned as Pastor of Brookins in August 1982. During his administration, the congregation of Brookins membership grew. The dedication and laying of the cornerstone for the building was held on Saturday, June 3, 1984 with Bishop Brookins presiding and Bishop H. W. Murph, the newly assigned Bishop of the Fifth Episcopal District, leading the ribbon cutting. The overflow crowd was estimated at eleven hundred persons. The opening-day services for Brookins were held on Sunday, December 9, 1984 at 3:00 p.m. A series of pastors have since been assigned to Brookins, including the Reverend Carmi Victor Woods and the Reverend Dr. Mark Smith. The Reverend Dr. Vernon Burroughs was assigned to pastor Brookins in November 2013 and continues to serve. Dr. Burroughs is no stranger to this area, having served as Presiding Elder.[45]

45. The History of Brookins African Methodist Episcopal Church www.http:// brookinsoakland.org/ChurchHistory.htm (accessed November 15, 2014).

Love Center Church, Oakland, 1972

The Love Center Church grew out of the music ministry of Walter and Edwin Hawkins, two brothers who are music geniuses that cannot be separated from their ministry and music. As a young student at the Elmhurst Junior High School and Castlemont High School, Walter's leadership ability and musical gifts surfaced. Edwin says we would sing at somebody's church almost every Sunday afternoon. They sang with other kid groups that traveled from church to church, which included future superstar Sly Stone and the Combs Family from Richmond. Edwin began attending Ephesian Church of God in Christ on Alcatraz in South Berkeley. He was impressed with the dynamic sermons of Bishop E. E. Cleveland and the choir director Ola Jean Andrews, whose jazz-imbued sense of harmony influenced Edwin's thinking. At the age of fourteen, Edwin landed his first paying job as a church pianist at Mount Pilgrim Church of God in Christ, a former movie theater on San Pablo Avenue near 27th Street. In May 1967, Edwin Hawkins organized a gospel choir and named it the Edwin Hawkins Singers. In his efforts to raise funds for the Edwin Hawkins Singers to attend the National Youth Congress music camp, he hastily recorded a gospel album in Ephesians Church of God in Christ, Berkeley, with a sound that fused jazz and gospel. Among the songs recorded was an eighteenth-century remake of "Oh Happy Day" featuring Dorothy Morrison. The song became the first major crossover gospel song that created a new contemporary gospel genre. Edwin's ultra-hip arrangement of an old song, fueled by a Latin-tinged soul groove, sold over a million copies. Though the song created controversy within the church it set the wheels into motion for the Edwin Hawkins Singers to tour nationally and internationally before Walter set out on his own. Breaking with tradition, Walter said he was glad to be part of contemporary gospel music's worldwide growth. "There's always been controversy around modern versus traditional gospel. What is tradition anyway?" Gospel music doesn't have a particular style. Gospel's got to progress. Walter Hawkins was performing in Europe with The Edwin Hawkins Singers when the seed was planted to start a church. After returning to the states, Walter organized lively biblical discussions in the home of his mother, Mamie Vivian Hawkins. These discussions grew into informal group meetings, which quickly evolved into regular, organized bible studies. These bible studies were radical at the time because they delved into topics that mainstream Christianity was quite reluctant to address. The Hawkins's were a musical family. Mother Hawkins often took her children to Good Samaritan Church of God in Christ in West Oakland. Walter received his ministerial license and was ordained by his pastor, Bishop E. E. Cleveland (the father of Bishop

Ernestine Cleveland Reems) of the Ephesians Church of God in Christ in Berkeley. Love Center Church was birthed in the flatlands of East Oakland in October of 1972 in a storefront at 8411 MacArthur Blvd., Oakland, near Castlemont High School. The membership grew rapidly and they relocated to another storefront, a few blocks away at 8901 MacArthur Blvd. Over the next ten years, the Love Center Church membership overflowed the small, one-room building because it welcomes all people. Pastor Hawkins had a simple yet practical approach to ministry; his message was, "The Fisherman." Today, this message is still an underlying principle of the Love Center Ministries. In 1975, "Changed" and "Goin' Up Yonder," both featuring Tramaine Hawkins, wife of Walter Hawkins and niece of Bishop Ernestine Reems, would become their first hit song by Walter Hawkins and the Love Center Choir. "Love Alive"topped the gospel record charts for months on end and remained on Billboard's gospel chart for more than three years, selling more than three hundred thousand copies. Two years later, Love Center sold its building and bought the old Cine 7 movie theater at 3814 MacArthur Blvd., which was in need of dire repair. Pastor Walter Hawkins and the Love Center membership worked diligently to refurbish the decaying structure and within a few months the newly renovated building opened. The Love Center Choir recorded "Love Alive III," which was the number-one, top-selling album on the Billboard Gospel Chart for thirty-four weeks. By now Love Center was known nationally for its outstanding music. Oakland Mayor Elihu Harris was so impressed he commissioned Pastor Hawkins to write an anthem for the City of Oakland: "Oakland Homeland." Within three years the membership of Love Center grew from three hundred to nine hundred members. Pastor Hawkins looked around and found a site at the old Concordia High School on Camden Avenue in Oakland, which had been vacant for nine months. To accommodate the nine hundred plus members, the church instituted two Sunday services, 8:00 a.m. and 11:00 a.m. Also, a building fund drive was launched to add a twelve-hundred-seat sanctuary and a kitchen.

On October 18, 1992 Pastor was elevated to the office of bishop by Bishop George D. McKinney and Bishop Wilbert L. Baltimore. In this same year the Love Fellowship component of the Edwin Hawkins Music & Arts Seminar was sanctioned. Nine affiliated churches from across the United States approached Bishop Hawkins for spiritual covering. To date there are twenty-five Love Fellowship pastors nationwide, including in Cape Town, South Africa. The ministry of Bishop Hawkins was to not be conventional. In 1997, Bishop Hawkins and the Love Center Choir recorded "Love Alive V" at the Paramount Theater, Oakland, with a seating capacity of 3,040. People from all races and walks of life were drawn to Love Center, which meant they needed to find a new location. In 1998, Bishop Hawkins made a decision to sell the site before finding a permanent church home. As a result, the church experienced a "wilderness period." Sunday church services were held at the Scottish Rite Hall and the weekly Bible study and prayer service were held at the Havenscourt Community Church on Havenscourt Blvd. in East Oakland. In February 1999, Love Center Miniseries purchased the property at 10400–10440 East 14th Street (later renamed International Blvd.), just a few blocks away from where Bishop Hawkins and his siblings grew up. Sadly, in 2008, at the height of his ministry, Bishop Hawkins announced that he had developed pancreatic cancer. His illness prevented him from preaching for over two months and traveling with his siblings on singing engagements. Later that year, in November, Bishop Hawkins underwent twenty-two hours of radical surgery followed by chemo and radiation therapy saying, "They removed a lot of stuff." On July 11, 2010, at the age of sixty, Bishop Walter Hawkins was called from labor to reward, leaving the church devastated, though they knew his illness was terminal. In January of 2011 the pastoral baton was handed off to Pastor Hawkins's son, Walter Jamie Hawkins Jr., who was ordained in a full ceremony at the church. It was a turbulent period in the church as Pastor Jamie Hawkins announced that he was leaving the church along with a number of members to start a new ministry. The very capable Reverend Sandy Coleman, who had stood by Bishop Hawkins through thick and thin, including his terminal illness, was finally appointed Interim Senior Pastor.[46]

Sojourner Presbyterian Church, Richmond, 1972

Sojourner Truth Presbyterian Church was organized by several people who were formerly members of the Faith Presbyterian Church in Oakland. In this endeavor they joined with others who had not been members of that congregation. One of the charter members fondly recalls how a group of young men, most of them neighbors in the Fairmede/Hilltop community, regularly biked to a restaurant in Berkeley for breakfast on Sunday mornings. Reverend Dr. Eugene Farlough Jr. became a visitor to the group. Before long, the conversation changed from hot biscuits, pancakes, eggs, and sausage to Christian ministry in their community. Out of these discussions came the idea to start a church whose mission would be centered on community service programs with a particular commitment to oppressed people in name

46. Hawkins Biography, Bishop Walter Lee Hawkins, obituary, June 21, 2010, History of Love Center on http:/www.lovecenter.org/church_hisory.html (accessed September 15, 2013).

and service. Lacking significant funds, and without a permanent facility, the initial meetings were held in individual homes. The first major task was to establish clarity of self-identification. It was decided to name the new church after a strong and exceptional black woman who refused to separate faith from action, who strongly believed in the salvation of the soul, who fought for the freedom of all God's people, and who struggled for the liberation of one's body. After much deliberation, the name "Sojourner Truth Presbyterian Church" was selected with the original five families becoming the charter/founding members. On March 12, 1972, twenty-six individuals gathered in the multipurpose room of the Fairmede Elementary School to hold the first worship service. Among the first worshippers were the Reverend H. Eugene Farlough, his wife, Arlyce, his son, Chris-Darnell Farlough, and Carolyn, Lisa, Stacey and Tami Anderson; Archie, Tracey, and Veronica Bush; Mary Burns; Ollie, Sonya, and Zephyr Cotton; Beatrice, Kenneth, and Terri Jett; Charles Jr., Charles, III, and Stella McHenry; Edward, Kimberly, and Sandra Phillips and Joe, Peggy, and Rasha Smith.

With the help from the Presbytery of San Francisco, the PCUSA General Assembly, and additional sources, funding was secured for the present site at 2621 Shane Drive was purchased. On April 15, 1973 the facility, originally constructed by Highland's Presbyterian Church became the newest predominately African American church in the Presbytery. The San Francisco Presbytery officially commissioned Sojourner Truth Presbyterian Church, with ninety-nine charter members and the Reverend Dr. Eugene Farlough Jr. as organizing pastor on September 28, 1974—Reverend Farlough was installed as permanent pastor one year later. The Reverend Farlough's benediction, "Get-to-stepping-out into the world where God is preceding you," epitomizes his tireless work in the community including mentoring numerous women and men in ministry. As Sojourner Truth Church continued its growth, on May 23, 1981 the congregation launched plans to build a new sanctuary and to use the "barn raising" approach. This massive project was done as a labor of love by dedicated individuals from within the church, sister churches, and community volunteers. On August 7, 1988 the first worship service was held in the new facility. On August 15, 1994, the Reverend Dr. Farlough ended his tenure as Pastor and accepted a position in Atlanta, Georgia at the Interdenominational Theological Center. Among the ministers who served as interim pastors during the search for a permanent pastor were the Reverends Arlene Gordon, Arthur Scott, Carmen Mason-Brown, Charles Tinsley, and Ophelia Manney. Dr. Farlough was called from labor to reward, May 28, 1996.

In 1997, a call was extended to the Reverend John Howard, who served for three years. In 2000, a call was extended to the Reverend Dr. James Noel, who served for seven years as interim pastor. In August 2009, the Reverend Kamal Hassan was called as Designated Pastor, and was installed as Pastor / Teaching Elder January 22, 2012. The Reverend Hassan has broadened the church's ministry and has said, "The task of the church is to be involved in social justice and social change. Part of what's happening is that churches have retreated from that role."[47]

47. Sojourner Truth Presbyterian Church History.

Epilogue

Facing the rising sun of our new day begun, let's march on 'til victory is won.

—JAMES WELDON JOHNSON

Black Church Beginnings in the Bay Area has attempted to shed light on the beginnings of Black Church history in the San Francisco Bay Area tracing the Gold Rush era, the First Migration, the Great Migration, and the Civil Rights era to 1972. The historical Black Church as we know it to be has come a long way from house meetings, church missions, storefronts, and tents to temples. This study has covered a vast range of subjects, which are a part of the reality of the black experience that range from the struggles of slavery after California was admitted as a free state in 1850, to the struggles of harsh discrimination laws including housing, employment, education, the Ku Klux Klan, voting rights, and other social barriers that were alive and well in "free" California. On the positive side, the Pacific Coast proved to be fertile ground for blacks relocating from the South during WWI and WWII. Indeed it was a step forward from sharecropping and slavery. Employment was plentiful at the shipyards. However, blacks were assigned to the lowest menial jobs and migrant workers were forced to live in the midst of decaying enclaves because racial covenants prevented them from living where they could afford. The building up of a rich religious black community in a foreign land was a testimony to the strength of black people who prayed, played, worked, and communed together toward the struggle for freedom. The Black Church became the center of hope within the Bay Area black communities. The church provided the first form of education because the laws prevented them from attending public schools. The Black Church provided social services during the Great Depression that were otherwise unavailable. The church was the host location where blacks strategized to fight racial oppression. A glance back in history reveals that blacks made little progress politically in the first decade of the twentieth century. By the end of WWII, blacks in the four metropolitan cities were living in ghettos as a result of severe housing discrimination and the deliberate neglect of the local governments that engaged in economic and social barriers. On the other side of the coin, black churches were growing by leaps in bounds. The growth and strength of the black church was reflected in the cohesiveness of black communities.

The twenty-first century reveals that times have drastically changed. The Black Church is challenged to rethink the way it delivers the gospel to the millennial generation without losing all of its base traditions. In 2010, Eddie Glaude Jr., PhD, a young professor at Princeton, created a firestorm in the black community when he announced that the Black Church was dead. His reasoning was that "the idea of his venerable institution as central to black life and as a repository for the social and moral conscience of the nation has all but disappeared. The idea of a Black Church standing at the center of all that takes place in a community has passed away. Instead, different areas of black life have become more distinct and specialized . . . black religious institutions and beliefs stand alongside a number of other vibrant non-religious institutions and beliefs. He further cited that a number of African Americans are attending churches pastored by non-black pastors. These non-denominational congregations often 'sound' a lot like Black churches."[1] In the 1960s, the Negro Church was challenged to reassess its relevancy to the demands of the Civil Rights and Black Power movements. The Negro Church had to come to grips with connecting faith and action as a result of the demands from both the Civil Rights and Black Power Movements. In the same fashion Negroes everywhere were redefining and renaming themselves from "Negro" to "Black" when Stokely Carmichael's slogan "Black Power" became the lighting rod in black communities. Malcom X said: "When we come together, we don't come as Baptists or Methodists. You don't catch hell because you're a Baptist, and you don't catch hell because you're a Methodist. You catch hell because you're a Black man. All of us catch hell for the same reason."[2] James Brown was dancing to the tune, "Say It Loud I'm Black and Proud," and puffy afros became the style of the day. A revolution had started. In the words of C. Eric Lincoln, "The Negro Church is dead because the norms and presuppositions . . . are no longer

1. Glaude Jr., *Huffington Post*, April 26, 2010.

2. Malcolm X, *Malcolm X Speaks*; Top 100 American Speeches of the 20th Century, Madison: University of Wisconsin-Madison December 15, 1999, p. 4.

relevant."[3] Professor Glaude's statement that the Black church is dead is a challenge fifty plus years later if the message of Black Church is to address the systemic problems that plague black communities. It was also during the 60s that black theologians wrestled with a gospel of liberation with a focus on black theology from the lens of oppressed black people. A new tension has erupted in the black community where the prophetic gospel message of social justice is competing with the prosperity gospel message that emphasizes individual wealth. To make matters worse, attendance at black churches that preach a social gospel message has declined significantly as congregants have fled in great numbers to hear a message that makes them feel good rather than challenge them to fight for the race. Did the message and challenge of social gospel die out? Is Professor Glaude's assessment of the Black Church an attack, or does it pose a challenge for the Black Church to reassess itself? Is the Black Church losing its prophetic edge in light of the prominence of prosperity gospel? Another challenge that confronts the Black Church is white pastors who are attracting black worshipers. Kaleo Christian Fellowship Church and Shiloh Church, both located in Oakland, and Hilltop Community Church in Richmond are pastored by white ministers with sizeable Black congregations. Across the country, pastors like Joel Osteen, Franklin Jenezen, and Ron Carpentier have attracted large crowds of black worshipers to their mega-churches while emphasizing a message of prosperity. Invariably, blacks rarely are part of the leadership of these churches and are usually supporting the music ministry or security. While storefront churches still exist, many have been replaced with mega-churches where congregants recline in comfortable padded seats and where the worship service has now become an experience of high technology. Equally important is the need to expand the role of women beyond service positions into leadership positions. It is estimated that women comprise over 75 percent of church membership, yet males hold the majority of leadership roles. The church is most challenged to bring women equally in the ministry as pastors, and in some cases co-pastors. In 2008, young people—white, black, Hispanic, and Asian—became energized and participated in voting in record numbers when it was evident that a young Barack Obama had a chance to become the first black man elected to the position of President of the United States, who held the position for two terms. The church is challenged to rethink its role with young people. These young people consider themselves out of the wilderness and have entered the Promised Land of mainstream America in a digital world. Church advertisements are generated via websites that are designed by persons who are more focused on

3. Lincoln, *The Black Church since Frazier*, 106.

technology and the glamor of the webpage than the message of the mission of the church. Upcoming events rarely focus on oppressive issues of economic and social justice that continue to plague black communities. As millenials enter into the vocation of pastors, they are drawing members from traditional staid churches. Younger pastors have opted to wear casual clothing in lieu of the black robe. Hymnbooks and Bibles have been traded in for digital-media big screens where words are displayed. Sermons are preached from transparent, plexiglass pulpits instead of the oak-stained, wooden pulpit. If one wants to reach the pastor, they use Twitter, Facebook, texting, or email. How does the Black Church prepare for this new world? The challenge for the black traditional church is to balance tradition with contemporary worship styles without losing the relevancy of an encounter with God as the world of tradition and contemporary adapt to each other. Warnock's message for the Black Church is that it struggles with a divided mind that struggles with a revivalistic piety and radical protest. The Black church needs to engage in serious and sustained self-examination, so as to clarify the theological content of its own message: Is it prophetic or pious?[4] Both are equally important in keeping the church grounded in its mission of saving souls and saving lives. Church membership has dwindled in many of the traditional churches that were founded over fifty years ago. Acts Full Gospel Church, which was founded in 1984 by Bishop Bob Jackson began as a Bible study in a rented dance hall, has grown to a membership that exceeds three thousand plus members with a strong evangelistic outreach ministry. While the Black Church that preaches a message of social gospel is certainly not dead, there are competing forces it must address.

Reverse Migration

A shift in demographics of Asians and Latinos moving into neighborhoods that once were occupied predominately by African Americans who have opted to move to suburban areas is a contributing factor in the declining membership of churches in the inner cities. Allen Temple and St. John Missionary Baptist Church, both of Oakland and Third Baptist, San Francisco, are examples of well-established churches in changing neighborhoods. The core neighborhoods once occupied by blacks have been replaced with gentrification. The Black population in San Francisco declined from 124,8221 in 1980 to 99,1999 in the year 2000 with the numbers continuing to decline. Oakland lost thousands of black residents from 2000 to 2010. The San Francisco Oakland metropolitan area lost 33,003 blacks, a decline of 8

4. Warnock, *The Divided Mind of the Black Church*, 15.

percent leaving Oakland with 106,637. By the end of the 1970s Blacks were relocating back to the South, creating a reverse migration. In addition to Blacks returning to the South, the suburbanization of blacks moving to bedroom communities in pursuit of the "American dream" of a new home with a cheaper price tag than inner city homes, blacks are looking for improved public schools for their children. Long commutes back into the metropolitan areas for work is not a deterrent.

On the other hand, all is not rosy for suburbanites: The dispersal of African Americans often bought with it a sense of isolation, of being disconnected from their past, their friends, and from any substantial numbers of other blacks and social contacts.[5] Commuter members, who live up to fifty miles away, commute back to the black community on Sundays to fellowship and to be in a familiar environment of good preaching and singing. By 1:00 p.m. on Sundays the pews are emptied, as commuter congregates leave the impoverished neighborhoods and return to their bedroom communities. Some pastors have addressed the issue of blacks moving to suburbia by building black mega-churches in those areas that appeal to middle-class blacks as well as whites, thus creating a multiethnic worship environment by blending traditional and contemporary worship styles. The Mount Calvary Baptist Church located in Solano County approximately fifty miles from the center of the Bay Area is an example of a new-style mega-church pastored by the Reverend Dr. Claybon Lea Jr. Blacks who live in the Solano County bedroom area no longer commute back into the inner city for worship. Mount Calvary is considered one church with two locations and three worship services that serve the communities of Fairfield and Suisun. The church even draws people from the Bay Area to partake of the worship experience. The out-migration of blacks has left a drain on inner city Black Churches. The institutional black church as we know it is being challenged to address declining membership, declining finances, and the fact that professionals who migrated away took their skills and knowledge with them; they no longer commute back to the church during the week.

The San Francisco Mayor's Task Force on African American Out-Migration convened in 2007 to develop action recommendations to discuss the causes of out-migration of the African-American population and find creative solutions to reverse the situation. The report published in 2009 revealed a number of historical trends. Most revealing was that the current median income of African-Americans in San Francisco was $35,200, which is nearly half that of whites, who make $70,800. The unemployment rate is 10.4 percent higher and mortgage rejection is above other groups.

5. De Graaf et al., *Seeking El Dorado*, 432.

Along with the economic barriers, African-Americans in San Francisco are arrested at more than twice the rate of any other racial groups combined. The recommendations were culled into three areas: Job and Economic Development, Cultural and Social Life, and Public Safety and Quality of Life.[6] Some called the "Out -Migration Report" a slap in the face of blacks in San Francisco, citing the "Unfinished Agenda" report that gathers dust on the shelf of San Francisco Human Rights Commission office. Dr. Amos Brown, pastor of Third Baptist Church, San Francisco said, "San Francisco has become a city of the rich, the immigrant poor, with a small number of black middle class." He sees the effects in his own church and in other black congregations. "For the past five years, no major church has put down extra chairs for Easter, Mother's Day or Christmas."[7]

With the exodus of black people and black churches, a transformation is taking place in Oakland and San Francisco. In San Francisco and Oakland, the neighborhoods that were occupied by blacks have been replaced with expensive lofts, apartments, and trendy boutique stores. On the other hand neighborhoods in the Hunters Point area of San Francisco and East Oakland below MacArthur Blvd. are declining into poverty enclaves, creating two distinct cities of the haves and the have-nots.

Eugene Robinson informs us that "Black America has shattered into four distinct categories: The mainstream middle class with a full ownership stake in American society the large abandoned minority with less hope of escaping poverty and dysfunction than any time since Reconstruction, the small transcendent elite with enormous wealth, power, and influence and emergent groups of mixed heritage and communities of recent Black immigrants. They have four different mindsets, different hopes, fears and dreams that make us wonder what black is even supposed to mean."[8]

No longer are we held together by the Black Church or confined to black-only neighborhoods. This class polarization among blacks has a major impact on black communities and most importantly, a decline in church membership. By the mid-70s, an influx of Latinos and Asians had moved to the East Oakland area. The new face for storefront churches are lettered with the words "Iglesias Baptisia," an indicator of the changing demographics. In the words of Rex Miller, "We cannot move forward by destroying or forgetting our heritage. In fact, the only way we can truly move forward is to

6. Report of the San Francisco Mayor's Task Force on African-American Out-Migration 2009

7. Judy Keen, "Blacks' Exodus Reshapes Cities," *USAToday*, May 19, 2011. http://usatoday30.usatoday.com/news/nation/census/2011-05-20-chicago-blacks-exodus_n.htm (acceseed March 17, 2016).

8. Robinson, *Disintegration: The Splintering of Black America*, 5.

honor openly those who served God during their time in history and within the spectrum of revelation they had. We are called to keep faith with their legacy and hold the continuity that demonstrates our common origins."[9]

9. Miller, *The Millennium Matrix*, 222.

Bibliography

Adkins, Jan Batiste. *Images of America African Americans of San Francisco*. Charleston: Arcadia, 2012.

Alexander, Michelle. *The New Jim Crow: Mass Incarceration in the Age of Colorblindness*. New York: New, 2010.

Aptheker, Herbert, ed. *A Documentary History of the Negro People in the United States*. New York: Citadel, 1951.

Baer, Hans A., and Merrill Singer. *African-American Religion in the Twentieth Century: Varieties of Protest and Accommodation*. 1st ed. Knoxville: University of Tennessee Press, 1992.

Bagwell, Beth. *Oakland, Story of a City*. Novato: Presidio, 1982.

Bastin, Donald. *Image of America: Richmond*. Charleston: Arcadia, 2003.

Beasley, Delilah L. *The Negro Trail Blazers of California*. Los Angeles: Kessinger, 1919.

Bell, Derrick A. *Faces at the Bottom of the Well: The Permanence of Racism*. New York: Basic, 1992.

Bennett, G. Willis. *Guidelines for Effective Urban Church Ministry: Based on a Case Study of Allen Temple Baptist Church*. Nashville: Broadman, 1983.

Bennett, Lerone, Jr. *Pioneers in Protest*. Chicago: Johnson, 1968.

Bergman, Peter M. *The Chronological History of the Negro in America*. New York: New American Library, 1969.

Blackwell, James E. *The Black Community: Diversity and Unity*. New York: Harper & Row, 1975.

Broussard, Albert S. *Black San Francisco: The Struggle for Racial Equality in the West, 1900–1954*. Lawrence: University of Kansas Press, 1993.

Chireau, Yvonne P. *Black Magic: Religion and the African American Conjuring Tradition*. Berkeley: University of California Press, 2003.

Cone, James H. *The Cross and the Lynching Tree*. Maryknoll: Orbis, 2011.

———. *For My People: Black Theology and the Black Church*. Maryknoll: Orbis, 1994. New Haven: Yale University Press, 1942.

———. *The Spirituals and the Blues: An Interpretation*. Maryknoll: Orbis, 1972.

Crouchett, Lawrence P., et al. *Visions toward Tomorrow: The History of the East Bay Afro-American Community, 1852–1977*. Oakland: Northern California Center for Afro-American History and Life, 1989.

Cruden, Robert. *The Negro in Reconstruction*. Englewood Cliffs, NJ: Prentice-Hall, 1969.

Davis, Gerald L. *I Got the Word in Me and I Can Sing It, You Know: A Study of the Performed African-American Sermon.* Philadelphia: University of Pennsylvania Press, 1985.

De Graaf, Lawrence B., et al. *Seeking El Dorado African Americans in California.* Seattle: University of Washington Press, 2001.

Dodson, Howard. *Jubilee: The Emergence of African American Culture.* Washington, DC: National Geographic Society, 2002.

Douglas, Daniels. *Pioneer Urbanites A Social and Cultural History of Black San Francisco.* University of California Press, 1990

Drake, St. Clair, and Horace R. Cayton. *Black Metropolis.* New York: Harper Torchbook, 1962.

———. *The Redemption of Africa and Black Religion.* Chicago: Third World, 1991.

Du Bois, W. E. B. *Prayers for Dark People.* Edited by Herbert Aptheker. Amherst: University of Massachusetts Press, 1980.

———. *Biography of a Race, 1868–1919.* New York: Holt, 1993.

———. *The Souls of Black Folk.* 1903. Reprint, New York: Barnes and Noble, 2003.

———. *W. E. B. Du Bois on Race and Culture.* Edited by Bernard Bell et al. New York: Routledge, 1996.

Etzioni, Amitai. *The Spirit of Community: The Reinvention of American Society.* New York: Simon & Schuster, 1993.

Festival (At the Lake). Guide 1988 Communities in Action. Oakland Public Library History Room.

Findlay, James F., Jr. *Church People in the Struggle: The National Council of Churches and the Black Freedom Movement, 1950–1970.* New York: Oxford University Press, 1993.

Flamming, Douglas. *Bound for Freedom: Black Los Angeles in Jim Crow America.* Berkeley: University of California Press, 2005.

Floyd-Thomas, Stacey, et al. *Black Church Studies: An Introduction.* Nashville: Abingdon, 2007.

Foner, Philip S. *Black Panthers Speak.* Philadelphia: Lippincott, 1963.

Frazier, E. Franklin, and C. Eric Lincoln. *The Black Church since Frazier.* New York: Schocken, 1974.

Franklin, John H. *From Slavery to Freedom: A History of Negro Americans.* 3rd ed. New York: Knopf, 1947.

Gates, Henry L. *Colored People: A Memoir.* New York: Knopf, 1994.

Gates, Henry L., and Cynthia Goodman. *Unchained Memories: Readings from the Slave Narratives.* London: Bulfinch, 2002.

Goode, Kenneth. *California's Black Historical Survey.* Santa Barbara: McNally & Loftin, 1974.

———. *California's Black Pioneers.* Santa Barbara: McNally & Loftin, 1973.

Harris, William H. *The Harder We Run: Black Workers since the Civil War.* New York: Oxford University Press, 1982.

Henri, Florette. *Black Migration: Movement North, 1900–1920.* Norwell: Anchor, 1975.

Higginbotham, Evelyn B. *Righteous Discontent: The Women's Movement in the Black Baptist Church, 1880–1920.* Cambridge, MA: Harvard University Press, 1993.

Hilfiker, David. *Urban Injustice: How Ghettos Happen.* New York: Seven Stories, 2011.

Hilliard, David. *Huey: Spirit of the Panther.* New York: Thunder's Mouth, 2006.

BIBLIOGRAPHY

Hine, Darlene Clark, ed. *Black Women in America: An Historical Encyclopedia*. Vol 2. Brooklyn: Carlson, 1993

Hopkins, Dwight N. *Being Human: Race, Culture, and Religion*. Minneapolis: Augsburg Fortress, 2005.

Irvin, Dona L. *The Unsung Heart of Black America A Middle Class Church at Midcentury* Columbia: University of Missouri Press 1992.

Jacobs, John. *A Rage for Justice: The Passion and Politics of Phillip Burton*. Berkeley: University of California Press, 1997.

Johnson, Marilynn S. *The Second Gold Rush: Oakland and the East Bay in World War II*. Berkeley: University of California Press, 1993.

Johnson, Paul E., ed. *African-American Christianity: Essays in History*. Berkeley: University of California Press, 1994.

Jones, LeRoi. *Blues People: Negro Music in White America*. New York: Morrow, 1963.

Jordan, Winthrop D. *The White Man's Burden: Historical Origins of Racism in the United States*. London: Oxford University Press, 1974.

Lapp, Rudolph M. *Afro-Americans in California*. 2nd ed. San Francisco: Boyd & Fraser, 1987.

———. *Archy Lee: A California Fugitive Slave Case*. San Francisco: Book Club of California, 1969.

———. *Blacks in Gold Rush California*. New Haven: Yale University Press, 1977.

Lee, Barbara. *Renegade for Peace and Justice: Congresswoman Barbara Lee Speaks for Me*. Lanham, MD: Rowman & Littlefield, 2008.

Lee, Shayne. *America's New Preacher T. D. Jakes*. New York: New York University, 2005.

Lemann, Nicholas. *The Promised Land: The Great Black Migration and How it Changed America*. New York: Knopf, 1991.

Lemke-Santangelo, Gretchen. *Abiding Courage: African American Migrant Women and the East Bay Community*. Chapel Hill: University of North Carolina Press, 1996.

Levine, Lawrence W. *Black Culture and Black Consciousness: Afro-American Folk Thought from Slavery to Freedom*. New York: Oxford University Press, 1977.

Lincoln, Charles E, and Mamiya, Lawrence H. *The Black Church in the African American Experience*. Durham, NC: Duke University Press, 1990.

———. *The Black Church since Frazier*. New York: Schocken, 1974.

———. *Race, Religion, and the Continuing American Dilemma*. Rev. ed. New York: Hill and Wang, 1984.

Malcolm X. *Malcolm X Speaks*. New York: Grove Weidenfeld, 1995.

Marable, Manning. "The Black Faith of W.E.B. Du Bois: Sociocultural and Political Dimensions of Black Religion." *Southern Quarterly* 23 (1985) 15–33.

McBroome, Nason Delores. *Parallel Communities: African Americans in California's East Bay 1850–1963*. New York: Garland, 1993.

McCall, Emmanuel L. *Black Church Life-styles*. Nashville: Broadman, 1986.

McMickle, Marvin A. *An Encyclopedia of African American Church Heritage*. Valley Forge: Judson, 2002.

Meyers, Eleanor S., ed. *Envisioning the New City: A Reader on Urban Ministry*. Louisville: Westminster John Knox, 1992.

Miller, Paul. *The Postwar Struggle for Civil Rights African Americans in San Francisco*. New York: Routledge, 2010.

Miller, Rex. *The Millennium Matrix*, San Francisco: Jossey-Bass 2004.

Mitchell, Henry H. *Black Church Beginnings: The Long-Hidden Realities of the First Years*. Grand Rapids: Eerdmans, 2004.

Montgomery, William E. *Under Their Own Vine and Fig Tree: The African-American Church in the South, 1865–1900*. Baton Rouge: Louisiana State University Press, 1993.

Moore, Shirley A. *To Place Our Deeds: The African American Community in Richmond, California, 1910–1963*. Berkeley: University of California Press, 2000.

Myrdal, Gunnar. *An American Dilemma The Negro Problem & Modern Democracy*. Volume 2. New York: Harper & Row, 1944.

National Advisory Commission on Civil Disorders. *Report of the National Advisory Commission on Civil Disorders*. Toronto: Bantam, 1968.

Nations, Opal Louis. *"It's So Nice to Be Nice": The Story of His Grace King Louis H. Narcisse*

Newman, Richard, ed. *African American Quotations*. New York: Oryx, 2000.

Newton, Huey P. *Revolutionary Suicide*. New York: Writers and Readers, 1973.

Olson, Lynne. *Freedom's Daughters: The Unsung Heroes of the Civil Rights Movement from 1830–1970*. New York: Touchstone, 2001.

Pinn, Anne H., and Anthony B. Pinn. *Fortress Introduction to Black Church History*. Minneapolis: Augsburg Fortress, 2002.

Praetzelis, Mary, and Suzanne Stewart, eds. *Sights and Sounds Essays in Celebration of West Oakland*. Cypress 1–880 Replacement Project, California Department of Transportation. Oakland: Caltrans, 1997.

Reed, Ishmael. *Blues City: A Walk in Oakland*. New York: Crown, 2003.

Rhomberg, Chris. *No There There: Race, Class, and Political Community in Oakland*. Berkeley: University of California Press, 2004.

Robinson, Eugene. *Disintegration: The Splintering of Black America*. New York: Doubleday, 2010.

Robinson, Louie. "The Kingdom of King Narcisse California." *Ebony*, July 1963.

Rosenburg, Bruce A. *Can These Bones Live?* 1970. Reprint, Oxford: Oxford University Press, 1988.

Ross, Roseta E. *Witnessing and Testifying: Black Women, Religion, and Civil Rights*. Minneapolis: Augsburg Fortress, 2003.

Self, Robert O. *American Babylon: Race and the Struggle for Postwar Oakland*. Princeton: Princeton University Press, 2003.

Sernett, Milton C., ed. *Afro-American Religious History: A Documentary Witness*. Durham, NC: Duke University Press, 1985.

———. *Bound for the Promised Land: African American Religion and the Great Migration*. Durham, NC: Duke University Press, 1997.

Shapiro, Nat, and Nat Hentoff, eds. *Hear Me Talkin' to Ya: The Story of Jazz by the Men Who Made It*. New York: Penguin, 1955.

Smith, J. Alfred. *Thus Far by Faith: A Study of Historical Backgrounds and the First Fifty Years of the Allen Temple Baptist Church*. Oakland: Allen Temple Church, 1973.

Smith, J. Alfred, and Harry L. Williams III. *On the Jericho Road: A Memoir of Racial Justice, Social Action, and Prophetic Ministry*. Downers Grove, IL: InterVarsity, 2004.

Smith, Jessie Carney, Ed. *Notable Black American Women: Book II*. Detroit: Thomson Gale. 1996.

Southern California Quarterly 46, March 1964.

Taylor, Clarence. *The Black Churches of Brooklyn*. New York: Columbia University Press, 1994.

Taylor, Martha C. "Pastoral Leadership Training & Mentoring African American Baptist Clergywomen." San Francisco Theological Seminary.

Taylor, Quintard. *In Search of the Racial Frontier: African Americans in the American West, 1528–1990*. New York: Norton, 1998.

Thompson, Jerry, and Duane Deterville. *Black Artists in Oakland*. Mount Pleasant: Arcadia, 2007.

Thurman, Howard. *For the Inward Journey: The Writings of Howard Thurman*. Edited by Anne S. Thurman. Richmond, IN: Friends United Meeting, 1984.

———. *Footprints of a Dream: The Story of the Church for the Fellowship of All Peoples*. New York: Harper & Bros., 1959.

———. *With Head and Heart*. New York: Harcourt, 1979.

Townes, Emilie M., ed. *Embracing the Spirit* New York: Orbis, 1997.

Tramble, Thomas, and Wilma Tramble. *The Pullman Porters and West Oakland*. Mount Pleasant, SC: Arcadia, 2007.

Walker, Clarence E. *We Can't Go Home Again: An Argument about Afrocentrism*. Oxford: Oxford University Press, 2001.

Walker, Wyatt T. *Somebody's Calling My Name*. Valley Forge, PA: Judson, 1979/1992.

Warnock, Raphael G. *The Divided Mind of the Black Church Theology, Piety & Public Witness* New York: New York University Press, 2014.

Washington, Booker T. *Up from Slavery*. New York: Dell, 1965.

Watkins, Walter F. *The Cry of the West*. Berkeley: Bridges, 1969.

Wenkert, Robert, John Magney, and Fred Templeton. *An Historical Digest of Negro-White Relations in Richmond, California*. Berkeley: University of California, 1967.

Wilkerson, Isabel. *The Warmth of other Suns*. New York: Random House, 2010.

Wilmore, Gayraud S. *Black Religion and Black Radicalism: An Interpretation of the Religious History of African Americans*. Maryknoll, NY: Orbis, 1998.

Wollenberg, Charles, *Berkeley A City in History*. Berkeley: University Press, 2008

Woodson, Carter G. *A Century of Negro Migration*. Washington, DC: Association of Negro Life and History, 1918. Mineola: Dover, 2002.

Yee, Shirley J. *Black Women Activists: A Study in Activism*. Knoxville: University of Tennessee Press, 1992.

Younger, George D. *The Church and Urban Renewal*. Philadelphia: Lippincott, 1965.

Zinn, Howard. *A People's History of the United States*. New York: HarperCollins, 2001.

Primary Sources: Unpublished, Church History

Bethel African Methodist Episcopal Church Anniversary Book, San Francisco.
Double Rock Baptist Church, History, San Francisco.
Bethany Baptist Church.
Bethel African Methodist Episcopal Church.
Church by the Side of the Road.
Cosmopolitan Baptist Church.
Davis Chapel Christian Methodist Church.
Double Rock Baptist Church.
Downs Memorial Methodist Church.

Easter Hill United Methodist Church.
Evergreen Missionary Baptist Church.
Faith Presbyterian Church.
First African Methodist Episcopal Zion.
First Union Baptist Church.
Galilee Missionary Baptist Church.
Liberty Hill Missionary Baptist Church, Berkeley, History.
Macedonia Missionary Baptist Church.
Market Street Seventh Day Adventist Church.
Mt. Carmel Missionary Baptist Church, Oakland.
McGee Avenue Anniversary Book, Berkeley.
McGlothen Temple Church of God in Christ.
Mingleton Temple Church of God in Christ.
Mt Zion Missionary Baptist Church Anniversary Book, Oakland.
New Providence Baptist Church.
Paradise Missionary Baptist Church.
Parks Chapel African Methodist Episcopal Church History.
Progressive Missionary Baptist Church.
Opal Louis Nations–(unpublished manuscript 2010 opalnations.com/files).
Obituary Reverend Benjamin F. Carroll, July 2, 1983.
Star Bethel Missionary Baptist Church.

Taylor Memorial Methodist Church.

Third Baptist Church San Francisco 150th Anniversary Book.
Marty Praetzellis and Suzanne Stewart "Sights and sounds: Essays in Celebration of
    West."
Oakland: Rohnert Park Anthropological Studies Center, Sonoma State University.
California Department of Transportation , District 4.
Carol Chamberland "Shaping San Francisco Fillmore Cultural Capital Historical Essay.

Periodicals: Newspapers, Magazines

Bay Area News Group.
Ebony Magazine, July 1963.
Sacramento Bee, Nov 11, 1950.
    San Francisco Chronicle 1946.
Oakland Tribune Newspaper,
———, Hollie West, July 1964.
———, Delilah Beasley. Activities among Negroes, 1923–34.
    ———, Lena Wysinger. Activities among Negroes, 1934-42.

Periodicals: Magazines

Southern California Quarterly 46 (March 1964).

Dissertations and Theses

Taylor, Martha C. "Pastoral Leadership Training, and Mentoring African American Baptist Clergywomen." DMin thesis. San Francisco Theological Seminary.

Journal Articles

Nations, Opal. "Festival (At the Lake) Guide: 1988 Communities in Action." Oakland Public Library History Room.

Interviews by Author

Shirley Taylor Adkins, August 11, 2014.
Beatrice Taylor Jett, August 11, 20124.
Kenneth Jett, August 11, 2014.
Lee Arthur Johnson, August 11, 2014.
Laura Taylor Johnson, August 11, 2014.
Billy Taylor, August 11, 2014.
Larry Taylor, August 11, 2014.
Rafe Taylor Jr, August 11, 2014.
Mary Thames, November 19, 2013

Archival and Manuscript Collections

African American Museum and Library, Oakland History Room.
Oakland Public Library History Room First African Methodist Episcopal Church 140th Year Anniversary, 1858–1998.
Sacramento Historical Society Golden Notes, Vol II No. l. pp 26–27.
Fifth Episcopal District African Methodist Episcopal Church, 138th Session.
California Annual Conference.
The Cry of the West; the story of the mighty struggle for religious freedom in California, Walter F. Watkins.
Hausler, Donald "Blacks in Oakland: 1852–1987."
———. "Blacks in Early Oakland: The Rise of the East Bay African American Community." 1850–1900, 2008.
Hunter, Floyd, *Housing Discrimination in Oakland, California: A Study Prepared for the Oakland Mayor's Committee on Full Opportunity and the Council of Social Planning, Alameda County* Berkeley 1963–1964.
National Register of Historic Places United States Department of the Interior, Oakland Public Library.

Internet

http://www.sfmuseum.net/hist5/ame.
http://www.episcopal.org/.
http://www.experiencebmc.org/.
http://www.mtchurch.org/mission.shtml.
http://www.nhbcoakland.com/history.html.
http://progressive4life.org/welcome/ourstory.
http://ilovejesus.co/myhome/lovealordhistory.html.
http://www.sjmbc.org/history.
http://www.galilee-sf.org/history.html.
http://www.spiritofdavis.com/hikstory.html.
http://wwwjonesumc.co/ages/history.html.
http://www.taylorchurch.org/churchhistory//id5.html.
http://www.providencecares.org/frame_pages/history_page.htp.
http://www.evergreenbaptistchurchsf.orgbc-history.
http://www.fouchesfuneralhome.com/obituares/Itolev-Hudson.
http://www.opalnations.com/files/Perkins_Odessa.pdf.
http://www.voiceofevergreen.org/index.cfm.
http://www.parchester_village_Richmond_California.

Index

as a major terminus point for
  Blacks, xxv
migrants settled in to improve their
  economic conditions, 91
not spared from economic plight of
  the Depression, 82
Bay Area Rapid Transit District (BART),
  58, 80, 90, 159
Bay Cities Political Club, 77
Beasley, Delilah, xxv, 6, 30, 54, 63, 69,
  100
Becker, Burton F., 66–67
Beckford, Ruth, 115
Beebe, Joseph Andrew, 77
Beebe Memorial Christian Methodist
  Episcopal Cathedral, 76–79, 109
Belcher, Charles H. (Reverend), 24,
  168–69, 181
Bell, A. Edward (Reverend Dr.), 164,
  169
Bell, A. O. (Dr.), 28–29, 139
Bell, Betty Taylor, photo, 154
Bell, Eola, 166
Bell, J. E., 166
Bell, James, photo, 154
Bell, Melvin J. (Reverend), 77–78
Bennett, Roy L. (Reverend Dr.), 13–14
Berkeley
  affected by the African American
    migration, 93
  first black church established in
    1919, 46
  founding of black churches, 45
  incorporated in 1878, xxiii
  middle class, 46–47
  not sharing in the limelight of jazz
    or black entertainment, 116
  removing "problem" families from,
    160
Berkeley, Thomas L. (Attorney), 166
Berkeley Baptist Church, 28
Berkeley Baptist Divinity School, 57
Berkeley Board of Education, 23
Berkeley Mission, 86
Berkeley Mt. Zion Baptist Church,
  74–75
Berkeley School Board, 23
Bernstine, Alvin C. (Reverend Dr.), 124

Bernstine, Willie L. (Reverend), 166
Berry, Alma, 24
Beth Eden Baptist Church, Oakland,
  20–22, 48, 55, 56, 71
  hosted a lecture by Captain E. L.
    Gaines of New York City, 63
  members disunited their
    membership from, 170
  Mother Club of the Black Women's
    Club founded in 1899, 53
  photo, 33
  photo of Reverend Dr. J. Hubbard,
    34
  photo of Reverend Hawkins, 33
Beth Eden Housing Corporation, 22
Beth Eden Women's Mission Home, 21
Bethany Baptist Church, Oakland
  (1960), 72, 172–74
Bethel African Methodist Episcopal
  (AME) Church, 11–12
  Pastor of, 15
  St. Cyprian renamed, 9
Bethel Church Job Placement Program,
  141
Bethel Missionary Baptist Church,
  Oakland, 75, 78, 138–141, 144,
  162
Bethlehem Lutheran Church, Oakland,
  84–86, 181
Bethlehem Missionary Baptist Church,
  Richmond (1945), 124, 165, 166
Bethune, Mary McLeod, 12, 54
Betts, Nicholas (Reverend Dr.), 110
Bible Fellowship Baptist Church, 138–
  39, 141
bible studies, radical, 185
Bibles, traded in for digital-media big
  screens, 194
"The Biblical Rules of Order," 170
Big Town label, Oakland-based, 126
Birmingham and Selma March, 155
The Birth of a Nation movie, 51, 65
The Bishop Clarence James Davis
  Educational Building, 81
Bishop Jones Literary Society, 68
"Black America," four distinct
  categories, 196
Black Americans, sending to Africa, 62

"What We Stand for" (speech), 27
wheelchair accessibility, 173
Wheelock, Todd (Reverend), 100
White, Alexander, Sr. (Elder), 183
White, L. S. (Reverend), 77, 109, 110
White, Lewis S. (Reverend), 78
White, W. F., 90
White, Walter A., 93
white flight, 92, 137, 161
white man, having the right of race
    prejudice, 101
white pastors, attracting black
    worshipers, 193
white racism and supremacy, Garvey
    denouncing, 63
white sailors, brought in to load
    munitions, 131
white women
    driving Negro passengers, 101
    as waitresses serving Negroes, 101
white workers, viewed black migrants as
    an invading mob, 95
Wigfall Mission in Haiti, 29
Wilcox, Mrs. Bessie, 84
"wilderness period," Love Center
    experienced, 187
Wildy, George W. (Reverend), 57, 162
William Clark Church Universal
    Theological Seminary, 73
Williams, A. E. (Reverend), 111, 172
Williams, Arthur (Reverend), 75
Williams, Barbara, Roberta and Shirley,
    168
Williams, Bernice and Fred, 168
Williams, Dorothy (Reverend), 24, 164
Williams, Guthrie John (Reverend),
    105, 157
Williams, Hazaiah (Reverend), 180
Williams, James (Reverend), 145
Williams, L. K. (Dr.), 21
Williams, Landon, 159
Williams, M. J. (Dr.), 173
Williams, M. K., 80
Williams, Mary, 168
Williams, Mrs. Mable, 141
Williams, Mrs. Tobe, 25
Williams, Samuel and Augustine, 163
Williams Chapel AMEC, 183

Williamson, Henry M., Sr. (Bishop), 79
Willis, C. W., 139
Willis, Maggie, 139
Wilmore, Gayraud S. (Reverend), 181
Wilson, D. Mark (Reverend), 49
Wilson, J. D. (Reverend), 56
Wilson, Jackey J., Sr. (Reverend), 125
Wilson, James Dee (Reverend), 48, 56
Wilson, Mary, 60
Wilson-Larche, Ruth, 60
Wiltz, James, 126
Winans, Joseph W., 3
Wishups, Georgia, 139
Wistar Redemption and Recovery
    Program, 175
women. See also black women
    commitment to ministry, 49
    contributions in society, 52–55
    Dr. Coleman a supporter of, 28
    expanding role into leadership
        positions, 193
    formed clubs to fight against racism,
        52
    mentoring in ministry, 188
    migrant, postwar unemployment
        and, 132
    ordination of, 17, 49
    sexism not allowing to hold pastoral
        positions, 48
    unemployment rates after WWII,
        132
    white, driving Negro passengers and
        working as waitresses, 101
Women's Choir, at Church by the Side of
    the Road, 168
Women's Chorus, of North Oakland
    Baptist Church, 29
women's club movement, 58
Women's Day, declared by Coleman in
    1914, 28
Women's League, 168
Women's Missionary Society, 58
Women's Missionary Union, at North
    Richmond Baptist, 50
women's movement, contributed
    to building a strong Black
    community, xxv
Woods, Carmi Victor (Reverend), 184